London: problems of change

Edited by
Hugh Clout and
Peter Wood

Longman

Acknowledgements

We are grateful to the following copyright holders for permission to make use of illustrations redrawn from published sources:

The Institute of British Geographers for Fig 2.3 derived from P D Nunn (1983) 'The development of the River Thames in central London during the Flandrian' *Transactions. Institute of British Geographers* NS8: 188.

The City of London Archaeological Trust for Figs 3.2 and 3.3 simplified from City of London Archaeological Trust (1980) *Archaeology of the City of London* Museum of London.

George Philip and Son Limited for Figs 3.4 and 5.5 simplified from R Clayton (ed) (1964) *The Geography of Greater London*.

The Cambridge University Press for Fig 4.1 redrawn from O H K Spate (1936) 'The growth of London AD 1660–1800' in H C Darby (ed) *An Historical Geography of England*.

The Oxford University Press for Fig 5.3 simplified from L D Stamp (1964) *Some Aspects of Medical Geography* and for Fig 6.2 redrawn from J M Hall (1976) *London: Metropolis and Region*.

The Office of Population Censuses and Surveys for Fig 7.1 simplified from E Gilje *et al* (1983) Demographic review of Greater London 1983 *GLC Statistical Series* 20 and for Figs 8.1 and 8.2 simplified from P Congdon (1983) A map profile of Greater London in 1981 *GLC Statistical Series* 23.

The Greater London Council for Figs 9.3 and 9.4 simplified from GLC (1966), *London Traffic Survey vol II*.

Professor Keith Clayton for Fig 13.1 updated from K Clayton (ed) (1964) *Guide to London Excursions* International Geographical Congress London.

The London Natural History Society for Fig 17.1 partly derived from London Natural History Society (1983) *The Flora of the London Area*.

The Essex Field Club and David Corke for Fig 17.2 simplified from D Corke (1978) *Epping Forest: the natural aspect*.

Dr J Shepherd for Fig 18.2 simplified from J Shepherd and P Congdon (1986) *A Social Atlas of London: aspects of change 1971–1981* Oxford University Press.

We are grateful to the following for permission to reproduce photographs:

Aerofilms, cover; Camera Press, page 140; Docklands Community Poster Project, page 166; Greater London Council, page 107; Punch, page 92.

All other photographs were supplied by the authors.

LONGMAN GROUP LIMITED
*Longman House, Burnt Mill, Harlow, Essex CM20 2JE, UK
and Associated Companies throughout the World*

First published 1986

ISBN 0 582 35491 9

Set in 10/12pt Times Roman, Linotron 202

Produced by Longman Group (FE) Limited
Printed in Hong Kong

Contents

List of figures

List of tables

List of abbreviations

DCP	Docklands Community Posters	LVSC	London Voluntary Services Council
DJC	Docklands Joint Committee	MGB	Metropolitan Green Belt
DoE	Department of the Environment	NCC	Nature Conservancy Council
GIAs	General Improvement Areas	NCWP	New Commonwealth and Pakistani-born
GLC	Greater London Council	NDHS	National Dwellings and Households Survey
GLEB	Greater London Enterprise Board		
HAAs	Housing Action Areas	odp	office development permit
idcs	industrial development certificates	OMA	Outer Metropolitan Area
JDAG	Joint Docklands Action Group	ROSE	Rest of South East
LCC	London County Council	SSSI	Site of Special Scientific Interest
LDDC	London Docklands Development Corporation	STOL	Short Take-off and Landing
		TRRL	Transport and Road Research Laboratory
LOB	Location of Offices Bureau	WHO	World Health Organization

Preface

In the mid-1970s a number of geographers at University College London decided to write a text-book that introduced sixth formers, their teachers and first-year undergraduates to selected aspects of the geography of London. That book was published in 1978 under the title *Changing London* (Hugh Clout ed, University Tutorial Press). Five years later members of the same Department agreed to collaborate on a second book that would fulfil a similar purpose but might also appeal to a wider audience of Londoners. In doing so, we had three main issues in mind. To start with, social and economic conditions in the capital had become far more 'problematic' than they had seemed up to the mid-1970s. Secondly, we had realized the need to include additional themes through our experience of using London as a 'laboratory' for teaching an integrated geography course to first-year undergraduates. Finally, the vigorous political debate surrounding the future of the Greater London Council had revealed even more clearly the importance of the city's changing geography for its administration, and the need for a clear and up-to-date exposition of the city's problems.

As editors of *London: problems of change* we must express our thanks to our colleagues for joining us in this venture; to Alick Newman, our senior cartographer, for drawing the maps and diagrams; and to Annabel Swindells, Claudette John, Kathryn Jones and especially Diane Abraham for typing and retyping many of the chapters.

Hugh Clout and Peter Wood

1 London: past, present and future

Peter Wood

There have always been problems of change in London. In the past these have generally been associated with its growth as the centre for many of the most successful components of British economic, administrative, social and cultural life. In recent years, however, the prospect has become one of decline. This decline is, nevertheless, apparently balanced by growth elsewhere in south-east England and adjacent regions to the west and north, in a more extended version of the pattern of decentralization that has been well established over the past century. So, has anything really changed? It probably has, since the continuing dispersal of urban development in the South East seems now to have reached a stage where the region's functional coherence is breaking down. London, which is defined in this book as the area of the Greater London Council (GLC), no longer dominates the region as it once did. The city no longer gains such sustenance from its surrounding areas and they are not so closely dependent economically and socially upon it. Instead, the wealth of many of the residents in the rest of the South East, the environmental qualities of life away from the city, the personal mobility that can be enjoyed there and the attractions of these areas for new investment both private and public, now pose direct challenges to the dominance of London. Modern economic and social change is undermining many of the foundations of high-density city life.

This modern dilemma of London has been compounded by increased administrative confusion and political conflict in the 1980s. Twenty years ago, rationalization of the administration of the capital and its surrounding region was much in vogue. The London County Council (LCC), established in 1888, and its 28 metropolitan boroughs were replaced by the more extensive GLC and 32 London boroughs in 1964 (Fig. 1.1). A year later, the South East Regional Planning Council was set up as part of a national programme for coordinated regional planning. The 'master plan' approach to solving the large scale problems of urban and regional planning in the UK was probably best exemplified by the 'Greater London Development Plan' (1969) and its modification (1975), and the various regional plans for the South East, including the 'Strategy for the South East' (1967), and the 'Strategic Plan for the South East' (1970), with its subsequent revision (1976). The technical justification for such exercises was that the needs of widely dispersed areas for transport provision, infrastructure investment, housing, industrial and office development, social and welfare services and environmental protection were increasingly interdependent. Thus strategic guidelines for local planning were needed either from statutory bodies, such as the elected GLC, or from appointed advisors, such as the members of the Regional Planning Councils and their associated Boards of civil servants. The perceived need for a large-scale perspective also lay behind such exercises as the Roskill Commission Inquiry on the siting of the third London airport (1972).

Since the mid-1970s, faith in such guidance has rapidly waned (see chapter 6). The Regional Planning Council was finally abolished in 1979, and the role of the GLC had been progressively diminished even before its proposed abolition in 1986. Of course, the rationale of metropolitan or regional-scale planning in and around London has not changed. In fact, it can be argued that as the urban system has continued to expand, while at the same time economic problems have intensified and

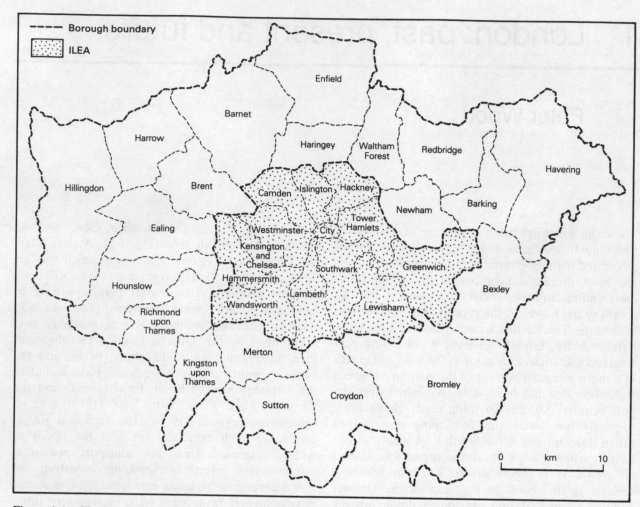

Figure 1.1   *The Boroughs of Greater London, 1964.*

resources become scarcer in the late 1970s, so the need for regional coordination has grown. What have changed are political attitudes, as the recession and disillusionment with planning have deepened. Cooperation between counties and boroughs has proved difficult to sustain, as all areas have begun to feel the threat of rising unemployment and rapid economic change. As the consensus has weakened, more influence has been transferred either to central government, ever suspicious of the power of London politics, through cuts and tighter control of local authority expenditure, or to local borough and community activity. Vociferous local reactions, for example, to oppose extension of motorways in London, building a third airport, changes in the green belt, or the policies of the Docklands Development Corporation have challenged the 'grand design' approach to metropolitan planning. The notion that planners, with their ability to see the 'wider interest', know what is best is no longer acceptable (chapter 19). As a result, in the mid-1980s there seems to be little agreement about the methods and agencies needed to influence the direction of change in London. The balance of power has moved to central government and will do so again decisively when the GLC is abolished. The contrasting policies and attitudes of the London boroughs will become more dominant, making agreement on critical areas of policy increasingly difficult. Local responses to the prospects of change have also become more active and will continue to add a further dimension of dissent.

In these circumstances, how can a book illuminate our understanding of London, when the future threatens to present more acute economic, social, ethnic, housing and transportation challenges than ever, and the system of planning and political decision making is in an unprecedented state of disarray? First, it can take a longer and broader view of the activities that make up the city, including its past (chapters 3–5, 16) as well as contemporary concerns, the successes in managing its environment (chapters 11, 12, 17) as well as stumbling attempts to devise an effective transportation or housing allocation system (chapters 9 and 10). It can also look at general themes of change such as population structure or the economy (chapters 7 and 8) as well as the ways whereby these come together in particular areas such as the city centre or the suburbs (chapters 13 and 14). It can give some emphasis to the views of ethnic and locality groups (chapters 18 and 19), to augment the perspectives of the planner or the academic. The pattern of London that emerges from our contributors is therefore much more diverse than an account by a single author would reveal.

Second, in all these respects the present book attempts to examine and explain the current scene in some detail. Each chapter reveals how rapidly both the factual situation and attitudes to change in London have been transformed during the last decade. Third, the book can identify some of the near certainties about the future, and their consequences, which must be given due attention in studying London. These include the continuing trend of decentralization of population and jobs from the city, the decline of manufacturing, a growing dependence on service activities, the inevitability of traffic congestion with increasing car ownership, the high cost of maintaining public transport, and the need to adapt and renew old areas, including many suburbs, through investment in infrastructure and housing. The migration process in and out of the city will raise the proportion of young workers in the population but the very old will also grow in importance. Ethnic minorities are likely to remain relatively concentrated in certain parts of the city while local residents generally will wish to have an increasing say in the changes that affect their lives. The considerable environmental improvements of the post-war years are likely to be sustained but new threats will emerge and regulation and investment will still be needed to maintain standards. The Green Belt will constrain building around London, although its detailed form and use will be modified in spite of locally-based opposition to change. The M25 orbital motorway, due to be completed in 1986/7, will give a powerful stimulus to development outside London rather than inside it (chapter 15). These types of pressure seem to be unaffected by changing fashions in planning or by economic recession. They arise from the changing use of the city inherent in late twentieth-century ways of life in Britain.

Finally, the book can reveal uncertainties about the future course of events. Many of these in London arise from the administrative confusion, already described, and from political attitudes towards making resources available for job creation, house construction, public transport, road building, infrastructure support, social services, and inner-city regeneration schemes. Unpredictable national economic fortunes, as we have seen, also affect the future of the city. Of major significance will be the relative rates of decline in London of jobs and the working population. In recent years, job loss has outstripped population decline, especially in the occupations that many Londoners are best equipped to fill. London's international status as a business and tourist centre is becoming increasingly important to its prosperity. Attitudes to living in the city are also likely to continue changing as new developments affect employment, housing and the living environment in general.

The following chapters fall into four groups of unequal length. The first includes chapters 2–6 and provides a broad view of the origins and development of London, from the geomorphological landscape that underlies it to its historic evolution up to a generation or so ago. Processes of expansion and renewal in the urban fabric recur as themes in chapter 6, which reviews events in the 1950s and 1960s and forms a prologue to the rest of the book. A second group of chapters (7–12) sets out the main elements of the contemporary pattern of change in London. In each, the varied effects of past planning are evaluated. These have been generally most successful in areas of environmental management, where technical and legal solutions have attracted widespread support. Significantly, however, solutions to economic and social problems have been less easy where goals are more controversial and underlying trends may be leading strongly in other directions.

The third group of chapters (13–15) discusses problems and prospects in three particular zones of the city: its commercial centre, its suburbs and its fringe. The focal themes in these chapters shift from the economy, to social change, and changing priorities in controlling urban development, and in so doing they demonstrate how elements discussed in earlier chapters have differing significance in various parts of the city. The final four chapters (16–19) take a more detailed look at facets of change that affect the lives of Londoners and are of growing significance for the future. Attention is first devoted to the varying ways in which London's rich and unique legacy of parkland has been used through time and subsequently to the mechanisms behind growing public awareness of change in the natural environment. After this the current experience and attitudes of ethnic minorities are explored and the book concludes by examining the reactions of local communities in general to the major changes taking place around them, and the problems of community participation that result.

London certainly faces many problems of change, not least those originating from the abolition after almost 100 years of a city-wide tier of government, but its size and diversity remain its chief attractions, making it unique among 'world cities'. The style and quality of life offered in the capital city are important because of its two distinct, if related, roles.

London houses almost seven million people, and their prospects and prosperity are of national significance in themselves; it also embodies the richness of British culture and is a symbolic focus of national life. The emphasis of this book may seem pessimistic; this is because we have chosen to examine *problems* of change and because the inevitability of change often causes alarm. Equally, we could have emphasized the *opportunities* presented by change, and we hope that many of the chapters may be read in this light as well. The overriding problem for the future is to adapt London to the changing needs of its inhabitants and to rise to the challenge inherited from its past. Problems of change in London may not be new but their resolution requires a modern understanding of its strengths and potentialities as well as of its needs.

Further reading

Individual chapters list appropriate books and articles but an excellent overall guide is provided by:
Dolphin P, Grant E, and Lewis E (1981) *The London Region: an annotated geographical bibliography* Mansell.
For a comprehensive reference book see:
Weinreb B and Hibbert C (eds) (1983) *The London Encyclopaedia* Macmillan.

2 Land under London

Eric Brown

Introduction

The benefits and hazards inherent in the physical site and situation of London, their attendant physical resources and aesthetic values are not and never have been of an obvious kind. So muted and subtle is their influence upon the totality of the urban geography of London it is no wonder that considerations of economic, social and political forces tend to dominate studies of the city. Nevertheless a full understanding of the location, character and functioning of the metropolis needs not only to consider the influence of the physical environment upon London but at least as importantly, the influence of London upon its environ-ment. For a radically new physical environment largely impervious in character, cellular in plan and rough in surface texture of tarmacadam, concrete, brick, stone, tile and slate has replaced the forests and marshes of prehistory and even the villages, farms and fields of historic times. There has also been an increase in the surface area of open water.

The underpinnings of London

The real foundation of London is a stable platform of old hard rocks of Palaeozoic age (p–m on Fig. 2.1, upper section) akin to those outcropping in the Mendips to the west and in the Nuneaton area to the north but beneath London buried by

Figure 2.1 *Generalized section across the London Basin: and section from Clapham Common to Pentonville.*

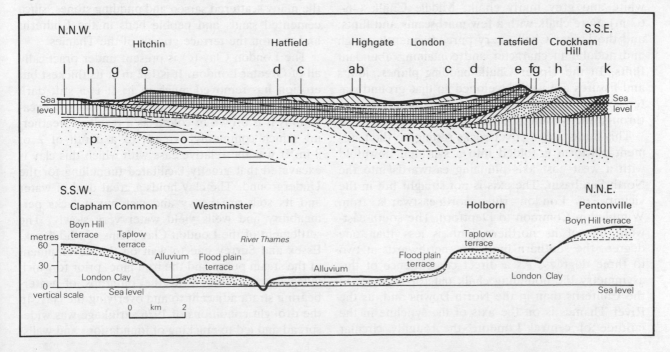

some 300 m of younger Mesozoic and Tertiary sediments. In 1870 a bore hole put down in Kentish Town by the Hampstead Water Works, in search of ground water in Lower Greensand strata (h), passed through the Chalk (e) and the expected layer of Gault Clay (g) beneath it but instead of then encountering the Lower Greensand, as the sequence of surface outcrops south of London in the Weald suggests would be the case, entered much older and harder Devonian rocks (m) at a depth of 250 m below sea level. A similar bore at Meux's Brewery in Tottenham Court Road did the same at a depth of 299 m below sea level and in 1911 at Stonebridge Park drilling below the base of the Gault at 295 m into the basement rocks showed traces of oil, gas and salt water. A buried coalfield like that discovered in a similar situation in Kent at approximately the same time has never been detected beneath London. South of London the basement slopes steeply to depths of over 1600 m below the Weald and 4000 m below the Isle of Wight.

A 50 m or so thick layer of Gault Clay everywhere rests on the basement platform and forms a waterproof bottom to the much more permeable 4 m of Upper Greensand (f) and 200 m of Chalk, a soft white limestone with flints. The Chalk is divisible into a relatively unjointed and unfissured Lower Chalk (55–67 m), a massively bedded, flintless, white and grey marly chalk; Middle Chalk (46–67 m), pure chalk with a few marl seams and flints; and the Upper Chalk, very pure, frequently rough and nodular in character and containing abundant flints. In the Upper Chalk bedding planes, joints and fissures are well developed so that ground water moves more readily through it than it does through the Middle and Lower Chalk.

This thick pile of cover rocks resting on the basement platform is folded into a synclinal downfold with a west–east axis plunging eastwards into the North Sea basin. The axis is not straight but in the vicinity of London runs north-eastwards from Wimbledon Common to Deptford. The south-eastward dip of its northern limb is less than one degree, the southern limb dips northwards at two to three degrees. As a direct consequence of this asymmetry the bounding chalk outcrop is wider in the Chilterns than in the North Downs and, as the River Thames is on the axis of the syncline in the latitude of central London, the roughly circular urban extent of Greater London spills south to the crest of the North Downs but only just laps against the southern limits of the Chilterns.

Preserved within the heart of the syncline is a sequence of clays and sands of Tertiary age which form the surface rocks under most of London and in which the foundations of most large buildings are excavated. The oldest of them resting directly on the Chalk are collectively referred to as the Lower London Tertiaries (d). Their outcrop forms a distinctive type of terrain along the north margin of the North Downs and the outcrop of their contact with the Chalk is marked by a line of springs and a string of settlements from Guildford through Leatherhead and Epsom. The component Thanet and Woolwich beds are predominantly sandy in character with subordinate clays. The sands were formerly worked as iron- and brass-moulding sands and their occurrence at Woolwich may have contributed to the location there of the Royal Arsenal. The Blackheath Beds limited to south-east London contain substantial pebble beds formerly much in demand for constructional purposes and locally cemented into conglomerates. Their edge is marked by a low escarpment between Croydon and Erith.

The outcrop of the Reading Beds, sands and clays of the same age resting on the Chalk of the Chilterns is less conspicuous but numerous small hilly outliers dot the Chiltern dipslope. They are the source of the many scattered sarsen and pudding stones, silica cemented sands and pebble beds in the Chilterns and even in the terrace gravels of the Thames.

The London Clay (c) is present under practically all of Greater London. It is 132 m at its thickest but erosion has removed much of it. It is a stiff dark grey or bluish-grey clay but seen in shallow excavations it is brown in colour as a result of weathering which commonly extends to a depth of 2 or 3 m. It was the relative ease with which this clay is excavated that greatly facilitated tunnelling for the Underground. The clay holds a great deal of water and its soils are heavy and wet but it lacks permeability and wells yield water very slowly. The settlement of the London Clay plains of Middlesex, Essex and Surrey had to wait on the development of the steam pump and the iron pipe, prior to which villages were limited to the outcrops of water-bearing strata adjacent to and overlying the clay. In the drought conditions of 1976 shrinkage was widespread and led to cracking of foundations and walls.

The sides of railway cuttings in clay, many now over 100 years old, have weathered and in wet weather have a tendency to slip. In its upper 20 m the London Clay becomes progressively more sandy in character and is mapped separately as the Claygate Beds (b) which have in the past been dug extensively for making tiles, pipes and pottery. The clay mixed with sand makes good bricks.

The youngest in the sequence of solid rocks are fine white and buff coloured sands with thin seams of clay and locally flint pebbles called the Bagshot Beds (a). They outcrop extensively south-west of London and cap the tops of numerous isolated hills farther east at Harrow, Hampstead, Highgate, Epping Forest and Brentwood. Springs, emerging at the base of the Bagshot and Claygate Beds on the flanks of the hills, are the sources of minor tributaries of the Thames such as the Fleet which are dammed near their sources to form Highgate and Hampstead ponds.

Minor folds and faults within the generally synclinal London basin are of sufficient magnitude to impress themselves upon the shape of the land. The straight north to south run of the Lea valley between Hoddesdon and Tottenham follows the line of a monocline down which the river has shifted uniclinally to the east undercutting and steepening the east side of the valley and leaving on the west a broad flight of gently sloping terraces. The broad flood plain of the Lea, the steep eastern side of the valley and the fact that ownership of Epping Forest was in the hands of the Corporation of the City of London served to hinder the north eastward spread of London and encouraged its south to north growth along the terraces on the western side of the Lea. The line of the Epping Forest ridge, Highgate and Hampstead hills and Hanger Hill marks the axis of a north-east–south-west syncline along which erosion has inverted the relief. In contrast Windsor Castle stands on an inlier of chalk on the line of a parallel anticline which north-eastwards brings chalk close to the surface in valley bottoms in the Pinner area. Along an east-west anticlinal axis through Cliffe, Purfleet and Grays, chalk is brought to the surface and the outcrop continues as far west as Lewisham, well within the built up area of London. In a complementary syncline to the south an extensive outcrop of the Lower London Tertiaries forms the basis of the distinctive terrains of the south-east Plateau and Lower Tertiary belt

of Kent. In south London two parallel faults, orientated north-east-south-west disrupt the rocks and throw the chalk outcrop down over 30 m to the north-east. There is no surface expression of the faults but by bringing impervious London Clay vertically against chalk they disrupt the movement of water through the chalk and change the level of the water table. Movements along extensions of the faults into Essex may have been the origin of the East Anglian earthquake of 1883.

Superficial deposits

An excavation almost anywhere in the London area below ground level reveals that the clays, sands and chalk of the solid rock succession are masked by a cover of superficial deposits of clay, silt, sand and gravel ranging in thickness from a scatter of a few pebbles to layers several metres thick. These have been laid down at various times during the past 2 000 000 years whilst the Thames and its tributaries have been cutting down into the solid rocks and excavating the hills and valleys which form the site of London. The deposits are therefore roughly altitudinally arranged and their varying nature reflects changes in the prevailing geomorphological and climatic environments.

Valley floors

The Thames enters the London basin obliquely in the north-west through a gap cut across the Chiltern Hills at Goring. Between Goring and its estuary the Thames pursues a due west to east course albeit in a markedly meandering fashion. It crosses obliquely right across the structural basin, the axis of which runs more nearly south-west–north-east. Upstream of Kew the Thames performs three very large meanders about its east–west axis. The first past Reading brings it on to the Tertiary outcrop but it then somewhat perversely turns its back upon the syncline and makes a large loop northwards past Henley back into the Chilterns, in a very attractive incised valley, before returning to the west–east line at Maidenhead. Downstream to Kew it then describes an even larger loop in the opposite direction reaching its most southerly point at the confluence of the Wey. Downstream through London and into the estuary the river continues to meander but never departs very far from its latitudinal course.

Three south bank tributaries of the Thames, the

Wey, Mole and Darent, have their sources in the Weald and cut across the North Downs in distinctive water gaps which, together with wind gaps at Farnham and Mersham, carry some of London's principal rail and road links with the south coast. Five other smaller tributaries, the Hogsmill, Beverley Brook, Wandle, Ravensbourne and Cray, have their origins in dip slope springs at the junction of the chalk and Tertiaries and drain most of the built up area south of the Thames. Only one north bank tributary, the Lea, breaches the Chiltern scarp but other Chiltern valleys drained southwards at their London ends by the Gade, Bulbourne and Misbourne head back into wind gaps which together with the Lea gap at Luton, carry most but not all, of the lines of communication by road, rail and canal from London to the Midlands. Other north bank tributaries, the Colne, Brent, the lower Lea and Roding owe their characters to the fact that at one stage in their histories they carried glacial meltwater from an ice sheet which invaded the Thames valley from the north-east.

The valley floors of the Thames and its main tributaries comprise their present flood plains together with two low gravel flood plain terraces a few metres above the floor plains (Fig. 2.2). In a later period of glaciation, when ice did not reach the London area, the Thames cut down the floor of its valley to a level 30 m below present sea level in response to a much-lowered sea level in the North Sea. Shallow trough-like valleys were eroded in the London Clay which later, as sea level rose, were filled with silts, clays, sands, gravels and brickearth 6–18 m thick in Westminster to a level up to 10 m above present sea level. Still later the Thames cut a channel in the gravelly deposits which was itself in turn later filled with alluvium.

During the past few thousand years the course of the Thames through central London has progressively migrated northwards across its flood plain, creating a series of *eyots* (or islands) and abandoned channels (Fig. 2.3). A place name ending *ey* or *ea*, as in Bermondsey and Chelsea, is descriptive of the local geomorphology. The flood plain alluvium varies in width but generally narrows upstream from the estuary. It was sufficiently narrow at the sites of London Bridge and Westminster Bridge, to be crossed in Roman times. In the latter case the crossing was facilitated by the existence of the Isle of Thorney, a small circum-alluviated knoll or eyot

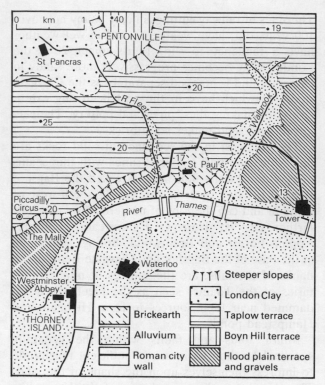

Figure 2.2 *Physiographic features of inner London.*

of flood plain terrace gravels, which became the site of the Palace of Westminster. The flood plain gravels contain much water and tunnels in the Underground have to be continuously pumped; between West Kensington and Temple stations, 6800 m³ of water are extracted daily. Isolated gravel-filled fissures in the London Clay below the flood plain gravels to depths of 23 m have been encountered in foundation works at Battersea and elsewhere, and these may be of a periglacial origin.

The construction of river embankments with deep foundations and building on the flood plains has not only prevented flooding but has completely transformed the natural scene. The prevention of the lateral spread of floodwater serves to raise the level of tide and flood peaks and so make necessary further raising of embankment levels. The weight of buildings on the flood plain and the abstraction of groundwater from below has resulted in consolidation of the ground and lowering of the surface.

The Thames terraces through London

The site of the Roman city of Londinium comprises

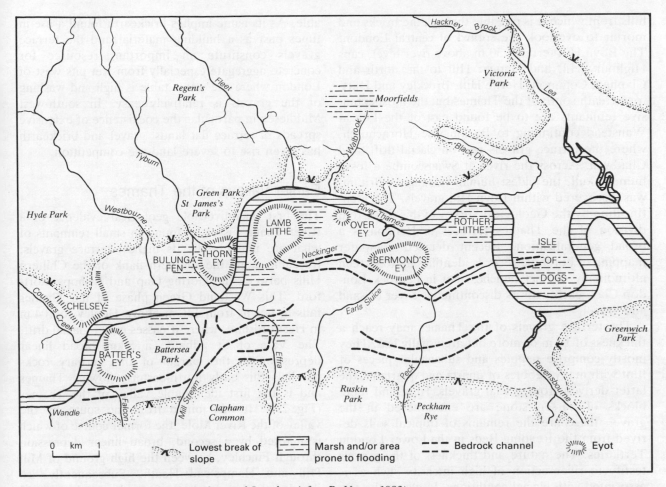

Figure 2.3   *The pre-urban setting of central London (after P. Nunn, 1983).*

three physiographic units. The east of the city, including the Tower, is located on the low flood plain terrace (Fig. 2.2), at the rear of which is the shallow incision of the Walbrook. Between Southwark and Blackfriars Bridges the Thames pushes against the north side of its valley floor. It has eliminated the flood plain terrace and directly undercuts a steep bluff, the flat top of which, some 15 m above the river is crowned by St Paul's Cathedral. This is a fragment of the Taplow terrace of the Thames, separated from a much more extensive spread of the same terrace throughout the West End, Hyde Park and Kensington by the valley of the Fleet river at Ludgate Circus. The Strand runs along the front edge of the terrace and Trafalgar Square is cut back into the bluff between the flood plain and Taplow terraces. Those familiar with the gradients of streets in the West End will appreciate that there is an upper and a lower Taplow terrace

but the distinction is not always easy to see because of the extent of building. North-eastwards the Taplow terrace underlies Hoxton. Shoreditch and much of Hackney, whilst Whitechapel, Stepney and Tower Hamlets are on the flood plain terrace. Upstream broad spreads of the Taplow terrace form the physical foundation of Hounslow, Heathrow Airport and Slough in the core of the great southward loop of the Thames. East of the Lea the same terrace is well preserved through Leyton, Wanstead Flats, Becontree Heath and South Ockendon. But south of the Thames the Taplow terrace is only preserved in scattered fragments, principally in the southwest at Putney and East Sheen.

Whilst extensive spreads of the flood plain terrace and Taplow terrace gravels remain relatively undissected and form well drained flat areas in the heart of London, the higher terraces through London are much more dissected and form flat-topped hills from which it is possible through the bricks and mortar to overlook the sprawl of central London. The Boyn Hill terrace, 30 m above river level, caps Highbury Hill and Hanger Hill to the north and Clapham Common, Herne Hill, Brockley and Dartford Heath south of the Thames but the most extensive remnants are to be found east of the Lea at Wanstead continuing to Barkingside–Hornchurch, where the terrace gravels rest on glacial drift, and Chadwell. Across the river at Swanscombe a fossil human skull, the oldest human remains in Britain, was discovered within Boyn Hill gravels. The identification by the Geological Survey of this three-fold division of the Thames terraces in London is a broad generalization. Recent detailed computer mapping of borehole records identifies up to sixteen altitudinally distinct benches, cut in bedrock London Clay, each with its discontinuous cover of sand and gravel.

The terrace gravels of the Thames may reach a thickness of 10 m or more but are usually less. They mostly comprise pebbles and subangular pieces of flint with many pebbles of quartz and quartzite, the latter derived from glacial gravels. Here and there blocks of Sarsen stone are encountered in the gravel, these are the remains of tropical soils derived from the Reading Beds in the Lower London Tertiaries. The nature and thickness of the gravels testify to river action of high intensity such as is associated with glacial conditions. In places the terraces are covered with brickearth, a mixture of silt and clay up to 6 m thick. Much of it is probably reworked London Clay transported by the Thames and redeposited in relatively still floodwaters but some may have been blown by the wind before deposition. Cappings of brickearth occur on the Taplow terrace in the City and around Covent Garden. Sir Christopher Wren described how it had to be removed in excavating the foundations for St Paul's. Similar spreads in south-west Middlesex and in the Lea Valley have constituted the pedological base of important market gardening areas.

Whenever holes are dug below the ground surface of the urbanized area of London the rubbish of man-made ground is exposed, not natural earth materials. In the City of Westminster this averages 3.5 m deep. The removal of soil and brickearth prior to building has in many areas counterbalanced this but the precise form and height of the natural land surface is in many areas no longer ascertain-

able. As its name implies brickearth found a use in times past as a building material and the terrace gravels constitute an important resource for concrete aggregate especially from wet pits west of London where the water table is high and washing of the gravels is relatively easy. In south-west Middlesex in particular the coexistence of extensive spreads of terrace flat lands, gravel and brickearth has given rise to severe land-use competition.

Earlier valleys of the Thames

The first unequivocable geological evidence of a River Thames is to be found in small remnants of what are undoubtedly its highest terrace gravels, traceable along the southern flank of the Chiltern Hills between the Goring Gap and Bishops Stortford. This Westland Green phase of the Thames falls in height from 146 m above Henley to 104 m in Hertfordshire, where it passes under glacial drift. The Vale of St Albans, a 5 km broad linear depression at the margin of the Tertiary rocks parallels this early north-easterly flowing Thames and is the first identifiable valley of the Thames (Fig. 2.4). It was joined from the south by the valley of the River Mole, the former course of which is marked by a second, broad linear depression through Finchley, between the high ground of Mill Hill and Hampstead Heath. Subsequently ice invaded the London basin from the north-east and diverted the Thames and Mole southwards into the present valley through London. The two abandoned valleys are prominent features in the relief of north London. Their floors are choked with glacial till and outwash gravels and it is evident from the distribution of the drift that ice tongues extended as far as Bricket Wood and Aldenham in the Vale of St Albans and Church End Finchley where a mass of boulder clay resting on the floor of the depression and pointing down the Brent Valley is probably the much eroded remains of a terminal moraine. The sub-drift floors of the two abandoned valleys are about 60 m above sea level and the Colne and the Brent are the descendants of the glacial meltwater rivers which drained from the ice tongues. The outwash gravels along the Colne, in the Vale of St Albans have been a valuable source of concrete aggregate since World War II. As the ice advanced up the valleys it dammed the Thames and Mole creating pro-glacial lake Hertford. It was overflow from this lake which probably initiated the breaches which led to the creation of the lower Lea, the Brent and the Colne and the diversion of the Thames. A smaller linear depression at Borehamwood, south of St Albans, may represent a course of the Thames during an earlier stage in the glacial diversion.

Three or more terraces appear to the west of the Colne, and seem to belong to the original valley through the vale of St Albans. They are the Winter Hill, Harefield, and Higher Gravel train, and together they form the distinctive, if subdued, staircase of the Beaconsfield gravel plateau, part of the Chiltern Hundreds. The three feature at a higher level than the flood plain, Taplow, Boyn Hill and Black Park terrace spreads (which belong to the diverted Thames valley through London) and lie between the Chiltern back slope and Slough.

The north-east of the London region is formed by the south-western fringe of the East Anglia boulder clay plateau, a thick series of glacial deposits drained to the Lea by the Rib, Ash and Stort. Along the latter, upstream of Harlow, run rail and motorway routes linking London with Cambridge via the Cam valley.

Hill-top gravels

The highest hills in and around London are all capped with variable thicknesses of gravel deposits. Hampstead Heath, Highgate Hill, Mill Hill, Totteridge, High Barnet, Shenley, in a line north from central London; Oxhey, Bushey Heath, Elstree and Arkley overlooking the Vale of St Albans; the Epping Forest ridge east of the Lea, Ongar, Brentwood, Billericay and the Laindon Hills in Essex; are all remnants of a plateau surface sloping north and east across the London basin at a height of approximately 120 m dating from a time when the proto-Thames was flowing north-eastwards along the line of the Vale of St Albans. Across this surface flowed south bank tributaries of the Thames, the ancestors of the Mole and Medway. Included in these hill-top gravels in north London are fragments of chert which could only have come from the Lower Greensand rocks of the Weald. Nothing of this plateau remains south of the Thames, where the highest hills form the Crystal Palace ridge and Shooters Hill.

During the last 2 000 000 years the Thames and its tributaries, under the influence of an episodically falling sea level and periods of arctic climatic conditions involving on occasions incursions of ice, have cut down from a height of about 120 m to their present levels, so creating the hill slopes and valleys on which London is built. The superficial deposits which characterize each stage in land form development from the highest, the Pebble Gravel, to the lowest terrace gravel have a tendency to move under gravity down valley and hill slopes. This was particularly so during cold wet glacial episodes. As a consequence most slopes in the London area are draped by a sheet of solifluction material, called head, about a metre thick comprising a trail of intermixed sand, gravel and clay derived from the hill-top deposits and the underlying clays which in slope-foot situations and in smaller valleys has accumulated to greater depths. It is this together with made ground which forms the present material of garden soils.

Landform regions

The combined influence of rock character, and erosion and depositional processes acting through time has produced in the London area a number of distinctive types of physical terrain (Fig. 2.4). They fall into four main categories, two highland and two lowland, in character. The lowlands comprise the valley lands of the Thames, its tributaries and former courses together with the clay plains of the London Clay outcrop. The hill lands comprise a great variety of dissected plateau and upland areas together with the bounding scarplands of the Chilterns and North Downs. Altogether there are some nineteen recognizable geomorphological regions over and into which the urban mesh of London extends.

At the core of the city is the floor of the Thames valley comprising its alluvial flood plain and the associated low gravel flood plain terraces. Similar valley floors characterize its main tributaries but that of the Lea is most extensive and merits recognition as a separate region. The broad spreads of the higher terraces of the Thames through London, especially the Taplow terrace, form the characteristic Thames-side gravel tracts. They are particularly prominent north of the river. The abandoned courses of the Thames and its tributary the Mole along the line of the Vale of St Albans and through

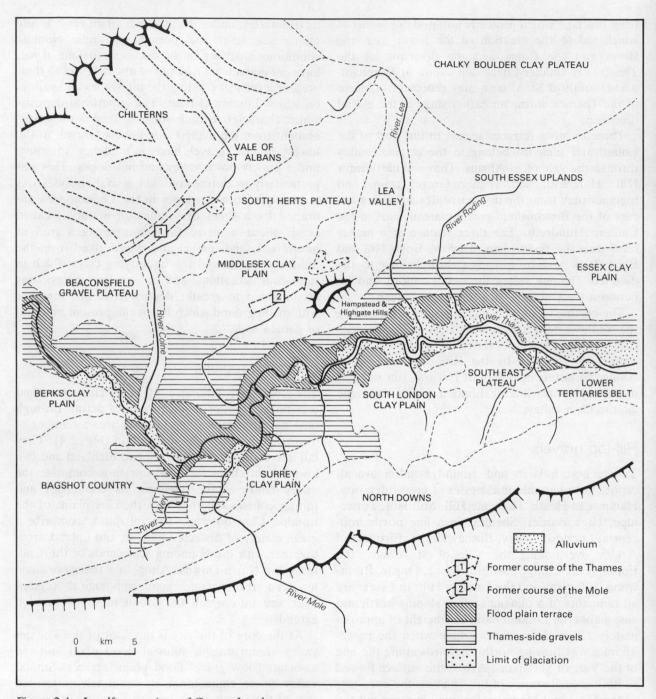

Figure 2.4 Landform regions of Greater London.

the Finchley depression constitute the remaining valley lands. There are five clay plains, which in detail are featureless, gently undulating regions but in places are studded with conspicuous residual hills such as Harrow Hill in Middlesex and the Norwood hills in south London. The clay plains in Middlesex,

south London and Essex were areas of great suburban expansion during the inter-war years.

The most prominent of the hill lands within the built up area of London are the north London heights of Hampstead and Highgate and their continuation north of the Finchley depression in the flat-topped hills of the south Hertfordshire plateau extending north to the Vale of St Albans. This high ground which rims the Thames valley to the north continues westwards through Bushey Heath to Harefield and thence across the Colne Valley, westwards into the staircase of higher terraces of the Thames in the Beaconsfield gravel plateau. East of the Lea the South Essex uplands extend eastwards from the Epping ridge to Brentwood giving way northwards to the boulder clay plateau of east Hertfordshire and Essex. The two plateau areas south of the Thames – the Bagshot country in the south west and that around Chislehurst and Bromley – owe their distinctive characters to the underlying outcrops of sandy Bagshot Beds and pebbly Blackheath beds respectively. Their surface characteristics contrast markedly with those of the adjacent clay plains.

The Chilterns and North Downs are chalk upland plateaux in a state of youthful dissection, trenched by sub-parallel valleys most of which are dry. The interfluves are mantled with a variety of clays, silts, sands and gravels of diverse origins and the valleys are floored with gravels and solifluction deposits such that the chalk bedrock is rarely to be seen exposed except on the steepest valley sides and on the bounding escarpments, the crests of which reach 240–50 m above sea level. The outcrops of the Lower London Tertiary rocks north of the North Downs form distinctive belts of subdued relief and relatively good and easily worked soils between the outcrops of the chalk and London Clay.

Prelude to London's growth

The physical site of London lacks spectacular features. But like most of the world's large cities it's growth and development has, in part at least, been in response to the subdued relief of its site which has not made that growth unduly difficult in terms of the character of its slopes, bedrock and surface drainage. Favourable elements in its situation have allowed relative ease of communication by water and land. Its nucleus was located near the tidal limit of the Thames where the alluvium of the flood plain narrowed and low gravel terraces on either side facilitated bridging. A steep bluff capped by a higher gravel terrace and undercut by the river provided the site of the core of what became the commercial city. Both it and the Royal City of Westminster on the lower gravel terrace upstream and linked to the City by the Strand along the top of the bluff, were able to extend northwards over the level well-drained surface of the Taplow terrace. Farther afield small villages grew up, invariably located on slightly higher ground within the sea of the London Clay outcrop, where permeable caps of sand and gravel provided at one and the same time well-drained soils and foundations and a source of water from springs and shallow wells in the capping. In the nineteenth and twentieth centuries these dry point villages have become the administrative and shopping centres of the suburban boroughs as the tide of bricks, slate, tile, concrete and tarmacadam flowed over the terraces and the clay plains of north and south London. The valleys of tributaries of the Thames served as avenues for London's expansion up valleys such as the Lea and Wandle, and lines of communication by road, rail and canal with the rest of England frequently, but not inevitably, made use of valley routes provided by the Thames and its tributaries through and beyond the bounding chalk uplands. The seemingly unchanging land has made its not unsubstantial contribution to changing London.

Further reading

British Regional Geology (1960) *London and the Thames Valley* HMSO

Davies G M (1939) *Geology of London and South-East England* Murby

Jones D K C (ed) (1980) *The Shaping of Southern England* Institute of British Geographers, Special Publication, Academic Press

Jones D K C (1981) *The Geomorphology of the British Isles: Southeast and Southern England* Methuen

Nunn P D (1983) 'The development of the River Thames in central London during the Flandrian' *Transactions, Institute of British Geographers* NS8: 187–213

Woodward H B (1922) *The Geology of the London District* Memoirs of the Geological Survey

Wooldridge S W and Hutchings G E (1957) *London's Countryside* Methuen

Wooldridge S W and Linton D L (1955) *Structure, Surface and Drainage in South-East England* Philip

3 London's beginnings

Hugh Clout

Environmental context

Modern London is a large and complicated city, with a bewildering variety of buildings, townscapes and neighbourhoods that have been brought into being over many centuries as a result of the actions of millions of decision makers. These individuals and groups evaluated conditions in the light of their own value systems and lived experience, which were very different from those of the world of today. They had varying degrees of wealth and political or social power to exploit land, labour and other resources in order to achieve their objectives, and thereby fashion the structure and appearance of their city. Over the centuries London has expanded outwards and numerous features have been added as old buildings and streets have been adapted or replaced to attempt to meet contemporary needs.

London has changed and continues to change with every day that passes, but the legacy of the past remains firmly imprinted in the present, not just in obvious ways, like the presence of historic buildings or the survival of old road systems, but also in hidden ways, such as the persistence of ancient rules and regulations, or of historic patterns of land ownership, corporate influence and administrative boundaries. In addition, London still displays interesting parallels between past and present in the relations between richer and poorer districts, whether in the context of the suburbs and the inner city or the 'East End' as opposed to the 'West End'. The present chapter and the two that follow seek to explore the evolution of London through two thousand years of history in the belief that evidence from the past may be used to help understand much of the geography of the present.

Two thousand years ago the landscapes of south-east Britain had been changed relatively little by human action. Technology was simple and the challenges of clearing the land of its natural vegetation and working it successfully for food production were formidable. However, there is no doubt that some stretches of relatively light soil had been cleared and brought into cultivation. For example, excavations near Heathrow have revealed the remains of circular huts, with pits, drainage ditches, pottery and bones of livestock, indicating occupation from before 2000 BC to Roman times (Fig. 3.1). Doubtless other patches of brickearth and gravel and terrace sites elsewhere in the London basin were favoured for early human occupation in a similar way.

By contrast, most of the rest of the region was clothed with woodland which was particularly thick and impenetrable on stretches of London Clay (for example in Middlesex) and in some parts of the Weald, where expanses of trees alternated with patches of marsh. Undoubtedly these wooded clay-lands presented substantial obstacles to movement but travelling across the well-drained river terraces would not have been too difficult. The damp alluvial flood plains of the Thames and its tributaries supported a variety of plant and animal life that could be exploited for food and for obtaining such commodities as reeds for thatching. As a general rule movement by river was easier than overland and excavations have discovered pottery and other artifacts that indicate that water-based trade operated between the Thames valley and a number of locations on the Continent.

Roman London

This array of environmental resources awaited the arrival of the Romans. Julius Caesar brought a military force to south-east Britain in 54 BC and met

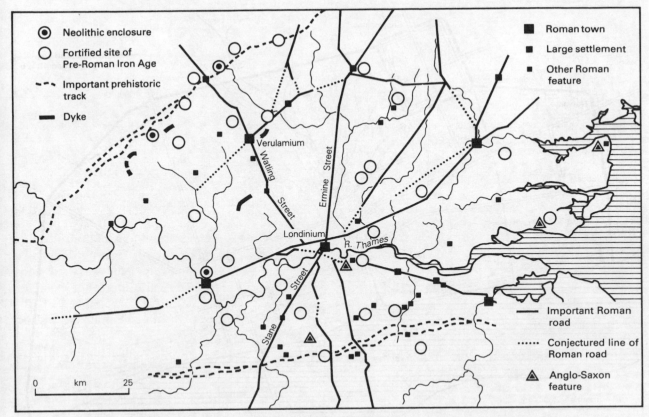

Figure 3.1   *Aspects of the archaeology of the London region (after F. Merrifield 1975).*

with fierce opposition from local tribes. By contrast, a second invasion led by Claudius in AD 43 was more successful. Colchester and other coastal ports provided suitable starting points for the Roman occupation of lowland Britain but other settlements were needed to command the interior and to control waterways that provided the essential links with territories across the Channel. Emperor Claudius' new possession needed such a control point and an area at the upstream limit of tidal navigation in the Thames valley appeared appropriate to satisfy these requirements.

This *situation* was well into the interior of the south-east but could also be reached easily by sea-going vessels. It was also an appropriate location to provide a river crossing for routeways on land. The Roman road, known as Watling Street, was laid out between Dover and Verulamium (St Albans), but how the Thames was first negotiated is not known (Fig. 3.1). There may have been a fording point through the marshes of Chelsea or Westminster but

very soon a rough wooden bridge was built just a little further to the east.

Despite legends to the contrary, there is no archaeological evidence that the sharply rising ground to the north of the bridgehead had been occupied before the Romans. In fact, it now seems indisputable that the location of London, while not completely deserted, had attracted no major settlement and was of no special importance until the Romans founded their town. The precise *site* comprised gravel-capped sections of the Taplow terrace, which formed twin hills with flattish summits, a little above 15 m in elevation. They were located between three small southward-flowing tributaries; the Fleet to the west, the Walbrook in the centre, and the Houndsditch (or Tower Brook) to the east (Fig. 3.2).

Of course the fundamental geomorphology of inner London has been modified by the debris of almost two thousand years of human occupation which has covered the 'natural' surface with a

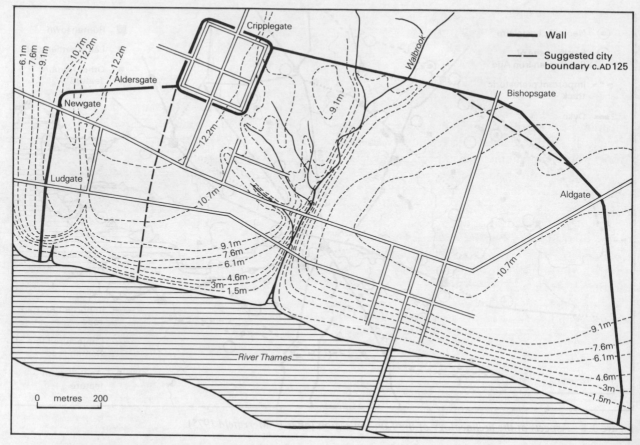

Figure 3.2   *Roman London (after City of London Archaeological Trust, 1980).*

mantle of 'made ground' of varying thickness. Land along the riverfront has been reclaimed and the three small tributaries and many others have long been culverted underground to function as sewers. The detail has certainly changed but anyone who takes even a short walk in central London soon becomes aware of the location of the valleys, the terrace levels and the rising ground between them. Considerable geographical imagination is needed, however, to begin to appreciate the opportunities that this site offered to the Roman invaders.

It is probable that they constructed a fort first of all, to which a civilian settlement was added. The eastern hill was chosen for this earliest phase of settlement and was given the name 'Londinium', which derived either from British settlers living in the district or from an earlier settlement across the Channel. East of the Walbrook two parallel east-west roads were laid out and soon after AD 50 a number of large timber framed buildings had been

constructed in the area that was to become the town centre. In AD 60 came the first definite mention of London, being described by Tacitus as a celebrated centre of commerce that was filled with traders. But despite such enthusiasm, the original Roman city was small and vulnerable to attack, indeed it was burned to the ground in the very same year during the revolt of the Iceni, led by the formidable Queen Boudicca.

The settlement was rebuilt and enlarged and by AD 125 the fort (to the north-west) and probably also the forum (with its basilica, court house and shops) had been built. In addition, Londinium was equipped with monuments, baths and appropriate buildings for the governor. A disastrous fire, probably accidental this time, devastated the greater part of the city in AD 130, which excavations have shown to have covered at least 25 ha, a substantially larger surface than in AD 60. The setback was only temporary and the settlement continued to expand, especially on its western side. A new boundary was formalized soon after AD 200 by a great defensive wall, 3 km long and incorporating the existing stone defences of the fort. The wall was built of Kentish ragstone (brought to London by river) and encompassed both hills and a total area of 130 ha.

Roman roads led through six great landward gates into the surrounding countryside and another stretch of wall defended the city along the waterfront, where embankments had been constructed to either side of the bridge. Contemporary writings and the results of archaeological excavations reveal that as well as being a military stronghold and a centre of government, Londinium was an important focus of trade and had its own mint for making coins. There is no way of knowing how many people lived in the area enclosed by its walls. Estimates (Table 3.1) suggest 20 000 in AD 200 (perhaps roughly 2 per cent of the population of what is now England and Wales) and 40 to 50 000 in AD 300 (maybe 4 per cent of the total).

From Londinium to Lundenwic

The greatness of Londinium was in fact established on a fragile base and the barbarian invasion

of 367–8 may have necessitated the city walls being strengthened. But when the Roman legions withdrew from Britain in 410 the city is believed to have entered a long period of decline. Very little is known of what happened during the next two hundred years but the town had certainly experienced a measure of recovery by the middle of the seventh century, with St Paul's Cathedral having been founded by the Anglo-Saxon king of Kent in 604. In more general terms, the return of the church of Rome revived other elements of Roman culture, such as a degree of literacy, construction of important buildings in brick or stone (often taken from Roman ruins), and an economy in which money was employed as a means of exchange.

During the troubled seventh, eighth and ninth centuries London was once again a major focus of trade and coin manufacture, and was a royal residence as well as an ecclesiastical centre. There is relatively little archaeological evidence relating to early Anglo-Saxon London within the line of the ancient defences. One theory has been that early Anglo-Saxon invaders by-passed the site of Londinium and established a number of smaller settlements in what is now suburban London. In mid-1984 a new interpretation was advanced from

Table 3.1   *The growth of the population of London (figures in thousands)*

	The City	Rest of London	Total London	England and Wales	London as % of England and Wales
*c.*200	20		20	1 000	2
*c.*1100	15		15	1 500	1
*c.*1400	45		45	2 250	2
*c.*1500	75		75	3 000	2.5
*c.*1600	186	34	220	4 500	5
*c.*1700	208	367	575	6 000	9.6
1801	128	831	959*	8 890	10.8
			(1 117)+		(12.6)
1851	128	2 235	2 363*	17 983	13.1
			(2 685)+		(14.9)
1901	27	4 398	4 425*	32 612	13.6
			(6 586)+		(20.2)
1951	5	8 188	8 193+	43 758	18.7

* = 'Total London' defined as the City plus the rest of the London County Council area
+ = City plus the rest of the Greater London Council Area

All figures prior to 1801 are estimates

Source: Mitchell B R and Deane P (1962) *Abstract of British Historical Statistics* Cambridge University Press

the evidence of a range of fragmented artefacts assembled from locations to the west of the Roman city. This identified a well-developed, eighth-century settlement, involving trade and industry, extending westwards from the old city. The place-name 'Aldwych' may evoke this 'old trading place', stormed in 851 and remaining in Danish control for thirty-five years until it was recaptured by the Anglo-Saxon King Alfred in 886. The new interpretation argues that at this time the Anglo-Saxons moved to the security of the ancient walls and indeed reconstructed them along the Roman foundations. New buildings were erected on the space that they enclosed during the following centuries of Anglo-Saxon peace. 'Lundenwic' supported markets to either side of the Walbrook, and a small settlement flourished on the bridgehead of the southern banks of the Thames (Fig. 3.3). The Danes launched further attacks, starting in 982, and the realm of England finally submitted to them in 1013. Half a century later London passed into the

hands of new masters following the Norman conquest of 1066.

Medieval London

Despite the upheavals of the preceding two centuries, William the Conqueror found London to be a flourishing port, with important trading links across the Channel and the North Sea. But the city probably housed substantially fewer people than at the peak of Roman times, with estimates for the year 1100 being no more than 15 000, by comparison with perhaps four times that number for the year 300. The newly-won prize needed effective defence and soon after the conquest a wooden castle was erected alongside the Thames at the eastern edge of the city, since any future enemy would probably approach along the river. By 1097 this simple compound had been replaced by a solid keep (the White Tower) using foundation stones from the Roman wall and special Caen limestone that had

Figure 3.3   *Anglo-Saxon London (after City of London Archaeological Trust, 1980).*

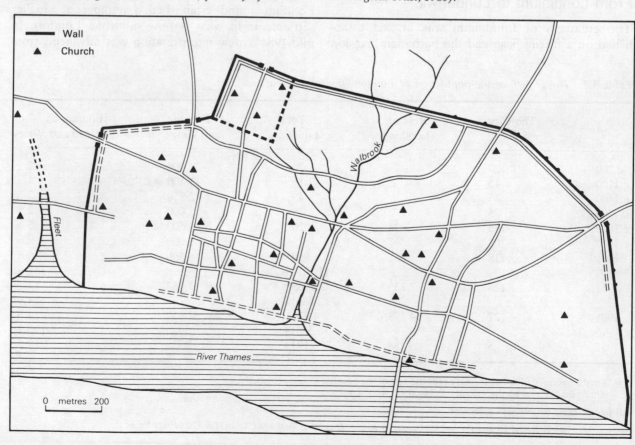

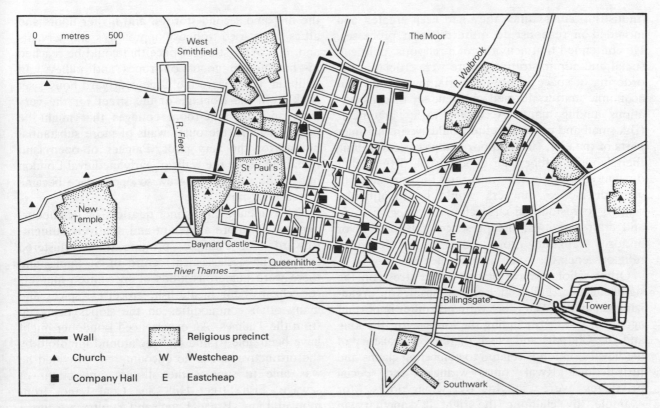

Figure 3.4   *Medieval London (after R Clayton, 1964).*

been carried by boat from France. This eastern castle remains at the core of the Tower of London. Two smaller strongholds were constructed on the western edge of the walled city, in the form of Baynard's Castle and Montfitchet Tower (Fig. 3.4).

Another nucleus of settlement was in existence a little way upstream on a patch of gravel, known as Thorney island, in the midst of marshland. The Saxon church of St Peter-on-Thorney had been founded in 785 and had been replaced by a great cruciform abbey by the pious Anglo-Saxon King Edward the Confessor. The Norman kings chose this place as their seat of residence and government, and a great hall was built adjacent to the 'church in the west' (Westminster). However, the population of this royal and ecclesiastical settlement was very small. Medieval London corresponded essentially with 'the City' within the line of the Roman walls but it increased its population from 15 000 in 1100, to perhaps 45 000 in 1400 (close to the estimate for the year 300) and 75 000 in 1500.

This expansion was, of course, during the 'pre-industrial' phase, long before factory-based mech-

anized production and at a time when the use of urban space was organized according to a logic quite different from twentieth-century ideas of economic rationalization. Historians characterize pre-industrial towns as possessing several of the following features: a marked concentration of population; specialist economic roles; a fairly sophisticated political structure; and an organizing function that extended beyond the immediate limits of the settlement. Charters defined the rights, privileges and freedoms of townsmen, in what was otherwise a feudal society; and guilds and other craft 'companies' were highly influential in the organization of urban life. The guilds worked to manage the production of goods and the operation of trade, to control quality and prices, and to safeguard business interests, especially those of their members. Apprenticeship and eventual membership of a guild endowed a man with status and privileges that he guarded jealously.

In 1960 the American scholar Gideon Sjoberg argued that pre-industrial cities did not display the kind of spatial pattern that was to be found in later 'industrial' cities, since they had been created and moulded in response to quite different processes. He contended that activities of a religious, political, social and administrative nature were crucial in the ordering of space in pre-industrial towns, and that economic matters formed only one set of considerations among many. According to his argument: (i) a small and powerful elite would live in the inner parts of the city, (ii) the poor and powerless (selling their labour, rather than goods) would live further out but still within the walls, and (iii) a number of very distinctive quarters would be identifiable, related to residential characteristics, specific trade and craft activities, the presence of foreigners or minority religious groups, and the existence of religious enclaves, such as monasteries.

Other scholars have placed added stress on the significance of guilds and city companies in organizing urban life. But there were also other important agents of power (including the lord mayor, the king and the Church) and much of the social history of medieval London is related to competing claims and jurisdictions. Rival courts wrangled and special privileges were sought by wrong-doers, for example, by claiming the right of sanctuary in church premises or fleeing across the bridge to Southwark or to other districts outside the jurisdiction of the guilds, companies and lord mayor. On a somewhat broader scale, there were fluctuating but serious tensions between the government of London and the national government, between lord mayors, guilds, parliament and the monarchy.

Comprehensive information is not available on the distribution of rich and poor households in medieval London but descriptions talk of concentrations of wealth close to the riverfront and statistics dating from the seventeenth century show that well-to-do households tended to cluster at two foci near the northern end of the bridge, and close to St Paul's Cathedral, with the poor living in outer parts of the walled city and beyond it. At least three types of house were found in the medieval city. The first and most common comprised tall buildings of three or more storeys that were packed on narrow elongated plots, with 'penthouses' or 'jetties' overhanging narrow streets and lanes, and sheds and outhouses squeezed into any available space behind the houses. Functions tended to be separated vertically, with retailing and craft activities on the ground floor, masters and their families living on the first and second storeys, and higher floors and attics being used to house apprentices and servants and to provide storage space that could be reached by hauling up goods on ropes and pulleys. In addition, there were the large courtyard houses set back from the frontage of the street for the very rich, and tiny one-room cottages that might be packed against the outer walls of more substantial houses for the very poor. Patches of open land remained inside the walls of early medieval London but as the population grew so open space became increasingly rare.

The evidence on distinct quarters or neighbourhoods is far more abundant and relatively straightforward. For example, printing trades clustered around the ecclesiastical centre of St Paul's and there were numerous kinds of specialized markets (or 'cheaps') for meat, fish, groceries, spices and many other commodities on the slopes rising up from the Thames. An experienced Londoner might have been able to find his way around blindfold by the distinctive smells he encountered, provided he was able to supress the all-pervading odour of sewage. Fish Street Hill, Sea Coal Lane, Ironmonger Lane, Bread Lane, and Poultry are just a handful of the scores of street names that recall their specialized functions. However, other traders, such as sellers of firewood and vegetables, tended to be relatively mobile and did not cluster in distinctive quarters.

Transportation by water was much easier and cheaper than along the poor roads and London's port handled large quantities of corn, fish and other foodstuffs, as well as timber and other building materials, and a great variety of precious goods. All dutiable merchandise imported into the City had to be unloaded at the 'legal quays' on the north bank of the river. Hence the port formed a very distinctive district, including marginal quays along the Thames, areas at the mouth of tributary valleys (for example the Fleet and Walbrook), and specially constructed docks or 'hithes'. Some foreigners lived in separate neighbourhoods, notably Jewish traders (who had come to England with the Normans but were expelled to the Continent in 1290) and Hanseatic merchants from northern Germany, who occupied the Steel Yard alongside the Thames until they too were expelled in 1598. By contrast, Flemings, Dutch, French and Walloons assimilated far more easily into the mass of the city's people.

Medieval London had over one hundred parish churches and these played important roles in organizing social, community and ceremonial life. In addition, the city had nearly a score of religious precincts that had been established in some profusion between 1100 and 1300 and covered extensive areas both within and immediately beyond the walls (Fig. 3.4). Many of these combined several functions, including that of a church, school, hospital and old people's home. Notable examples of enclaves include St Bartholomew's priory and hospital at Smithfield (founded in 1123), Charterhouse monastery (dating from 1371), the nunnery and hospital of St John of Jerusalem, the Templars' church, and the religious house of Blackfriars established by the Dominicans in the thirteenth century. These enclaves provided very real obstacles to house building but they were to become ripe for redevelopment following the dissolution of the monasteries in the sixteenth century. The marshy area of the upper Walbrook known as Moorfields, to the north of the city wall, formed another impediment to expansion until effective drainage was introduced in the seventeenth century to replace culverts that had been installed in Roman times. However this district provided important recreation space for Londoners.

Not all functions were welcomed by the city fathers, the guildsmen or the great companies, and were either removed or kept outside the walls. For example, slaughterhouses and livestock markets were relocated at Smithfield beyond the walls, although these functions had been carried out in the heart of the city in early medieval times. Noxious industries were banned with, for example, the tanners of the lower Fleet valley being forced during the fourteenth century to relocate at Bermondsey on the south bank of the Thames. Other polluting activities were established near the port, while beyond the eastern walls of the city many migrants and refugees settled, bringing their skills and trades to the incipient 'East End' but not to the City. This caused considerable disquiet among the guilds and companies since their rules and regulations normally did not extend that far, despite numerous and repeated attempts to extend their jurisdiction.

The city fathers also tried to control the economic challenge that the inflow of large numbers of migrants represented to their established interests, by ruling that new buildings should not be put up beyond the walls. As a result of this prohibition, old buildings inside the City were patched up and extended by digging cellars and tacking on back rooms and additional attics. Many more one-room cottages were pushed on to any available scrap of land. All this activity served to increase the density of population in the City. But the prohibition on building outside the walls was defied, and cheap, poorly-constructed housing was installed on the eastern side where the demand for somewhere to live was particularly great. This stemmed from the large numbers of migrants who reached London along the Thames, docking either at its legal quays or further downstream or travelling overland from the rich, fertile and densely populated agricultural areas of south-eastern England and East Anglia.

Not surprisingly the intensity of farming activity and land fragmentation was greater to the east of London than to the west, where land tended to be held in large blocks or estates that were often in the hands of powerful and tenacious religious institutions, such as the abbey of Westminster. With housing demand being concentrated there and farmland being fragmented into convenient small parcels, important medieval suburbs developed to the east of the City and provided housing for large numbers of humble workers as well as more comfortable traders. The social contrast between 'East End' and 'West End' was already established but was to become much more pronounced in later centuries.

A different world also existed across the Thames, beyond the complex rules and regulations of the City. The ancient patched timber bridge had been replaced by a stone structure in 1209. Houses, shops and even a chapel were built on the new bridge and the taxes levied from them helped to pay for its upkeep. At curfew the bridge was closed until morning and hence a range of distinctive functions developed at Southwark where a causeway cut through riverside marshland to link the southern end of the bridge to dry land. Numerous inns and hostelries catered for travellers who arrived too late to enter the City, and pleasure grounds, brothels and places of entertainment were also found on the south bank, sometimes in properties owned by the Church (for example the estates of the Bishop of Winchester, the Archbishop of Canterbury, and the Abbot of Bermondsey). Such goings-on provoked consternation among the City fathers, who eventually succeeded in having Southwark declared a ward of the City of London in 1550. But the rules were not enforced strictly and vagrants and 'marginal' members of medieval society continued to live in close proximity to more respectable people in Southwark.

Medieval London grew impressively to reach 75 000 inhabitants in 1500 but it remained a remarkably fragile city in both physical and human terms. Its densely packed houses were usually constructed of timber and they remained vulnerable to fire, even though thatch had been banned in 1189 in favour of tiles. Stone from south-eastern England (for example Kentish rag and Reigate stone) or from France (Caen stone) was incorporated in many of the City's churches but their structures also included a great deal of timber. The Anglo-Saxon cathedral of St Paul's had been burned down in 1087 but its vast medieval replacement was also made predominantly of timber, with a massive spire dominating the whole City.

Medieval London was also vulnerable in human terms. Mortality rates were high, and constant in-migration was necessary for the city to maintain its population numbers, let alone experience any growth. Every year large numbers of young people came to London as apprentices and servants. Most came from south-east England but more distant parts of the kingdom also made their contribution as the fame of the city spread far and wide. Some married and produced families of their own, but many died young because of poor hygiene and the onslaught of epidemics.

As well as this diet of human beings, the monster that was medieval London needed to consume humbler fare, and the satisfaction of these requirements stimulate very important economic and social changes in the English countryside. More and more villages geared at least a share of their farming activities to the needs of the London market and large quantities of perishable food were daily sent by road and especially by water. Good supplies of drinking water were also essential if London's citizens were to survive. Local springs, shallow wells sunk into gravels overlying clay, and the Thames itself provided the earliest supplies but each of these sources became polluted with the passage of time as a result of seepage and the rudimentary disposal of human waste and domestic and industrial garbage.

Foreign visitors complained about the pollution of the Thames and the odour coming from clothes that had been freshly laundered in it. Far more serious than the smell were the micro-organisms that were entering human bodies through ordinary drinking water! As early as the thirteenth century conduits had been made of elm trunks to bring fresh water to the City from the Tyburn (near Marylebone) and later schemes brought supplies from Hackney and Hampstead. But these projects were tiny in relation to the drinking-water needs of the rapidly increasing population. For most medieval Londoners, simple survival was an unrelenting, harsh and very real struggle against the forces of death.

Further reading

The historical evolution of London is presented in various popular accounts:

Barker F and Jackson P (1974) *London: 2000 Years of a City and its People* Macmillan

Dalzell W R (1981) *The Shell Guide to the History of London* Michael Joseph

Gray R (1978) *A History of London* Hutchinson

Hibbert C (1980) *London: the Biography of a City* Penguin

Kiek J (1984) *Everybody's Historic London* Quiller Press

Archaeological findings are summarized in:

Biddle M (1973) *The Future of London's Past* Rescue

Merrifield F (1975) *The Archaeology of London* Heinemann

Information on aspects of the site, situation and early growth of London is found in:

Barton N (1962) *The Lost Rivers of London* Phoenix House

Clayton R (ed) (1964) *The Geography of Greater London* Philip

Nunn P D (1983) 'The development of the River Thames in central London' *Transactions, Institute of British Geographers* **8**: 187–213

Schofield J (1984) *The Building of London from the Conquest to the Great Fire* Colonnade

The classic discussion of pre-industrial urbanization is:

Sjoberg G (1960) *The Pre-Industrial City* Free Press, New York

4 London in transition

Hugh Clout

Toward the first 'million' city

During the three centuries between 1500 and 1800 London experienced a long but far from uninterrupted period of population growth, with the number of Londoners rising from 75 000 (some 2.5 per cent of the population of England and Wales) in 1500 to 1 000 000 by 1790 and 1 117 000 at the time of the first official census in 1801, when one out of every eight residents in England and Wales was living in the London area (Table 3.1). In the words of the report that accompanied that census, London was '. . . the Metropolis of England, at once the Seat of Government and the greatest Emporium in the known world'. In the next fifty years the city's population was to more than double to reach 2 600 000, some 15 per cent of the total.

Over the same span of centuries the spatial extent of London increased enormously. The City became linked to the historic nucleus of Westminster by a line of housing along the Strand (where the legal quarter occupied a kind of neutral ground between the forces of commerce and the Crown) and by blocks of new construction further north. New building was taking place in other directions as well, as Fig. 4.1, which depicts conditions at the middle of the eighteenth century, shows very clearly. The pattern and timing of expansion occurred in different ways in different districts and it is helpful to recognize five main components within the London area.

(i) The City of London itself had to contend with and recover from two massive disasters in the 1660s, namely the Great Plague (1665) and the Great Fire (1666). Many rich City-dwellers subsequently moved to new accommodation further to the west.

(ii) In this western area a wave of new, 'planned' building occurred on former Church-owned estates, following the dissolution of the monasteries which started in 1536–8 and the sale of Church lands to the nobility and to other rich purchasers.

(iii) By contrast, expansion to the east of the City continued in a rather more piecemeal fashion, in response to continued in-migration and the remarkable dynamism of the port.

(iv) In addition, the development of the south bank was made possible after 1750 by the construction of new bridges which opened the way for a less lopsided pattern of growth than in earlier centuries.

(v) Finally, large numbers of surrounding settlements were drawn increasingly into London's orbit, functioning as recreation space for its citizens and as food-supply areas.

All this expansion was made possible and indeed necessary by the rapid advance of Britain as a trading and colonial nation. As well as being national capital and major port, London flourished as the leading nerve centre for British commercial activities (being truly a merchants' city) and as administrative headquarters for the whole empire. Its growth and vitality between 1500 and the early nineteenth century was truly remarkable and was all the more striking since it was achieved before mechanization of any kind had become generalized or widespread.

Under such circumstances, to guarantee adequate food supplies and to attempt to provide fresh water continued to represent major challenges. For example, in 1582 a tidal water wheel was installed at the northern end of London Bridge to pump water from the Thames into conduits whence it was distributed by carriers. The pump continued to function until 1817 despite the fact that river water

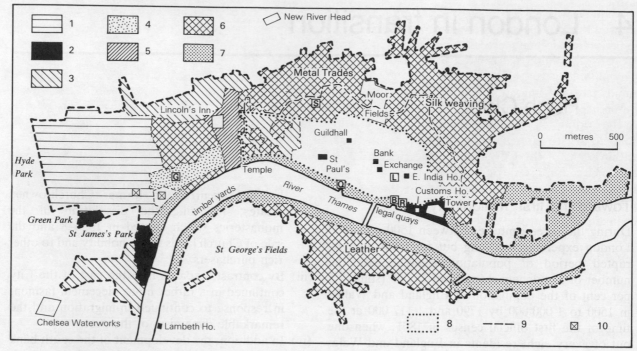

Figure 4.1 *London, c. 1750 (after O. Spate, 1936).*

1. Aristocratic residential quarter;
2. Government;
3. Middle-class and professional residences;
4. Amusements;
5. Legal quarter;
6. Industrial areas and artisans' dwellings;
7. Wharfs, warehouses, waterside trades and labourers' dwellings;
8. Commerce and finance in 'the City';
9. Boundary of the City Liberties;

10. West End shopping, around Haymarket and Charing Cross.

Main markets:
S, Smithfield (meat, malt);
L, Leadenhall (meat, provisions, leather);
G, Covent Garden;
Q, Queenhithe (corn, meal, malt);
B, Billingsgate (fish);
R, Roomland (coal).

was seriously polluted and there was no provision for purification. Hugh Middleton's New River project of 1613 was far more satisfactory and brought water 65 km from the clean upper stretches of the Lea valley to Islington, whence it was carted, carried, or very unusually, piped to a minority of the inhabitants of the City. Several other water-supply companies were formed during the eighteenth century; some took fresh water from the lower Lea and from springs at Hampstead but others made use of water direct from the Thames. The Chelsea Water Company (established in 1723) had the specific objective of serving the new western estates and made early use of iron pipes and filter beds to attempt to purify the supply. Other companies were less concerned about water quality, with the south bank being served by three that took water direct from the Thames between Vauxhall and Southwark.

The City of London

The City itself was growing rapidly, with its population rising from 75 000 in 1500 to about 208 000 in 1700. Thereafter the number of its residents declined and the real growth of the capital occurred in outer areas. The dissolution of London's monastic houses freed land for new building activities within the walls and enabled former Church property to be converted for housing and other purposes, at a time when extra accommodation was needed desperately. By about 1550 a veritable 'building boom' was underway and before the end of the sixteenth century the old walled City was pretty well saturated with housing. By 1600 its population was not far short of 200 000 (Table 3.1) and it is clear that the massive increase of the preceding century had been made possible by much subdivision and extension of buildings as well as new construction.

John Stow's great *Survey of London* (1598) showed that the City walls and gates were generally in good repair and gave clear evidence that the growth of London had spread well beyond them. City authorities and the Crown were alarmed at the rapid rate of migration to the capital and an outbreak of plague in 1563 was attributed in part to overcrowding. A royal proclamation was issued in 1580 to try to stop building on new foundations within 5 km of the City in order to safeguard law and order, improve living conditions, and reduce the galloping demand for more food supplies. Other proclamations followed in 1593 and 1602 but to no avail. In addition, the City fathers tried to halt the subdivision of old houses into small units (a process known as 'pestering') but they were equally unsuccessful. Unlike many Continental cities, no new walls were built around London at a later date but a temporary ring of earthworks, forts and ditches was established in 1642–3 during the Civil War, running from Wapping to Westminster and from Lambeth to Rotherhithe.

As we have seen, London life was remarkably unhealthy and periodic outbreaks of disease, of varying impact, were very much a characteristic of the capital. For example, it has been estimated that the Black Death of 1349 had claimed up to half the city's population, with up to 200 victims being shovelled each day into the plague pits of Smithfield at the peak of the epidemic between February and April. Later outbreaks of plague claimed 30 000 London victims in 1603 and perhaps 40 000 in 1625. However, the Great Plague of 1665 was of quite a different magnitude, with about 100 000 people dying as a result of the disease.

The second major disaster to befall Restoration London came with the Great Fire of 2–5 September 1666, which began in a bakery in Pudding Lane but spread quickly to riverside cellars and warehouses where inflammable materials were stored. Sparks even drifted across the Thames to cause damage on the south bank but the real effects were in the City itself. Human losses were minimal, but as Samuel Pepys and other observers recorded, enormous devastation was caused to the fabric of London (Fig. 4.2). In just four days the work of centuries

Figure 4.2 *London's transition from medieval to Georgian times.*

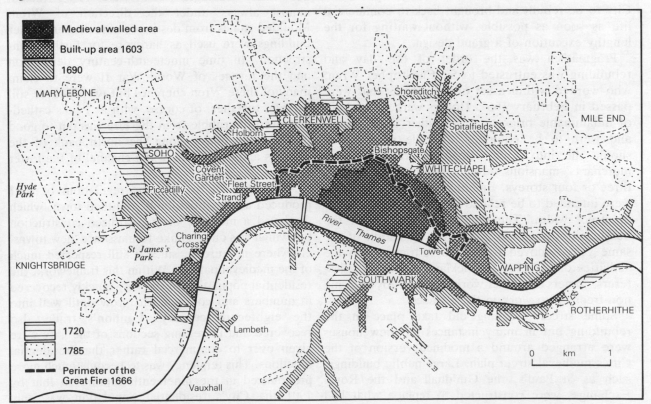

was destroyed over a large area, stretching for 2 km along the Thames and for almost 1 km back into the heart of the City. No less than five-sixths of the walled area was destroyed, eighty-six churches were lost, together with the cathedral of St Paul's, and almost 11 000 dwellings.

Numerous designs were put forward for rebuilding the devastated area varying from the idealistic to the severely realistic. With the wisdom of hindsight it might seem that this was a great opportunity to reorganize London into an elegant, functional and well-ordered city. But there were other important matters to be considered. First, the burned-out city only appeared to be an empty space; in fact the land on which it had stood was still owned by many individuals and organizations whose property rights and potential claims for compensation would have to be respected in any rebuilding scheme. Second, the devastation of London and the decline of its population caused by the Plague and temporary out-migration after the Fire was of great concern to the city fathers, since it worked to the advantage of England's trading rivals, most notably the Dutch. Not surprisingly there were strong pressures from London merchants and other power groups for the City to be rebuilt and brought back to commercial life as soon as possible, without waiting for the lengthy execution of a grand design.

Pragmatism was the order of the day and rebuilding was entrusted to Sir Christopher Wren, who worked within a set of regulations that were passed in February 1667. Houses were to be built of inflammable brick or stone rather than timber, and were to be equipped with tile roofs. They should fit into four categories, ranging from merchants' mansions through residences with two, three or four storeys. Buildings of different heights were intended to be related to appropriate varieties of street width. The demand for labour in the building trade was so great that legislation of the same year removed traditional restrictions on the activities of carpenters, bricklayers, masons, plasterers, joiners and other workmen, thereby allowing non-freemen to work in these trades.

Some street widening did take place in the rebuilding but in many instances the new houses were arranged around a modified version of the City's medieval street plan. Large public buildings, such as St Paul's, the Guildhall and the Royal Exchange, were constructed to replace what had

St Paul's Cathedral.
Modern Office blocks crowd in on Wren's masterpiece, built after the Great Fire.

been lost. Some fifty-one churches were built afresh and many damaged ones were reconstructed, almost always under the direction of Wren. Moulded stones from destroyed churches and other buildings were used as hardcore for further construction. In time nineteenth-century demolition and the ravages of World War II were to claim many of these Wren churches but twenty-three still survive, together, of course, with St Paul's cathedral. Even the rubble from the Fire was put to good use to build quays along the north bank of the Thames and to straighten the channel of the lower Fleet.

Application of the building regulations of 1667 produced a trim, brick-built, red-tiled town, which displayed a measure of standardized construction but which was quite unlike Renaissance 'new towns' elsewhere in Europe, since it still respected much of the medieval pattern. Within this framework, the residential population of the City quickly recovered in numbers and continued to grow until well into the eighteenth century. London's trade also recovered and increasing sections of the City were given over to commercial rather than residential functions. This tendency was to become much more pronounced in the nineteenth century so that by 1901 the City's residential population was only about one-fifth of what it had been in 1801. London's rich and poor were moving to live in other parts of the capital that were growing fast. Well before 1700 the population of London 'beyond the walls' had surpassed the number of residents in the City (Table 3.1).

The West End

The link between the City and Westminster was provided along the line of the Strand, where the Savoy Palace had been built as early as 1248 and was followed by many other fine houses owned by noblemen and rich merchants (Fig. 4.1). Further west, the Tudor palace of St James (1528) formed a nucleus of royal residence around which many aristocratic families had their own mansions constructed. The process was accelerated by the disposal of former Church estates that were sold to wealthy purchasers or were given to supporters of the Crown after 1536. In addition, the western side of London had the advantage of being upwind from the domestic and industrial pollution that came from the City and its port. John Evelyn (1661) stressed that '. . . because the winds blow near three-quarters of the year from the west, the dwellings of the west end are so much the more free of fumes, steams and stinks of the whole easterly pile; which, where seacoal is burnt, is a great matter'.

The fourth Earl of Bedford was the first great landowner to capitalize on the growing demand for comfortable housing outside the City by allocating part of his estate, the former convent garden north of the Strand, for urban development. The royal surveyor and architect Inigo Jones had already designed the Banqueting House in Whitehall (1622) and now turned his energies to prepare a plan for what came to be known as Covent Garden (1631), which comprised a central piazza surrounded by arcades and housing, with a church on the western side. Leading courtiers duly poured in their applications for gracious houses overlooking the square. Had the Civil War not intervened, this kind of development might have spread immediately across many other parts of the West End. But Cromwell insisted that such activities should be controlled and only a few schemes slipped in until the Restoration of 1660. Ten years later the fifth Earl of Bedford obtained a licence for holding a market to sell fruit and vegetables and the Covent Garden piazza

acquired the commercial role it was to perform for the next three centuries.

By 1670 work had also started on developing Bloomsbury Square, where the fourth Earl of Southampton had a mansion built for his own use, together with comfortable houses for affluent residents, a network of secondary service streets and a market. John Evelyn described the whole scheme as being 'a little town'. These were just the first of many projects to be implemented on large estates to the west of the City. Speculative builders, of which the most remarkable was Dr Nicholas Barbon, collaborated with landowners to develop their property. Thus during the last four decades of the seventeenth century and throughout the eighteenth century the Grosvenor, St James's and many other estates underwent fashionable urban development (Fig. 4.3). Special leases specified the style and quality of the houses to be built and also served to fix the level of rents. The detail of construction was controlled by a number of eighteenth-century building acts which sought to reduce the chance of another great fire occurring in London. For example, housing had to be built of brick and timber frames concealed or sunk well behind the facade of the new building.

Growing demand for fashionable housing and the success of earlier ventures meant that these schemes continued well into the nineteenth century. The best known example involved Marylebone park, where tenants' leases expired in 1811 and the land reverted to the Crown. A number of schemes were prepared to make use of the property but a rather surprising design by John Nash was judged to be the most acceptable. The initial plan proposed a large number of villas and a palace for the prince regent. These were not built and only a few large villas were constructed in what came to be known as Regent's Park. The park was surrounded on three sides by elegant terraces and was flanked to the north by the Regent's Canal. Park Villages East and West represented the first attempt to construct modest semi-detached villas and the formula was subsequently adopted on other estates. More ordinary dwellings for humbler people were built further away from the park, with barracks and a market being installed on the eastern side. To the south a new thoroughfare (Regent Street) was laid out through Crown land (1817–23) and followed a curving route to reach Westminster, where St

James's Park was remodelled as the counterpoise to
Regent's Park, and triumphal Trafalgar Square was
created on the site of former royal stables
(Fig. 4.3). Additional objectives of the Regent
Street project were to clear the Old Swallow Street
slums and to make a clear break between untidy,
squalid Soho and the expensive housing that had
been built on noble estates further west.

In the 1820s land on the Grosvenor estate started
to be converted into a fashionable district close to

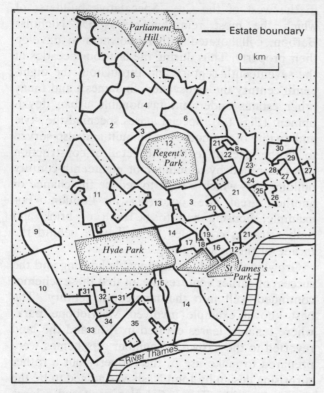

Figure 4.3   *The great estates of West London in the early
19th Century (after S. Jenkins, 1975).*

1. Maryon Wilson
2. Eyre
3. Harley/Portland
4. Eton
5. Dean of Westminster
6. Fitzroy
7. Agar
8. Aldenham
9. Ladbroke
10. Holland
11. Bishop of London
12. Crown
13. Portman
14. Grosvenor
15. Lowndes
16. Jermyn
17. Berkeley
18. Albemarle
19. Burlington
20. Berners
21. Bedford
22. Somers
23. Tonbridge
24. Foundling
25. Rugby
26. Bedford Corp.
27. Northampton
28. Lloyd-Baker
29. New River
30. Penton
31. Alexander
32. Harrington
33. Gunter
34. Smith's Trustees
35. Cadogan

Buckingham Palace, to which George IV had
recently moved (Fig. 4.3). Thomas Cubitt was
entrusted with this project that was to become
known as Belgravia. He was the first large-scale
building contractor to employ his own specialist
craftsmen, instead of subcontracting the work as
previous builders had done, and to run his own
workshops where standard products such as door
and window frames were prefabricated. The land
that was to be developed on the Grosvenor estate
was damp, and part had been occupied by the
reservoir of the Chelsea waterworks. The total area
needed to be reclaimed. In 1823 the Grosvenor
Canal was built to enable vast quantities of building
materials to be transported with relative ease to a
wharf on the present site of Victoria Station. Cubitt
came to an agreement with the Grosvenor estate to
drain the whole area (using earth from St
Katharine dock which his firm was involved in
excavating), reconstruct the local main sewer, and
build fashionable houses, although the detailed
designs were left to individual architects. After
numerous financial difficulties, Belgravia proved an
enormous success and Cubitt turned his energies to
Pimlico, which was also part of the Grosvenor
estate. This kind of development catered largely for
rich members of London society but not exclusively
so; humbler schemes, such as those at Camden
Town and Somers Town to the north, provided
houses for people of rather more modest means.

The broad sweep of development in the West
End embraced a succession of 'building booms' that
occurred after the successful conclusion of warfare,
with intervening phases being rather less active. For
example, Mayfair was developed after the Treaty
of Utrecht (1713) had ended the Wars of Spanish
Succession; the New Road (between Paddington
and Islington) and bridges across the Thames were
constructed after the Peace of Paris (1763); and
after the victory of Waterloo (1815) much government money was invested in public building (for
example, along Whitehall, the National Gallery, the
Houses of Parliament). In addition, many new
churches were constructed and the first building of
the University of London (now University College).

As well as massive urban extensions and the erec-
tion of public buildings, a start was made on
improving the quality of life in the capital. Between
1720 and 1745 five major hospitals had been built
and that trend continued for the next hundred

University College, Gower Street, London.
The portico was designed by William Wilkins, architect of the National Gallery.

years. The Westminster Paving Act (1762) was instrumental in improving street surfaces and providing oil lamps for illumination in some parts of the West End. Foreign visitors were duly impressed by the magnitude of all these innovations to the west of the City and would surely have echoed the words of the German Puckler-Muskau who observed in 1826 that London '. . . now, for the first time . . . has the appearance of a seat of government, and not an immeasurable metropolis of shopkeepers'.

The East End

Changes operating to the east of the City were very different in character from what was happening on the fashionable West End estates. The port's volume of trade more than doubled during the eighteenth century and attracted large numbers of workers to handle cargoes and to work in associated industries, like shipbuilding and repairing. Dutiable cargoes had to come through the 'legal quays' where customs dues were levied, but in addition great quantities of coal from north-eastern England and other bulky commodities were handled. All of this activity occurred alongside the Thames and it was clear that new arrangements were necessary to cope with a series of mounting pressures.

New types of mooring facility were needed to deal with the growing traffic and the much larger vessels that were coming to London, with the average size of ship docking in the city doubling during the eighteenth century. Enclosed basins would avoid having to cope with water levels that changed with the state of the tide, while secure, walled handling facilities and special warehouses would reduce problems of theft and damage to cargoes stored in the open air. Above all else, new docks were needed to reduce the incredible congestion that occurred when large numbers of vessels arrived at the same time and in some instances had to wait in the Thames for up to three months before unloading. During periods of warfare vessels arrived in convoys and even under normal circumstances most ships came in the summer, including the great West India fleets that carried sugar, rum, dye-woods and other tropical produce. There were sometimes 1200 or even 1400 ships waiting to unload in the Thames above Limehouse. The wastage rate for perishable goods was enormous.

The need for new docks was both great and obvious, with West India merchants forming the leading pressure group. But for many years the City authorities showed great reluctance to favour any schemes for new downstream docks that would be located on land beyond their jurisdiction. Between 1796 and 1800 a series of parliamentary committees enquired into the problem of congestion and recommended that the port be improved. The opposition of the City authorities was somewhat eroded and a start was made on excavating dock basins in the soft alluvium of the Thames flood plain. In 1802 the West India Dock was cut on the northern side of the Isle of Dogs to cope with up to 600 ships at a time (Fig. 4.4). With the opening of Commercial Road in the following year Limehouse and Poplar became dockland settlements and this achievement was followed by the London Dock at Wapping (1805), the East India Dock (1806), a series of docks on the south side of the river (starting in 1807), and Saint Katharine Dock (1828). This latter scheme brought the new docks as close as possible to the City and involved the demolition of 1250 dwellings and important church buildings, and the dispersal of the 11 000 people who were made homeless. Visitors to these new docks fully appreciated the weight of commercial and colonial power that they represented. To quote Puckler-Muskau again: when visiting the port '. . . the spectator must feel astonishment and a sort of awe at the greatness and might of England'.

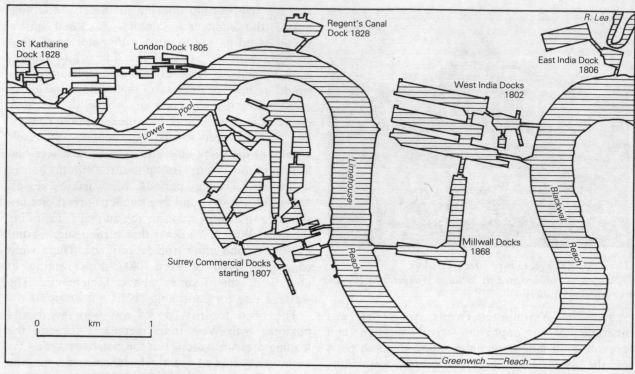

Figure 4.4   *London's upstream docks.*

To function efficiently the docks required a large supply of casual labour that could be called upon when cargoes needed to be handled but could also be laid off during slack periods. The basis of dock employment was far from secure and this fact contributed to the serious poverty that was encountered among many sections of East End society. Rich merchants had their fine houses to be sure, but they were greatly outnumbered by far more humble folk. As in earlier times, large quantities of cheap housing were pushed up to provide shelter for the labouring classes. As early as 1598 John Stow had described the stretch of waterfront from the Tower of London to Wapping as '. . . a continuous street, or filthy straight passage, with alleys and small tenements or cottages . . . inhabited by sailors and victuallers'. Alehouses, pawnshops, brothels and 'dens' catered for the needs of passing mariners but this district also contained a variety of respectable workshops.

Although there were exceptions, the general quality of housing on the eastern side of London was not high and had not been improved by an act of parliament in 1617 which stipulated that only leases of less than thirty-one years should operate

in the manors of Hackney and Stepney. Some attempts were made to bring religion to the working people of the East End and a number of fine churches were constructed following the Church Building Act (1711). For example, Nicholas Hawksmoor designed elegant churches for Spitalfields, Stepney, Limehouse and Greenwich, as well as Bloomsbury and parts of the City. But in the East End these vast edifices were rarely if ever filled, unlike the fashionable churches that flourished in residential districts to the west of the City.

The East End continued to perform its traditional function as a reception area for immigrants, with Jews and Huguenots (French Protestants) being the most notable groups during this period. Cromwell allowed Jews to return to England and numbers of Sephardic Jews settled in Whitechapel during the seventeenth century. They were followed by members of Jewish communities from central Europe who brought their trades and skills to districts beyond the eastern fringe of the City. Huguenots fled from France after religious toleration was removed by the revocation of the Edict of Nantes in 1685. They moved to two main districts, setting up silk-working establishments in Spitalfields and also opening craft workshops in Soho. In addition, the East End absorbed many other minority groups in dock work, commerce and various trades, often in the poorest of conditions. Sweated labour was already prevalent and was to become even more characteristic as the nineteenth century wore on. The reception function has continued ever since, with Jews fleeing from persecution in central and eastern Europe during the hundred years after 1850, and immigrants from the Indian sub-continent arriving after World War II (see chapter 16).

South of the Thames

After the mid-eighteenth century, important changes started to occur on the right bank of the Thames following the construction of new bridges. Until 1750 there had been only one (London Bridge) and most crossings were made by ferry with numerous boatmen operating from land points or 'stairs' along the river. Westminster Bridge was opened in 1750 and was followed by Blackfriars Bridge (1769) and four others (Vauxhall, Waterloo, Southwark and the new London Bridge) between 1816 and 1831. As a result a much needed supply of additional building land became easily accessible from the city and Westminster. Marshy stretches, such as St George's Fields, were drained and new turnpike roads were built, forming the framework into which new housing was inserted. However, pleasure grounds, such as Vauxhall (Fox Hall) Gardens continued to flourish and gain in notoriety, being patronized by all groups in society, from the nobility to pickpockets, prostitutes and high-waymen. Vauxhall Gardens were finally closed down in 1859 and other pleasure grounds suffered the same fate because of the profligacy of the company that frequented them. Some of their owners were imprisoned for keeping 'disorderly houses' on their property.

London's environs

Beyond the expanding built-up mass of London, scores of villages and small towns were being drawn into the social and economic space of the capital. Springs at Hampstead, Epsom and several other places attracted well-to-do visitors to sample the waters and enjoy their real or presumed medicinal

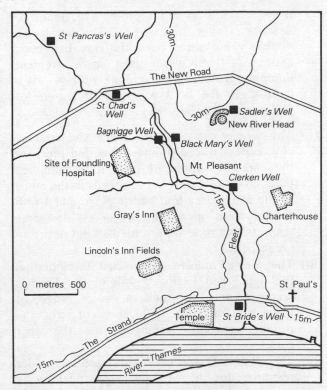

Figure 4.5   *Wells and resorts in the Fleet Valley, c. 1800.*

qualities, while numerous 'wells' close to the northern fringe of London supplied recreational areas that appealed to humbler sections of urban society (Fig. 4.5). The agricultural villages of Dulwich, Islington, Muswell Hill, Richmond, Streatham and Sydenham acquired additional functions as weekend resorts.

Farming activities in the London basin had long been geared to providing food for the capital's growing human and animal populations. The land-use pattern corresponded to some extent to the kind of distance–decay model proposed by Von Thünen but was complicated by local variations in soil quality, the survival of old traditions (for example on commonland), and the attribution of high social status to some districts. However at the beginning of the nineteenth century, five generalized land-use zones could be distinguished from detailed maps produced by Thomas Milne (1800) and information gathered by Henry Hunter (1811).

(i) The *zone of claypits* was located in immediate proximity to the built-up urban fringe, and its brickearth deposits provided raw material for making bricks and tiles. The light that came from its kilns at night prompted Hunter to describe it as a 'ring of fire'. The pits had a double value since once the clay had been extracted they were used as convenient dumping grounds for London's rubbish. At a later stage the land was sold or leased for building in the usual way.

(ii) The *zone of cattle pastures* was in the hands of cowkeepers whose animals provided much of the capital's supply of fresh milk; although dairy cows were also kept in sheds in the midst of the urban area and had to be supplied with fodder from more distant areas. In some respects this zone represented a kind of proto-green belt.

(iii) The *zone of market gardens* had developed on the light, well fertilized soils of the Thames terraces and supplied a wide range of vegetables and fruit. Its location cut across the roughly concentric arrangement of the other zones.

(iv) The *zone of hay* provided essential fodder resources for the capital's large and growing population of horses at this age of horse-drawn carts and carriages.

(v) The *zone of mixed husbandry* formed the outer component in the pattern and produced various crops and animal products for the London market. The precise combination differed in response to local conditions of soil, accessibility, farm size and entrepreneurial skill.

However, London's food requirements could not be met from south-east England alone and by as early as the seventeenth century a wide supply network had been set up whereby cattle raised as far afield as Scotland, north Wales and Lancashire were shod and sent 'on the hoof' to farmers in the Midlands and the south-east where they were fattened before being sold to London's butchers.

Early nineteenth-century London was very much larger than its medieval ancestor but important similarities remained, largely in response to the fact that London remained a 'walking city', with most citizens relying on their own feet to move around and only a minority being able to afford the luxury of a horse and carriage. In the 1820s London had not yet become exposed to the opportunities for mass suburbanization that mechanization and public

transportation would start to offer during the second half of the nineteenth century when the railway age was firmly established.

Further reading

Useful discussions of London in transition are found in:
Clark P (ed) (1976) *The Early Modern Town* Longman
Clark P and Slack P (1976) *English Towns in Transition 1500–1700* Oxford University Press

The great description of late sixteenth-century London is:
Stow J (1956) *A Survey of London, 1598* Dent

This has been analysed recently in:
Power M J (1985) 'John Stow and his London' *Journal of Historical Geography* 11: 1–20

Models of early urban growth are examined by:
Jones E (1980) 'London in the early seventeenth century: an ecological approach' *The London Journal* 6: 123–33

An excellent summary of the historical geography of London across two centuries is found in:
Spate O H K (1936) 'The growth of London, AD 1660–1800' in Darby H C (ed) *An Historical Geography of England before 1800* Cambridge University Press pp 529–48

The role of London in the context of the nation as a whole is discussed by:
Wrigley E A (1967) 'A simple model of London's importance in changing English society and economy 1660–1750' *Past and Present* 37: 44–70

London's varied society is examined by:
George M D (1951) *London Life in the Eighteenth Century* Penguin

The development of great estates is examined in:
Jenkins S (1975) *Landlords to London: the story of a capital and its growth* Constable
Olsen D J (1964) *Town Planning in London* Yale University Press
Summerson J (1962) *Georgian London* Penguin

The construction of the upstream docks is examined in:
Pudney J (1975) *London's Docks* Thames and Hudson

5   Prologue to the present

Hugh Clout

Power and prestige

In 1851 greater London housed 2 685 000 people, 14.9 per cent of the total in England and Wales (Table 3.1). One hundred years later it contained 8 193 000, 18.7 per cent of the national total. The various areas of London experienced strikingly different functional trends during the intervening period. More and more land in the City became converted to commercial uses as the residential role of this 'central business district' continued to dwindle. Merchants, shopkeepers and tradespeople were moving out and their property was taken over by banks, insurance companies and other types of office. The City's night time population remained roughly stable at about 128 000 during the first half of the nineteenth century but by 1901 it had fallen to 27 000 and was to slump to 5 000 in 1951, having been helped dramatically on its way by war damage in the early 1940s, when 40 ha were razed to the ground. By contrast, the rest of greater London increased its population three and a half times between 1851 and 1951, as successive waves of Victorian and twentieth-century suburbanization extended the built-up fringe further into the London basin.

Victorian London was a potent symbol of British might in the world at large but, even more than in earlier times, it was a nerve centre of commercial and colonial power literally without rival. It was the supreme money market and the most commanding concentration of people, trade, industry and administration to be found anywhere on the globe. London was *the* focus, nourished in the widest sense by the gains of imperialism and in a more direct way by the food and other commodities supplied to it by railways and in steel plated steamships. It was also a self-stimulating centre, with new ideas and trends being sparked off in this supreme assembly of wealth, fashion and political and economic power.

During the 1840s and 1850s large numbers of impoverished Irish workers moved to London as they fled from famine conditions at home. The capital's Irish-born population increased to over 100 000 by 1860, many of whom were attracted to the East End by the availability of casual work in the docks. At the end of Queen Victoria's reign, greater London housed one-fifth of the entire population of England and Wales, and during the 1890s and early 1900s it had absorbed no less than one quarter of the nation's total natural increase, being sustained by important flows of migration from all parts of Britain.

The power of British industrial capitalism and colonialism fuelled the growth of London's economy, which provided the driving force for its changing geography. The rapidly expanding urban area acquired new commercial buildings, especially in the City and the West End; new churches, stations, schools, theatres and museums proliferated; and the district around Whitehall was remodelled to house the administration for the nation and the empire, with London having no fewer than 160 000 civil servants by 1900. New markets were built to handle the ever-growing quantities of foodstuffs that were essential to sustain the capital. For example, in the quarter century after 1850, the Metropolitan cattle market was opened for sale and slaughter of live beasts, and the meat and fish markets of Smithfield and Billingsgate were remodelled. On a rather more lofty plane, the Great Exhibition of 1851 was held in Hyde Park to display the glories of imperial Britain and the profits derived from this spectacle were used to purchase

35 ha of South Kensington where museums, colleges, headquarters of learned societies (including the Royal Geographical Society) and the Albert Hall were duly installed.

All round London the tide of bricks and mortar continued to surge forward and swamp existing agricultural settlements as estates large and small were covered with housing to cater for every respectable level of society (Fig. 5.1). Although the age of town and country planning had not yet dawned, the expansion process was not completely haphazard or random but was linked to the aims and policies of individual landlords and developers and the possibilities afforded by a variety of new means of transport. For example, the Dukes of Bedford sought to ensure an air of gentility and temperance on their estate of new housing in Bloomsbury, which was developed in the first half of the nineteenth century, by having gates and watchmen positioned at strategic access points and, of course, expressly forbidding the construction of public houses or other outlets for the sale of alcohol. Similar policies were operated by the Dukes of Westminster on their property further to the south. By contrast, small landowners catering for an emphatically working-class housing market rarely took steps to control the

'demon drink'. Not surprisingly, the distribution of alehouses and bars showed very striking spatial variations in Victorian London (Dyos and Wolff 1973).

The geographical pattern of housing development during the hundred years after 1850 was intimately linked to the opportunities offered by new rapid modes of communication. Railways, trams, underground trains and latterly motor buses and private cars enabled London to be transformed from a 'walking city'. As Olsen (1976) explained: 'To a great extent what happened to London happened to all big cities, but happened sooner and more intensely here than anywhere else' (p 323).

The railway: accommodation and expansion

Britain's railway lines were established by numerous companies operating in competition with each other to capture a share of trade. As far as London was concerned their initial objective was to link the capital to the nation's growing industrial regions and to the main channel ports, with movement of goods being primarily in mind. Penetration of the existing built-up area and provision of a cross-city link were quite different matters which aroused strong opposition from many influential groups of Londoners who feared that the demolition of housing and the installation of railway lines would lower the value of their property. Indeed, in 1848 a Royal Commission made a firm recommendation to Parliament that lines through the heart of the City should not be permitted.

Some companies opened temporary terminals beyond the main built-up area but at a later stage constructed stations a little closer to the city centre. For example, Liverpool Street replaced a more distant terminus at Bishopsgate, and Euston replaced one at Chalk Farm (Fig. 5.2). Several lines from the south terminated on the right bank, with special bridges being built. Left bank termini were opened later on, for example at Victoria, Charing Cross and Cannon Street. On the northern side of London the railways penetrated no further than the New Road and its extensions, with termini being aligned along an arc from Paddington, through Euston, St Pancras, King's Cross and Broad Street to Liverpool Street. (Marylebone was added as a late-comer in 1899.) Passengers wishing to travel

Figure 5.1   *The growth of London during the 19th century.*

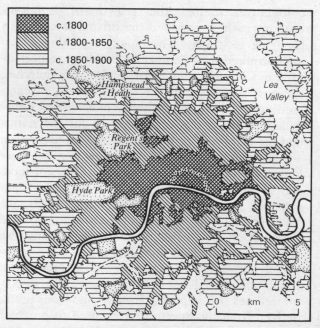

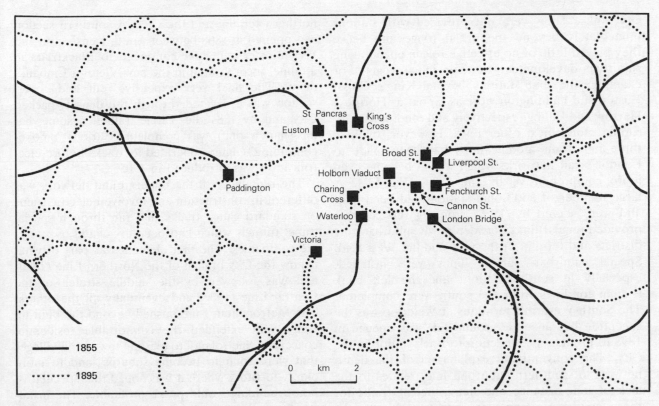

Figure 5.2   *London's railway network, 1855 and 1895.*

between terminals had to make use of horse-drawn carriages, horse buses (which had been introduced in 1829) or, later, the underground railway.

The site and situation of London posed both difficulties and opportunities for the railway builders. On the south bank of the Thames they had to contend with damp low-lying ground and several tributaries and canals. In order to cope with these problems and the presence of extensive built-up areas the London and Greenwich Railway (1836) was constructed on a lengthy viaduct between London Bridge and Deptford, which kept demolition to a minimum and provided usable space beneath the arches that could be rented out for warehouses, workshops or stables.

The lines coming into Euston, King's Cross and St Pancras had to cope with two obstacles, namely the Northern Heights of Hampstead and Highgate, and the Regent's Canal, which had been completed in 1820 to link the main canals from midland England with London's docks. Costly tunnels provided a solution to the first problem but each company adopted a different response to the pres-

ence of the canal. The westernmost London and Birmingham Railway (opening its Euston terminus in 1838) had to cope with a particularly steep incline and then bridged the canal, whose level rose from east to west through a flight of locks. The Great Northern built a tunnel under the canal for its lines into King's Cross (1852), while the Midland constructed a bridge and then adopted the novel idea of raising the ground floor of St Pancras (1868) well above the surrounding street level. Once again, the space beneath the station and its access arches was used for storage. Lengthy bridges and complex engineering solutions were also required to accommodate lines from the south on the north bank of the river.

By contrast with these difficulties, the level land in the tributary valleys of the Lea and the Stort to the north-east of the capital were ideal for railway building, while the wide sweep of flat land on the Taplow terrace was very convenient for the line between Paddington and Maidenhead that was opened by the Great Western in 1838.

These early railway lines were designed as 'inter-city' links. They were not provided with stations immediately beyond the urban fringe and hence they played little or no effective role in encouraging suburban development in their initial years. For example, the first stations beyond King's Cross, Euston and Paddington were as far out as Hornsey, Harrow and Ealing respectively and conditions were similar along most other lines. However, by 1870 three important modifications had been made to London's rail network, which was to become even more comprehensive by the 1890s (Fig. 5.2). A large number of additional stations had been built and were served by 'local' stopping services that provided regular links between newly suburbanizing districts and termini in the City and the West End. Special suburban surface lines were installed, especially in south London; and the left bank termini for lines from the south were completed. The South-Western's terminus at Waterloo was the exception but an underground line was opened in 1898 to provide a connection to Bank station in the City. The conventional explanation of the dense network of southern suburban lines relates to the lack of long-distance and heavy freight traffic for these southern companies; perhaps also to the removal of the Crystal Palace to Sydenham. Whatever the reasons, this fact has important implications for London's transport system today, with a London-controlled underground system predominantly north of the Thames, a nationally-controlled network of British Rail lines especially to the south, and profound complications of integrating the two.

The difficulty of travelling between terminals and through the City and the West End demanded a radical solution, which came in the form of underground railways. Once again the lines were installed and operated by a number of separate companies. The first service was provided by coal-burning locomotives of the Metropolitan District Railway which ran from Paddington to Moorgate through a tunnel that had been created by the 'cut and cover' method between 8 and 20 m beneath the surface of the New Road. Excavation work had started in 1860 and made good progress west of King's Cross, where the tunnel ran through gravel and had to negotiate only one sewer, the Tyburn. But further east it ran through clay and the Fleet sewer had to be crossed three times and actually burst as the tunnel was being built. However the trains started to run in 1863 and provided a useful connection between the

northern termini and the City. A southern section was opened in 1868 between South Kensington and Westminster and later continued to Blackfriars in a tunnel incorporated in the new Victoria Embankment. The final very expensive 'cut and cover' section was excavated through the densely-packed City and by 1884 the 'Circle' (albeit a somewhat mis-shapen one) was complete. Curious 'smoke-consuming' engines operated its tracks before electrification was introduced in 1905.

The remainder of the underground network was different in construction and involved electric trains on standard gauge tracks that ran through special 'tube' tunnels which had been excavated by separate companies. The first element was part of what is now the City branch of the Northern Line (1890) and was followed by the middle stretch of the Central Line (1900) and eventually all the others. The Metropolitan Line pushed beyond the built-up fringe and extended the comfortable residential concept of 'metroland' to existing towns and villages that were soon to become suburbs, and to more empty territory where it was hoped that speculative house building would prove profitable. The installation of the tubes proper produced comparable results in other areas. Of particular importance was the tunnel beneath the Northern Heights of Hampstead which enabled the Northern Line to reach Golders Green in 1907 and opened the way for the suburbanization of the clay plain of central Middlesex during the 1920s and 1930s. Most underground lines were installed north of the river but a comparable role was being performed south of the Thames by suburban lines which were electrified between 1909 and 1932.

Surface railways and underground lines represented formidable engineering achievements in their own right and served to 'shrink' space within greater London, thereby enabling more people to live in pleasant suburban surroundings away from their places of work, whether in factory or office. Urban tramways started operating in 1870 and were followed by motor buses in 1905. Both modes of transport contributed further to the suburbanization process and also facilitated movement in the West End and the City.

On the western side of London new bridges eased communications between the two banks of the Thames, and Tower Bridge was opened at the eastern edge of the City in 1894. This essential role was performed by pedestrian and vehicle tunnels further east in docklands where the river is appreciably wider. The first of these was the Thames Tunnel of 1843 (which was later used for the East London branch of the Metropolitan Line) followed by pedestrian tunnels at Woolwich (1889) and Greenwich (1902) and vehicle tunnels at Blackwall (1897) and Rotherhithe (1908). Tunnel entrances, stations, new roads and other large engineering works almost always involved substantial demolition of existing properties and pushed their residents on to the capital's already desperate housing market. Many of these urban 'improvements' were targetted on slum neighbourhoods and we must not forget that their poor and relatively powerless residents had virtually no chance of making their voices heard to argue the case for replacement accommodation.

The quality of life

Despite the glories of Empire, the profits of trade and the enormous wealth of some Londoners, disease, deprivation and poverty intertwined to form a critical problem in the capital throughout the nineteenth century. In 1829 the Metropolitan police force was set up to tackle the problems of crime and civil disturbance which threatened middle-class sensibilities and raised the danger of working-class London challenging the 'establishment' of parliament, monarchy and the church. In 1832 cholera had led to the deaths of over 5 000 Londoners and typhus and smallpox killed thousands more each year in overcrowded tenements and slums. In 1842 an official *Inquiry into the Sanitary Conditions of the Labouring Population of Great Britain* was collated by Edwin Chadwick and described the conditions of London's slums in horrifying detail. These were certainly not all in the East End but were also found on the margins of fashionable districts further west, which housed a large and varied service population whose labour was needed to ensure the comfortable living standards and growing profits of the upper and middle-classes. More important still, the *Inquiry* established the scientific connection between squalor and disease, but its critical findings failed to generate much response.

In 1846 a general board of health was established but had very few real powers; and in 1847 a Royal Commission on the health of the capital gave rise

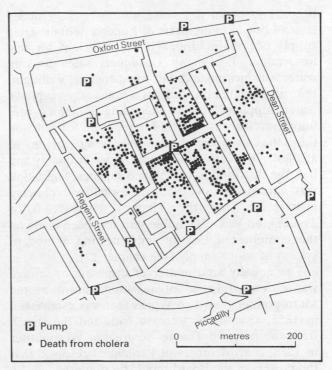

Figure 5.3 *Outbreaks of cholera in Soho, mapped by Dr. John Snow (after L. D. Stamp, 1964).*

to an administrative reform of London's sewers. New cemeteries were established in outer London, thereby avoiding the regular re-use of plots in inner-city burial grounds, and in 1855 the market for live cattle was moved to Islington, with only carcasses being sold at Smithfield from that time onward. But cholera remained a desperate problem in London and there was no real means of combating it. As many as 14 000 lives were claimed in 1849 and further serious outbreaks continued in the 1850s.

Some feeble attempts were made to clean up conditions, such as flushing ancient blocked sewers into the Thames. But this may have made matters even · worse since many Londoners were still obtaining their drinking water in untreated form direct from the river. Not until 1859 did Dr John Snow manage to demonstrate that the cholera germ was carried in water by analysing water quality in the pumps of Soho and correlating it with the local pattern of the disease (Fig. 5.3). The use of flushing lavatories, which had started in 1810, added to the pollution of the Thames and the problem was intensified when urban cesspools were banned in 1848. Flushing lavatories – and efficient sewer pipes – had become essential if disease was to be kept under control but in many parts of London neither water supply nor mains drainage was sufficient for this innovation. For many Londoners safe drinking water was lacking and one commentator, writing in the mid-nineteenth century, found the capital's water supplies '. . . so abounding in animal life, unfit even for washing, and so repellant for drinking that the working classes are being driven to alcohol'. In an attempt to improve water quality and halt the distribution of polluted supplies, legislation was introduced in 1856 to forbid water being abstracted from the Thames downstream of Teddington lock. A humble start had been made on the complicated task of implementing a modern system of water supply (see chapter 12).

The equally vital matter of disposing of sewage was entrusted to an organization known as the Metropolitan Board of Works that was established in 1855. Conditions were so bad, and the stench from the polluted Thames so great at Westminster in 1858, that Members of Parliament resolved that the powers of the Board should be strengthened. By 1865 some 130 km of intercepting sewers running from west to east had been installed to capture effluent that would normally have drained through London's 'lost rivers' and other channels into the Thames or would have reached it through simple runoff or seepage. The new sewers carried the liquid and solid wastes of the capital beyond the built-up area to two major outfall points at Barking and Crossness on the north and south banks respectively. The solution was sophisticated for the 1860s but now seems sadly deficient, since treatment was lacking.

The chief engineer for the schemes was Joseph Bazalgette who was also responsible for the Victoria Embankment which was constructed over a length of 2 km between Blackfriars and Westminster during 1864–70. This operation followed many other embankment schemes implemented in central London in earlier years; for example, part of the new Houses of Parliament (1839) had been constructed on recently reclaimed land. The Victoria Embankment embraced many objectives. Land was reclaimed; the channel of the Thames was confined and thereby deepened, giving it a very different cross-section from earlier times; and a new highway was installed to link Westminster and the City, via the Embankment and Queen Victoria Street. The scheme also created plenty of space on which impressive public buildings could be constructed, functioning both as centres of administration and symbols of British power; while beneath ground level there was a tunnel containing the District Railway, and a great pipe which accommodated an intercepting sewer.

The opportunity for reclamation of new land was distinctly limited in Victorian London but there was abundant scope for slum clearance, which was often combined with the construction of new roads, railways and stations. For example, many overcrowded tenements were demolished when Shaftesbury Avenue (1877–86) and Charing Cross Road (1887) were sliced through the parish of St Giles, while Victoria Street was positioned along a route that had been selected for its effectiveness in puncturing the slums of 'Devil's Acre' in Westminster. After a postponement of more than sixty years, the building of Kingsway and the Aldwych at the beginning of the twentieth century and the installation of triumphal administrative buildings did away with 12 ha of mean housing in scores of streets.

Railway building also had the dual effect of enhancing access and 'improving' the environment. If such schemes were positioned in an appropriate way they could also be used to disperse concentrations of the poorest of the poor, of whom middle- and upper-class Londoners were remarkably fearful, since in their minds the labouring classes were also dangerous classes. It has been estimated that as many as 100 000 people lost their homes in nineteenth-century London as a result of building of new stations and sections of line. Not surprisingly these features of technological innovation were always inserted through patches of cheap housing; large landowners and rich residents had the means to resist.

Despite all this activity, London still contained many slum areas. Charles Dickens described conditions in the former brickfields of Notting Dale potteries in north Kensington that evoke life in modern third-world shanty towns. Charles Booth's great survey of *Life and Labour of the People of London* (1889–1903) underscored the widespread existence of appalling housing and human degradation in the East End, in mews and mean streets fringing fashionable West-End estates, and in many other parts of the city – the largest and richest in the world!

Slum clearance associated with railway development and new road schemes often served to make conditions worse in adjacent neighbourhoods, since rehousing rarely if ever figured in these urban 'improvements'. A correspondent contributing to *The Times* wrote about what had happened in the parish of St Giles after New Oxford Street (1845–7) had been cut. His report summarized effectively the dilemma of many working people at that time. '. . . The poor are displaced, but they are not moved . . . They are shovelled out of one side of the parish only to render more overcrowded the stifling apartments in another part . . . The dock and wharf labourer, the porter and the costermonger cannot remove. You may pull down their wretched homes; they must find others – and make their new dwellings more wretched than the old ones. The tailor, shoemaker and other workmen are in much the same position. It is a mockery to speak of the suburbs to them.' That view was certainly correct at mid-century but circumstances were to change significantly as the century wore on.

New forms of urban transportation and rising real wages made suburban living a realistic possibility for at least some members of the 'respectable' working class. If workingmen's trains operated early and late, to cater for long working days, and if the cost of travel were pegged at a reasonable level, then a house in the suburbs was not unthinkable. For example, as early as 1864 the Great Eastern Railway Company had agreed to charge particularly low fares for up to 16 km on some of its suburban lines as part of an arrangement which had enabled Liverpool Street station and a stretch of line to be built on the site of a patch of poor housing. The spread of working-class suburbia as far out as Edmonton, Tottenham, Walthamstow and Leyton had much to do with this agreement. In 1883 all railway companies were obliged by the Cheap Trains Act to offer special workmen's fares and this enabled large numbers of better-off workers to move to London's suburbs.

Closer to the core of the city the challenge to provide new homes for the respectable and deserving poor was being tackled by philanthropic individuals and organizations. For example, the American millionaire banker George Peabody donated £500 000 to found a trust to improve the living conditions of London's 'poor'; and Baroness Burdett-Coutts, also of banking stock, provided

Cottages on the LCC's Totterdown Estate in Tooting. Built between 1903 and 1911, this pioneer example of suburban council housing compares favourably with much modern housing for low income families.

assistance. Both her scheme (Columbia Square) and the Peabody estates were among the first blocks of purpose-built flats in London and provided a very new way of accommodating Londoners.

The housing problem was, of course, intimately linked to problems of poverty and contributed to the desirability of devising a more 'centralized' and relatively efficient form of local government that might promote schemes to relieve the misery of many Londoners. Powerful vestries in the West End opposed such an idea but it gained support in the East End. The 'centralists' eventually won, with the London County Council being founded in 1888. Radical liberal groups wanted a single London authority that would incorporate the police force but this was opposed and prevented by the Home Office. Elections were held in 1889 and the LCC came to operate within the area of the Old Metropolitan Board of Works and took over its functions. But opposition to a centralized London authority remained strong and ten years after the LCC's creation a number of boroughs were established, with the partial intention of curbing the new organization's powers.

At the end of the nineteenth century the LCC started to establish its own important housing schemes. Sometimes a proportion of the deserving

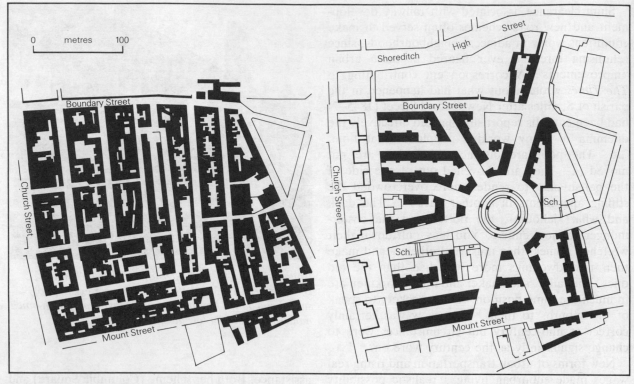

Figure 5.4 *Redevelopment of the Boundary Street estate.*

poor was rehoused close to where they had lived before, as in the case of the LCC Boundary Street estate in Bethnal Green which replaced the slums of the Nichol in 1895 (Fig. 5.4); but soon after the turn of the century a start was made on rehousing workers on new 'cottage estates' in suburban locations such as Acton, Norbury and Tooting that were accessible to central London by railway or electric tram. However, the housing needs of the poorest of the poor remained beyond the scope of such schemes.

Looking outwards

Londoners with savings to invest or the financial security to raise a loan were, of course, in a far more privileged position on the capital's housing market. Suburbia was being established for them and in a sufficiently diverse way to cater for a wide range of tastes and pockets. Indeed European observers commented on the low density and low height of so much of London's new housing, in contrast with conditions in their own cities. The

suburbanization process was well under way by the 1890s and continued without any major physical controls until the introduction of fundamental town and country planning legislation in 1947 (Fig. 5.5).

The two world wars brought serious interruptions but suburbanization certainly forged ahead during the 1920s and 1930s. Greater London managed to escape the worst effects of the economic depression that hit old industrial regions so harshly between the wars. Indeed the capital attracted a range of new activities in the mechanical and electrical industries and acted as a great 'magnet' for workers from other parts of Britain who were desperately seeking jobs. By the mid-1930s the drift to the South East was in full flow and London's economy was flourishing as never before, with the manufacture of innovative products being grafted on to its long-established base of commerce and administration.

The growth of suburbia brought unquestionable benefits to its new residents (see Chapter 14). 'Finding a house within their financial reach, many thousands had their living standards transformed; in a few short years, the sum of human happiness was

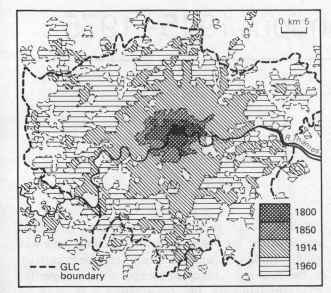

Figure 5.5   *The suburban spread of London during the 19th and 20th centuries (after R. Clayton, 1964).*

immcasurably incrcascd' (Jackson, 1973, p 363). But the process also had negative aspects which Jackson captures as he describes 'the sudden, wide-ranging onslaught of the private builders across outer London in the 1920s and 1930s . . . little affected by the pitifully inadequate planning measures . . . Both the waste of opportunity and the resultant ugly monotony are appalling to contemplate' (p 363). It is open to debate whether this was chaotic urban 'sprawl' or necessary urban 'spread', interspersed with existing settlements and structured by railways, main roads and property boundaries. But certainly vast quantities of open land were being converted to urban use, as the economy of greater London progressed, many would argue, at the expense of other parts of Britain. These dual themes of land conversion and regional imbalance were critical in the elaboration of town and country planning and the formulation of regional development policies in the post-war years. Their implications will be explored in many later chapters of this book.

Further reading

The growth of London in the nineteenth and early twentieth centuries is examined in:
Coppock J T and Prince H C (eds) (1964) *Greater London* Faber

Weightman G and Humphries S (1983) *The Making of Modern London 1815–1914* Sidgwick and Jackson
Weightman G and Humphries S (1984) *The Making of Modern London 1914–1939* Sidgwick and Jackson

A rich and varied exploration of Victorian London is contained in:
Dyos H J and Wolff M (eds) (1973) *Victorian City: images and reality* (2 vols) Routledge and Kegan Paul

Aspects of suburban development are presented in:
Dyos H J (1961) *Victorian Suburb* Leicester University Press
Jackson A A (1973) *Semi-Detached London* Allen and Unwin
Olsen D J (1976) *The Growth of Victorian London* Batsford
Tindall G (1980) *The Fields Beneath* Temple Smith
Thompson F M L (ed) (1982) *The Rise of Suburbia* Leicester University Press

Working-class London, housing problems and improvement schemes are discussed in:
Fried A and Elman R M (eds) (1971) *Charles Booth's London* Hutchinson
Jones G Stedman (1971) *Outcast London: a study in the relationship between classes in Victorian Society* Penguin
Port M (1981) 'Metropolitan improvements' *The London Journal* 7: 194–206
Wohl A S (1977) *The Eternal Slum: housing and social policy in Victorian London* Arnold
Yelling J A (1981) 'The selection of sites for slum clearance in London 1875–1888' *Journal of Historical Geography* 7: 155–66
Yelling J A (1982) 'LCC slum clearance policies 1889–1907' *Transactions, Institute of British Geographers* 7: 292–303

Detailed aspects of changing transportation are presented in:
Falk N (1981) 'London's docklands: a tale of two cities' *The London Journal* 7: 65–80
Hoyle S R (1982) 'The first battle for London: a case study of the Royal Commission on London Termini 1846' *The London Journal* 8: 140–55
Kellett J R (1969) *The Impact of Railways on Victorian Cities* Routledge and Kegan Paul

6 Decentralizing London, 1945–1975

Gerald Manners

Economic and employment growth

After the Second World War, the London conurbation resumed its inter-war growth. Its industries
were characterized by their diversity in the manufacturing and service sectors. They were biased
towards new, innovative and what were, in the
national context, rapidly growing activities. London's

economy was increasingly buoyant, provided
employment for some 4.3 million people, and was
by far the largest single centre of economic activity
in the country. As a consequence of this prosperity,
the population of the conurbation continued to
increase, and by 1951 some 8.3 million people were
living there. In turn, the built-up area, which
already extended well beyond the administrative

Figure 6.1 *The extent of London, 1945.*

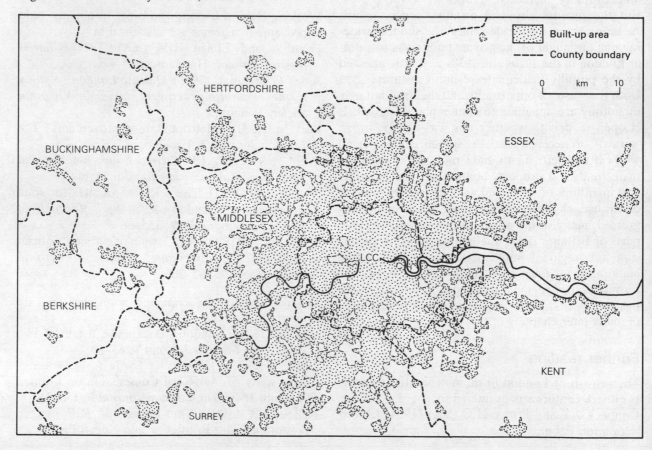

area of the London County Council, was spreading still further into the neighbouring Home Counties (Fig. 6.1).

In those early post-war years, manufacturing activities were by no means evenly spread throughout the capital. They had a quite distinctive geography. One major concentration of productive capacity was in what Peter Hall (1962) termed the 'Victorian Manufacturing Belt', a broad zone that encircled the central area of the capital but lay mainly to the north of the Thames. Here were to be found, often in geographically distinctive 'quarters', many of the older trades such as clothing and furniture manufacture, printing and publishing activities, and specialized engineering, such as the famous clock and instrument firms of Clerkenwell. Production was generally in the hands of quite small enterprises making components and/or finished products; often they were closely linked with each other, trading partly finished materials and sharing a common pool of skilled labour; and they tended to occupy small workshops in old, multi-storey premises.

A second zone of post-war manufacturing was located in the conurbation's outer suburbs, in such places as Harrow, Barnet, Bexley and Croydon. The industries in this zone were the product of more recent developments, a response to twentieth century technologies and market opportunities, and their specialisms included electrical, mechanical and instrument engineering, motor-vehicle components and assembly, and the manufacture of pharmaceuticals. Production tended to be housed in comparatively large, single-storey factories that were clustered along the conurbation's major radial roads, to a lesser extent along its railways, around the North Circular Road, and on such inter-war industrial estates with common services and good transport connections as Park Royal, Purley Way and Slough. The manufacturing companies in this zone tended individually to be much larger than those in the inner areas; and in some instances, typified by the Ford Motor Company at Dagenham and the Hoover factory on the Great West Road, they were part of a national or international complex of production facilities.

A third and very distinctive component of the capital's post-war manufacturing base was to be found on Thameside, downstream of Tower Bridge. Besides having such port-related activities as ship

and marine engine construction and repair, this was a zone in which advantage was taken of the low costs of water transport, where coal was transformed into town gas and electricity, and where other bulk materials such as lead, sugar and grain were processed advantageously, close not only to their docks of import, but also to the large London market.

In their scale and geography, London's service industries – providing the capital with utilities, transport, education and health care, for example – reflected the needs and the importance of the capital's resident population and its many manufacturing activities. They were also a function, however, of London's role as the seat of national government, as the locus of many national institutions – cultural, educational, medical and political – as the centre of the country's banking and financial system, and as the location of many company headquarters. They further reflected the international role of London as the focus of the Empire and Commonwealth. Together, the service industries provided nearly sixty per cent of the conurbation's jobs. Many were scattered throughout the conurbation, but the largest concentration was to be found in the cities of London and Westminster where a major complex of office activities was steadily expanding. It was a concentration of employment that was particularly dependent upon the public transport system for assembling its workforce from within and beyond the conurbation.

The growth of London's economy in the post-war years was partly the result of its favourable industrial structure. In addition, however, London's success was a reflection of innovations, a feature that was in part related to the existence, in and around the capital, of many private and government research establishments, the country's largest university and many other institutions of higher education. The spirit of innovation affected the provision of services as much as manufacture – London's retail trade spawned the first clothing boutiques, and its airports first provided for the development of package holiday tours on a large scale. It was also the case that the conurbation provided the largest consumer market in the country which inevitably reduced the risks of launching new products and services. A further element in London's post-war success was its nodality within the South East region (which housed nearly one-third of Britain's population), its accessibility to the country as a whole, and its exceptionally good physical and telecommunication links with the rest of the world.

Between 1951 and 1961, the number of jobs in the conurbation grew from 4.29 to 4.46 million, the increase being in both manufacturing and, more especially, the service industries. After 1961, however, although service employment growth continued unabated, jobs in manufacturing stabilized and then began to decline. This growth, and the changing economic geography of the London conurbation in the two post-war decades, can best be understood through an appreciation of two parallel processes – decentralization and renewal. These are processes which have in fact shaped the evolution of all major cities for centuries.

The accommodation of economic growth

In the modern period, London has always expanded outwards. As its wealthier inhabitants have sought more attractive and often larger homes with gardens on the edge of the built-up area, so have a widening range of activities found it advantageous to operate from locations further away from the centre of the city. Economic functions have benefitted from the physical space available for expansion in the suburbs, by the lower price of land there, and by a growing supply of local, suburban labour. Just after World War II, the country's main international airport was transferred from a cramped site near Croydon to the more distant but open space of Heathrow. Almost simultaneously the activities of the seaport of London began to move downstream from the up-river docks to more convenient and modern facilities at Tilbury, Felixstowe and Dover. After 1945, with gradually rising living standards and increasing personal mobility, inner London's population fell, while that of the adjacent counties steadily rose. Successful firms either expanded *in situ* or sought more extensive accommodation on sites in suburban locations. Sometimes, less profitable firms moved out to lower their costs and ensure survival. Unsuccessful firms contracted or closed, but in so doing allowed others to use their factories or offices, or facilitated the physical redevelopment of their former sites. Thus, the pattern of land use in the capital was modified as individuals, manufacturing companies, devel-

opers and local authorities built new housing, more factories and warehouses, additional office space and public buildings to accommodate the conurbation's economic expansion.

As it decentralized, manufacturing industry showed a growing preference not only for peripheral sites near the main arterial roads but also for locations beyond the conurbation, where land and labour costs were lower, and access to the national market often easier. This was especially the case once the construction of the national motorway network began in the 1960s. More reluctantly in the first instance, but eventually in increasing numbers, office employers also began to move away from the expensive central area, to lower cost and often more attractive locations in the outer suburbs. Harrow, Kingston and especially Croydon were typical reception areas for offices. It was in these outer suburbs, outside the area of the LCC, that pressures for further development were at their greatest in the 1960s, particularly along the major radial lines of communication, and in the north-west and western segments of the conurbation.

Meanwhile, higher value activities consolidated and strengthened their hold on the centre. Offices, especially for insurance, banking and finance, corporate headquarters, the provision of information and advice, and central government grew relentlessly. Tourist activities, cultural amenities and the entertainment industries expanded and prospered. Employment opportunities in the professions, especially the law and accountancy, multiplied. And the institutional role of London, as the home of learned societies, professional and trade associations, and pressure groups of all sorts, grew steadily. In finding accommodation in or near to the conurbation centre, office activities could enjoy and exploit an information-rich environment that was unparalleled both nationally and in some respects internationally. It was an environment that considerably enhanced the effectiveness and the efficiency of their operations.

There was one element in the process of metropolitan growth and adaptation after 1945 that was different from previous decades, however. This followed the establishment of a comprehensive land-use planning system under the 1947 Town and Country Planning Act, and a willingness by central government for the first time to intervene in the process of spatial economic development. In particular, successive governments committed themselves to the objectives of both regional planning (where the goals of intervention concern the broad pattern of physical and economic develoment throughout a region) and regional development programmes (through which government sought to steer some activities away from the more prosperous southern parts of the country to assist other, less prosperous regions in the north and the west).

Plans and policies

Under the 1947 Act, counties were charged with drawing up land-use plans. Superimposed upon these plans in the South East was a much grander planning scheme that related to the whole of the metropolitan area and the less urbanized territory surrounding it. This was the 1944 Plan for Greater London, drawn up by a team under Patrick Abercrombie. The planners took the view that the sprawling, relatively uncontrolled, inter-war growth of London was unsatisfactory, that the size of the conurbation was already too large, and that government should develop policies designed to achieve four ends.

The first of these was to restrain the growth of London and its population by resisting the geographical spread of the capital and holding back and diverting its economic expansion. The second policy was to redevelop, where appropriate, the central and especially the inner parts of the conurbation at lower residential densities, to provide better accommodation and improved environmental standards for the people living there. The third was to accommodate the population thus displaced from the inner parts of the conurbation and the activities unable to expand there, not only in the outer suburbs but also in planned developments in the Home Counties beyond. Finally, it was accepted that some of the economic and employment growth of the capital should be encouraged to move away from the South East altogether, into the less prosperous regions of the country where unemployment rates were persistently high and local growth limited.

This plan for London, after public discussion and some modification, was formally adopted by the government (Fig. 6.2). To contain the physical expansion of London, a green belt was designated around the conurbation. Around London, housing

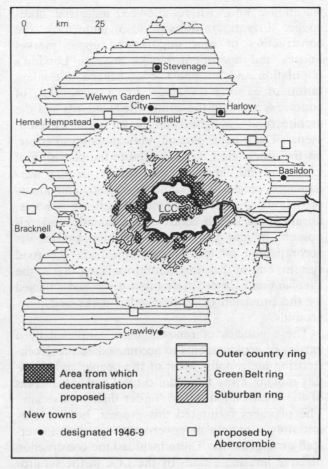

Figure 6.2   *the Plan for Greater London, 1944 (after J. Hall, 1976).*

and other developments not related to the perpetuation of an essentially rural economy and environment were severely restrained. To control economic growth, all proposals for new and enlarged industrial premises above a minimum size had to receive the approval of the Board of Trade (the predecessor of the Department of Trade and Industry) before local planning permission could be given and construction begin. These 'industrial development certificates' (idcs) were granted only sparingly in the immediate post-war years and in the 1960s, although their administration was more relaxed during the intervening period.

The policy of encouraging central and inner area renewal for commercial purposes was left primarily to private individuals, developers and companies who continued to provide new and adapted office, warehouse and, where allowed, industrial floor-space. Private initiatives also undertook the construction of new middle and upper market houses and apartment blocks and, as London's population and housing needs changed, the adaptation of existing dwellings. Local authorities, of course, supervized the siting, the standards and the architectural characteristics of all these developments. The greater part of public money and effort, on the other hand, was devoted to the provision of lower income housing, particularly in the war-damaged areas of London's East End, and to the provision of social amenities such as schools, libraries and health centres. Occasionally, redevelopment in and near the conurbation centre was accompanied by local improvements in the road system, one of the more ambitious being that at the Elephant and Castle; more often it was accompanied by the provision of badly-needed parks and play-grounds.

These policies of renewal were paralleled by a variety of arrangements to accommodate the decentralizing metropolis. Most of the people and activities moving away from the central and inner areas of the conurbation did so 'under their own steam'. The planners facilitated this process, however, by initiating a variety of government-sponsored over-spill arrangements. These included the construction of large housing estates by the LCC in the suburbs of the conurbation, but within the surrounding counties, at such places as Roehampton, St Mary's Cray and Erith and Plumstead Marshes (adjacent to the site that became Thamesmead). Planned overspill also involved deliberate 'town expansion' of some smaller centres in and beyond the rest of the South East – places such as Ashford, Basingstoke, Bletchley, Dunstable, Thetford and Swindon – the LCC carrying some of the organizational, architectural, building and population displacement costs.

By far the most important component of the planned overspill arrangements, however, was the designation and construction after 1947 of new towns. In the first instance, eight new towns – Crawley, Basildon, Harlow, Stevenage, Hitchin, Welwyn, Hemel Hempstead and Bracknell – were developed in a ring beyond the metropolitan Green Belt. Some of these, like Harlow, were located on essentially green-field sites; others, like Hemel Hempstead, were grafted on to quite substantial existing communities. In each case, a Development

Corporation was appointed by the government and charged with the task of not only preparing a plan and acquiring the necessary land, but also laying out the roads, building much of the housing, shops and commercial premises, establishing industrial estates and negotiating with the local authorities for the provision of schools and other social services. The Development Corporations also had the task of attracting employers from the inner areas of the conurbation or elsewhere, simultaneously offering accommodation to their employees who were willing to move out of London. The achievements of this approach to planned overspill led the government to designate Northampton, Peterborough and Milton Keynes as a second phase of new towns for the South East in the 1960s. Not only were these sited substantially further away from the capital, but their planned size was very much larger, in the case of Milton Keynes some 250 000 compared with the 50–80 000 originally planned for the first generation new towns.

By these means the natural tendency of the metropolis to spread progressively was endorsed and encouraged, while its equally natural tendency to sprawl over an ever-increasing area was controlled. The decentralizing forces of the city region were diverted and channelled to produce an urban form that, in the judgement of many, was environmentally more attractive than would have been the product of unconstrained market forces.

Certainly, by the early 1960s, when the Plan for London had almost run its course and further decisions were required about the planning of land-uses and the location of population and economic activities in and beyond the conurbation, it was judged that the broad strategy for the city region should remain unchanged. Indeed, to the measures restraining the growth of manufacturing industry in the conurbation were added a government agency to encourage office decentralization – the Location of Offices Bureau – and an administrative device to arrest the pace of new office construction, the 'office development permit' (odp). Moreover, a succession of plans – such as the 1964 South East Study, the 1967 South East Strategy, and the 1970 Strategic Plan for the South East (Fig. 6.3) – continued to be based upon the assumption that considerable environmental benefits could be won through a planned decentralization strategy without unwarranted public or private costs. All three plans

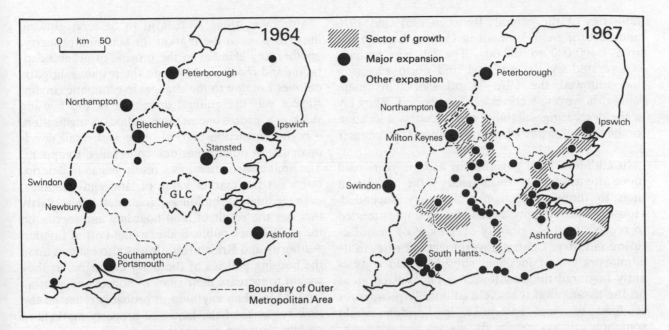

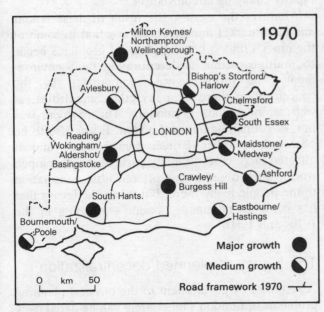

Figure 6.3   *Plans for the South East, 1964, 1967, 1970.*

urged the strengthening of green belt and country-side policies; all three advocated the provision of more planned overspill facilities. In the 1970 Strategic Plan for the South East, to the new and expanded towns programme, six major and five medium growth zones were added within which overspill population and economic activities from the London conurbation could be accommodated at minimum public expense.

Changing circumstances

The decentralization of London's population and activities was given expression not only in the succession of plans for south-east England, but also through a major change in the organization of local government. In 1964 the LCC was abolished. It was replaced by a larger authority, the Greater London Council, whose responsibilities extended over what in essence was the whole of the conurbation. Parts of the surrounding Home Counties passed into its control. Middlesex disappeared (except for the purpose of the Post Office and the game of cricket). The area was divided into 32 new London boroughs (Fig. 1.1).

Soon after its creation, the GLC recognized that it had inherited a number of serious problems, some of which had a geographical dimension. The process of decentralization, which was causing the population of the Greater London area to decline from 8.2 million in 1951 to 7.4 million in 1971, was not in itself a serious concern. Many people welcomed it, and the opportunities it provided for giving the remaining population more living space and re-developing the poorer parts of Victorian London. Behind the figures, however, lay a cluster of economic and social problems for the capital which were being made worse by government policies.

Central to these problems was the increasingly rapid employment decline in the manufacturing industries of the capital. Between 1961 and 1976 manufacturing employment in Greater London fell from 1 400 000 to 790 000. The fall was perhaps exaggerated by the national and world recession that followed the 1973–74 oil shock. Its main causes, however, were more deep-seated. They lay in the decreasing suitability of London as a location for nearly all types of manufacturing (see chapter 8).

In addition, local government had for years paid more attention to the social needs of the population than to the economy on which they depended. Housing and amenity needs, for example, tended to receive land-use priority over those of manufacturing industry. Central government likewise, in its administration of idcs and subsidies, had consistently favoured the new towns or the assisted areas on the assumption that the traditionally prosperous seedbed of new enterprise in London would somehow always retain its vigour and strength. Together, local and central government had also failed to improve the road system of the capital to retain its attractions for manufacturing enterprise (see chapter 9).

In parallel with the decline of London's manufacturing role, the Port of London and the railways also steadily shed jobs. The story was different, however, in other sectors of the capital's economy. Employment throughout most of the service sector continued to expand and was particularly buoyant in banking and insurance, in accountancy and the law, in education and health care, and in both central and local government. By 1976, services provided 2.73 million jobs in the capital, nearly three-quarters of total employment. The continuing growth of higher-order services in particular reflected the dominance of London as the most important and unrivalled 'central place' in the British economy.

By the end of the 1960s, however, the evidence began to mount that the labour force of the capital was failing to adapt quickly enough to changing economic circumstances. Skilled workers were in short supply. Unskilled workers found it increasingly difficult to find a job. The problem of unemployment was especially concentrated in the inner areas of the conurbation. Conditions there appeared to diverge increasingly from the prosperous central area, on the one hand, and the relatively prosperous outer suburbs, on the other.

Moreover, there were also to be seen growing imperfections in the market for land and property, another key element in the process of urban adaptation and renewal. Although the response in parts of inner London to the changes in economic circumstances was the gradual upgrading of the housing stock – a process sometimes called 'gentrification' – or the attraction of new office and retail developments, in other areas new roles failed to appear. The built environment, as a result, began to deteriorate. Yet the market value of land and buildings, even redundant buildings, remained high. Partly this was the result of land hoarding and inertia on the part of such public bodies as the Port of London Authority and British Rail. It was also blamed upon the housing policies of the inner boroughs, as they sought to increase their stock of houses and housing land. More than anything, it probably reflected the slow response of the land and property markets to rapidly changing circumstances.

Whatever the causes, the result of these labour and land-market imperfections was that in some of the inner London boroughs' social problems began to multiply within a deteriorating built environment. The problem was compounded by the concentration there of many ethnic minorities, as well as indigenous Londoners. The problem was not, of course, unique to London. It was also to be observed in other British conurbations, and it afflicted large cities in many parts of the developed world. Such observations offered little consolation to the people living there, but this is the legacy that has come to dominate London's planning in the 1970s and 1980s.

The legacy of planned decentralization

A response by government to the physical planning problems of London's inner areas can be dated back to the draft Greater London Development Plan in 1969. For the first time in an official publication, questions were raised about the medium and longer-term vitality of the capital's economy and the assumptions which had underlain government actions since 1945. The GLC argued for changes in the administration of idc and odp policies; it questioned the role of the Location of Offices Bureau; it expressed concern about the future employment prospects of many who lived in the inner parts of the conurbation. Partly in response, various urban aid programmes in the fields of education and housing were developed by central government to ameliorate at least some of the capital's persistent and worsening social ills. It was only in the middle 1970s, however, that a reasonably comprehensive set of policies was gradually pulled together under the umbrella of the 1978 Inner Urban Areas Act. It was from that date that most of the 'traditional' policies that were designed to encourage decentralization were set aside, and government became increasingly concerned with attempts both to slow down that tendency and also to promote more vigorously the complex process of inner area adjustment and renewal (see chapter 8).

The first 30 years after World War II, therefore, should be seen as a distinctive phase in the development and planning of London and its surrounding city region. It was a period when market forces were increasingly encouraging the decentralization not only of people but also an increasing number of economic and social activities. It was also a period when these tendencies were endorsed, to some degree accelerated, and in part guided by public initiatives and policies. What lessons can be learned from it?

In evaluating the experience of what has sometimes been called 'planned decentralization', four fundamental realities must be faced. First, Britain has a mixed economy; the evolution of the country's economic geography is influenced predominantly, therefore, by private rather than public decisions. The vigour and the location of economic and social activities are substantially determined by individuals, private companies, private institutions and (relatively independent) public industries, all of which take their decisions within the context of market circumstances and prices. The role of central and local governments, especially at the regional and sub-regional scales in matters concerning employment and urban change, is in reality quite modest.

Moreover, and this is a second point, the role of government is substantially passive in nature. Apart from the designation and establishment of New Town Development Corporations, the negotiation and implementation of town expansion schemes, decisions about the location and construction of new investments in transport infrastructure, and the provision of local authority housing and other building, Government either gives approval to private ambitions or denies them. It permits the construction of offices and factories in some places, and forbids them elsewhere. It delineates green belts and establishes conservation areas, and within both it restrains discordant developments. In essence, it provides the framework within which private interests and initiatives can express themselves; but it takes relatively few development initiatives itself.

Third, the urban system is steeped in inertia. The built environment, and the communications system that serves it, change relatively slowly. Adaptation and growth occur only 'at the margin', in a non-geographical as well as a geographical sense. The larger the urban area, and the more sluggish the pace of economic growth, the slower the rate of overall change. Since public policies influence only part of that change, governments are inherently limited in what they can achieve. Finally, judgements about policy effectiveness are inevitably constrained by the fact that in most situations it is difficult, if not impossible, to know what would have happened with different policies, or in the absence of policy. The evaluation of government actions is, as a consequence, as much an art as it is a science.

Nevertheless, the planned decentralization of the 1950s, 1960s and 1970s has clearly left a distinctive mark upon the broad physical expression of London's development during those decades. Urban sprawl was substantially arrested. An extensive green belt – admittedly of variable character, multiple uses and complex value (see chapter 15) – was established around the capital. The distinctive built environment of formal overspill schemes in the out-of-town estates, new towns and expanded towns appeared in the outer suburbs and the outer metropolitan area. Simultaneously, redevelopment in the inner areas of the conurbation promoted the movement of people and activities act of London and gave the local planners more room to manoeuvre. As a result of these policies, the residual residential densities were beneficially lower. In all these respects, the plans met their goals and were successful.

At the same time, it has to be remembered that the decentralization of people and activities in the post-war years was increasingly a market-induced process. By the middle 1970s, as has been noted, only some 13 per cent of the population that had moved out of Greater London since 1945 were accommodated in planned overspill communities. The other 87 per cent had moved away following their own initiatives. This does not undermine the logic of the formal plans; they made their distinctive contribution to the overspill process; they certainly accelerated its pace in the early post-war years; and they beneficially influenced the origin of some of the movement, permitting, for example, some less well-off families who might have been locked into the inner city to leave the capital. The modest size of voluntary overspill, however, is a reminder that the government's plans were endorsed by, and an endorsement of, powerful market forces. This experience suggest that London's planning today, in which the provision of assistance to the inner areas has become the dominant theme (see chapter 8), can only have comparable success if it acknowledges the need for economic renewal, based on new roles and new activities, rather than the restraint of market forces. The latter continue to encourage many people and activities to decentralize.

Another lesson comes from the attempt to manage urban form. The 1944 Abercrombie Plan confirmed a settlement pattern in which the primacy of London in South East England remained unchallenged, even though the capital's geographical extent was deliberately contained. The subsequent plans of the 1960s and 1970s, on the other hand, began to replace that notion with the idea of promoting 'countermagnets' – the second phase of new towns and the major growth areas – and implicitly accepted the goal of promoting a more diffused, poly-nuclear urban form throughout the region, focused on a number of major and medium growth areas (Milton Keynes, Reading and Southampton/ Portsmouth are but three examples). Some progress was made towards this objective. But by the late 1970s, a much more diffused pattern of settlement than was originally intended had also begun to emerge, as private preferences for living and working in small towns and villages – rightly or wrongly – overrode the goals of the planners.

In addition, the planners themselves could not always agree on their objectives. A classic example can be seen in the case of airport development. The regional plans of the 1950s, 1960s and 1970s generally ensured the timely provision of infrastructure to support the changing urban form of the London region. However, at no point was a proposal for a third international airport produced at the same time as a regional plan. Either the plans were announced without the various relevant authorities having decided on the need for, or the location of, such an airport; or the airport was proposed without provision for its effects upon the pattern of regional development.

A final lesson to be derived from the experience of planned decentralization concerns its effects upon the economy of the capital itself. Nobody knows whether or not government policies improperly weakened the economy of London in the short or longer term. Planned overspill undoubtedly provided accommodation for people and activities that would have left London in any case, and many jobs were lost through the structural contraction and closure of firms *in situ*. It is nevertheless inescapable that the use of controls (idcs and odps) prevented some development in the capital. At the very least, some new factories and offices were not built and the environment for production and commerce came to be poorer than it might otherwise have been. This must have had significant but unquantifiable effects upon the capital's overall output and productivity. It could also have affected the extent and the expression of enterprise. Moreover, emphasis of policies upon planned decentralization encouraged the London boroughs to be broadly indifferent to their economic bases for several decades, as they put their greatest efforts into housing and social welfare improvements.

The policy of planned decentralization had a sound logic and acceptable justification, but its implementation imposed both short and longer-term costs as well as benefits upon the metropolis and country. It was the costs which were for so long overlooked. In the immediate post-war years, they were relatively small and quite properly incurred. From the mid-1960s, however, it can be argued with hindsight that public policy should have become rather more conscious of a changing balance of advantage. Why did this not occur? The answer lies partly in the inertia of long-established planning priorities, focusing on the legacy of both Victorian inner-city slums and inter-war suburban sprawl. Controlled decentralization succeeded to a degree in alleviating both of these problems, and so was little challenged as the correct strategy until the late 1960s. The lack of research on London, the poor quality of detailed information available to policy makers, and the delay in making it accessible also prevented the planners from recognizing the symptoms of new ills. In developing an acceptable response to the modern problems of London, one of the major constraints remains the paucity of up-to-date and authoritative information. Nevertheless, the aim of the ensuing chapters will be to explore the aftermath of the era of planned decentralization in London, using the best evidence that is available.

Further reading

The general context of regional planning for London is discussed in:

Hall J M (1976) *London: metropolis and region* Oxford University Press

Hall P (1974) *Urban and Regional Planning* Penguin

Manners G *et al* (1980) *Regional Development in Britain* 2nd ed, Wiley

The main planning documents are:

Abercrombie P (1945) *Greater London Plan 1944* HMSO

Department of the Environment (1978) *Strategic Plan for the South East, Review, Government Statement* HMSO

Ministry of Housing and Local Government (1964) *The South East Study* HMSO

South East Economic Planning Council (1967) *A Strategy for the South East* HMSO

South East Joint Planning Team (1970) *Strategic Plan for the South East* HMSO

South East Joint Planning Team (1976) *Strategic Plan for the South East, 1976 Review* HMSO

The industrial background of the capital is analysed in:

Hall P G (1962) *The Industries of Greater London since 1861* Hutchinson

Martin J E (1966) *Greater London: an industrial geography* Bell

A useful cartographic presentation is:

Shepherd J, Westaway J and Lee T (1974) *A Social Atlas of London* Oxford University Press

7   Population trends

John Salt

Patterns of change

A city is like a living organism, kept vital by its population. People are born, live and die in it; they flow in and out; they circulate within it, conveying and conferring life and character. London is no exception. This chapter will focus on change in the population of the GLC area over the last decade or so. First it will review the patterns of change and then examine its two leading components, the processes of natural change and migration.

Total population

Britain's major cities have undergone large scale population decline in recent years but the causes and consequences of this trend are only partly understood. Decentralization, of course, is not new. Inner areas of most British cities have been losing people for a century. Greater London's population peaked at 8.6 million in 1939; inner London (the old LCC) had its maximum population in 1901 (4.53 million), falling to 2.3 million in 1981; outer London peaked in 1951 at 4.85 million. In the decades since the last war decline has accelerated (Table 7.1). Analysis of borough populations over time shows a series of population peaks moving steadily outwards in concentric fashion. For example, the City of London had its maximum population in 1801 (129 000), falling slowly until 1861, then more than halving to 51 000 in the next 20 years. Westminster peaked at 500 000 in 1871, subsequently declining continuously to 191 000 in 1981. Further out, Kensington had its heyday in 1901 with 250 000 inhabitants. The result of these trends is that London's population total is now similar to that of the early twentieth century; inner

Table 7.1   *Intercensal population change in London (per cent)*

	Inner London	Outer London	London total
1951–61	− 5.4	0	−2.5
1961–71	−13.2	− 1.8	−6.8
1971–81	−17.6	− 4.6	−9.9

Source: Censuses

London has its lowest population since 1841 and outer London is down to its 1931 level. However, there is some evidence that the rate of loss may be slowing down, largely because of a fall in annual net outward migration from 117 000 in 1970–71 to under 40 000 in 1980–81.

What has been the geographical pattern of recent population loss? Figure 7.1 shows what happened in London during the decade 1971–81. With the minor exception of the City, where the Barbican development provided new housing, all boroughs lost population. The average in the inner boroughs was 17.6 per cent, reaching 28.9 per cent in Kensington and Chelsea, the highest loss of any local authority in the country. All outer boroughs also lost population, with Brent and Richmond faring worst, though none exceeded a rate of 10 per cent.

Closer analysis shows a concentration of the heaviest losses in wards in the central boroughs, although even there not all wards were losers. Such inner area gains were usually the result of local authority redevelopment schemes, for example, in Islington and Tower Hamlets.

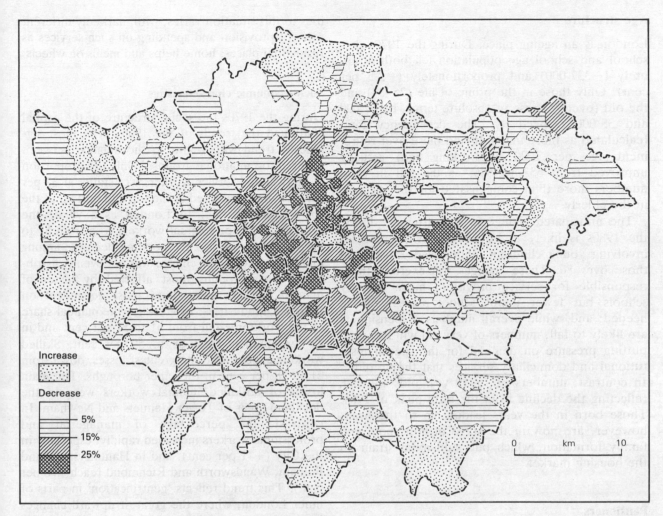

Increase

Decrease

- 5%
- 15%
- 25%

0   km   10

Figure 7.1   *Population change in Greater London, 1971–81.*

Households

For the purpose of assessing housing need (see chapter 10) changes in household numbers and structure are more important than simple population numbers. Unfortunately a change in census definition between 1971 and 1981 makes assessment of household change difficult. A simple comparison shows a loss of 144 000 households during the decade, though the GLC's own calculations suggest a lower rate of loss of 57 000, while Department of the Environment figures indicate a net gain of the same magnitude. These differences appear to be due to changes in the definition of one person households, for which the census indicates a 56 000 increase (26.5 per cent) over the decade, the GLC a rise of 135 000 and the DoE 199 000.

The census suggests that in 1981 single-person households were the most common size in seven boroughs (the central four, plus Hackney, Hammersmith and Fulham, and Islington). In contrast, ten outer boroughs and outer London as a whole now have more households with four persons than three. A polarization in household structure, therefore, seems to be developing, since in Greater London four-person and single-person households were the only categories to increase between 1971 and 1981. Although single-person households are concentrated in the centre, analysis at ward level indicates some outer London areas where they are dominant, usually in the central parts of boroughs like Harrow, Croydon, Richmond and Kingston where flats are concentrated.

Age structure

London is an ageing place. During the 1970s pre-school and school age population fell both absolutely (−337 000) and proportionately (−2.5 per cent). Only those in the prime of life (25–34) and the old (over 75) rose in absolute terms, by 67 000 and 38 000 respectively. The dependency ratio (calculated as those under 16 and those over retirement age per 1000 of working age) actually improved from 632 to 606, as the fall in child numbers more than compensated for the increase in the elderly.

The anticipated change in age structure during the 1980s is likely to be uneven, with increases involving young children, adults aged 25–49, and those over 80. These changes will exercise those responsible for service provision: more primary schools but fewer junior school places will be needed; and, while overall numbers of pensioners are likely to fall, numbers of very old will increase, putting pressure on demand for the special institutional and domiciliary services that they require. In contrast, numbers of 15–19 year olds will fall, reflecting the decline from the birth peak of 1964. Those born in the years leading up to the peak, however, are now in the stage of household and family formation, which puts additional strain on the housing market.

Pensioners

The existence of large numbers of elderly people creates its own social problems. By 1981, 18 per cent of Londoners were pensioners and 29 per cent of the capital's households were headed by them. The vast majority (97 per cent) live in private households but as the number of very old people increases more will require institutional care. Because of higher life expectancies for women, single elderly women living alone constitute a particular problem: in 1981 there were 293 000 households in Greater London containing only a single female pensioner. The difficult situation for pensioners living alone is compounded by the low level of amenities, especially for the very old. They are less likely to live in self-contained accommodation, with good access to baths and lavatories and, among women especially, may have virtually no access to cars. The response of the local author-

ities to this situation varies, with markedly different rates of provision and spending on such services as residential places, home helps and meals on wheels.

Socio-economic characteristics

During the 1970s the social structure of the capital continued the trends of the 1960s. The most significant trend was a shift in the balance between different occupational groups. While the proportion of clerical and service workers was static, at 37 per cent, change continued at the top and bottom of the socio-economic pile. In London as a whole the proportion of non-manual workers rose from 51 to 54 per cent, with a corresponding decrease among manual workers. The change was not evenly distributed. The boroughs most affected by losses of manual workers were those most dependent on traditional industries. In Hackney the manual share of the workforce fell from 61 to 51 per cent and in Tower Hamlets from 68 to 59 per cent. Skilled workers experienced the greatest losses, down from 21 to 18 per cent in the inner boroughs. The main losses of unskilled manual workers were in the dockland areas of Tower Hamlets and Newham. In contrast, the percentage of managerial and professional workers increased rapidly, especially in the City (+11 per cent), and in Hammersmith and Fulham, Wandsworth and Richmond (each + 6 per cent). This trend reflects 'gentrification' in parts of inner London, where the greatest upward changes in social structure have occurred.

Components of population change

The trends described above result from the interaction of processes of natural change and migration. The latter has been the principal and increasingly significant component. During 1961–71 a net increase through natural change of 5.6 per cent was offset by a migration loss of 12.4 per cent to give an overall loss of 6.8 per cent; in the next decade, natural increase was only 1.1 per cent and net migration loss 11.3 per cent, giving an overall loss of 10.1 per cent.

Again, the situation varied widely across London (Fig. 7.2). There was a clear distinction in the contribution of natural change and migration between the inner and outer boroughs, but local variations occurred within these two broad group-

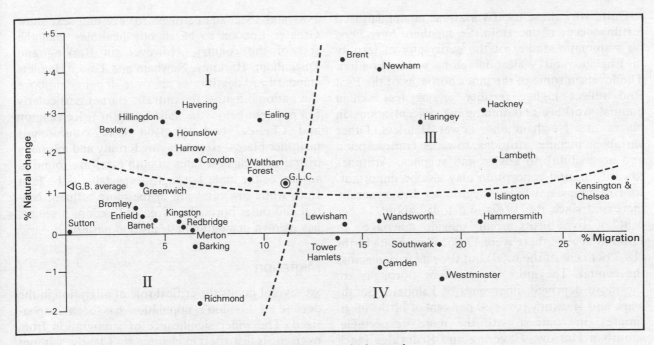

Figure 7.2   *Typology of natural change and migratory change, by borough.*

ings. Four types of experience emerge. *Group I* includes outer boroughs with relatively high rates of natural increase and low net out-migration. Most of these, therefore, had low levels of decline. *Group II* also had low net out-migration, but also very low natural increase (or decrease in two cases). These outer boroughs also had low overall decline and were generally stable in population terms. *Group III* includes those inner boroughs (and Brent) with high rates of both net out-migration and natural increase, the latter affected by high concentrations of immigrants. *Group IV* includes boroughs where high net out-migration is compounded by low natural increase or even decrease, leading to rapid population decline. This analysis indicates that while migration is the most important factor of population change in London, the local relationship between births and deaths varies significantly. What then are the trends in natural change in London?

Natural change

Fertility

The number of births in London fell from 113 068 in 1971 to 91 379 in 1982, though decline was irregular. Matching the rest of the country, a trough was

reached in 1977 when there were only 82 519 births. These trends were not even across the capital; in outer London births declined less than in the inner boroughs. Greater London as a whole proves, after standardization for age and sex structure, to be less fertile than England and Wales. London's fertility average for 1981–2 is 5 per cent below the national figure. Some boroughs, especially in the East End, are considerably more fertile than the capital's average: Newham, for example, is 22 per cent above the national rate. In contrast, standardized birth rates are around 10 per cent below average in some inner boroughs (Camden, Hammersmith and Fulham, Kensington and Chelsea and Westminster) and some outer ones (Bromley, Kingston and Richmond).

In a number of cases the pattern of high fertility correlates positively with a high proportion of births to immigrants. The highest proportions of births to New Commonwealth and Pakistani-born (NCWP) mothers were in Newham (41 per cent), Tower Hamlets (45 per cent) and Brent (46 per cent). Clearly the presence in these boroughs of NCWP populations has a dramatic effect on fertility levels. Births to Irish mothers occur especially in Brent, Islington, Hammersmith, Camden and Haringey, where they make up 5–8 per cent of the total.

Quite why these local variations in standardized fertility occur is uncertain. So far there have been no systematic studies of the geography of fertility in England and Wales, let alone within London. The levels in some of the inner boroughs of the East End reflect higher fertility among less skilled manual workers and immigrant concentrations in places like Newham and Tower Hamlets. Other variables include attitudes towards contraception and accessibility to advice and supplies. Attitudes towards marital conception may also be important. In Britain as a whole, illegitimacy has generally increased since the 1970s and today about 14 per cent of live births occur outside marriage. In London in 1982 there were 17 061 illegitimate births (18.7 per cent of the total) but the rate varied across the capital. The most 'promiscuous' boroughs are the more deprived inner ones of Lambeth, Southwark and Hackney (over 30 per cent of births illegitimate), in contrast with the more 'respectable' suburban Harrow, Havering and Redbridge (each with 9 per cent). Perhaps not surprisingly illegitimacy is more prevalent in the inner city, partly reflecting the larger numbers of single people coming there to live, partly also the presence in central London of several large teaching hospitals with maternity provision.

Mortality

Londoners are more equal in returning to their maker than leaving Him in the first place. The capital's death rate has been steadier than its birth rate, the general trend being to decline as the population falls through out-migration and the survival rate of those left behind increases. During the 1970s the Crude Death Rate remained fairly constant at around 11.4 per thousand, with slight annual fluctuations reflecting epidemics, such as that of influenza in 1976. The number of deaths in 1982 (76 804) was the lowest recorded since World War II. In contrast to child and adult mortality, which have changed little, infant and perinatal mortality have fallen steadily, from 2 000 to 900 deaths during 1971–81, in response to improved childbirth practice and neonatal care. London, in short, has become a safer place in which to be born.

Despite generally even mortality rates, there remain some spatial inequalities in the incidence of death across the capital. Average death rates for 1981 and 1982, standardized for age and sex, show Greater London to be slightly healthier than the rest of the country. However, in Barking and Dagenham, Hackney, Newham and Tower Hamlets standardized death rates are over 10 per cent above the national figure. In contrast, Barnet particularly (13 per cent below the national figure), Kensington and Chelsea, and Kingston were considerably healthier places. Hence, taking fertility and mortality overall, the highest rates in both cases are found in several of the inner boroughs, especially in the East End, while low rates are in the more affluent central and outer boroughs. Greater London, it seems, has its own demographic transition pattern.

Migration

At several points the critical role of migration in the decline of London's population has been emphasized. The wider significance of immigration from overseas is discussed in chapter 16. Clearly, without immigration from the NCWP, population decline in London would have been even greater. Internal migration within Britain has nevertheless brought about the main changes. London is the hub of a national migration system and is engaged in a complex series of population exchanges with the rest of the country. These exchanges involve a variety of people, and over time selective migration by different types tends to bring about change in the characteristics of the capital's residential population, as well as its numbers.

Scale and geographical pattern

Many people can claim that at some time they have been Londoners and a multitude passes 'through' the capital each year. The census records that in 1980–81, 107 457 moved to London from the rest of Great Britain, while 146 797 went in the opposite direction (Table 7.2). Thus, the net loss of 39 340 masked a very large gross flow. Data from NHS registrations paint a similar picture, gross numbers being rather higher than the census. They clearly indicate a falling net annual loss from London between 1979 and 1983, from 57 000 to 34 000. Analysis of the flow pattern for 1983 is revealing (Table 7.3), indicating a general tendency for London to gain from all regions except southern England, the only large deficit being with the rest

Table 7.2   *Migration between London and the rest of Britain, 1981*

Age	Numbers to GLC	Numbers from GLC	Net migration
0–16	12 963	23 744	−10 781
17–19	10 952	5 544	5 408
20–24	35 799	25 745	10 054
25–29	18 587	25 114	−6 527
30–34	10 016	17 302	−7 286
35–39	4 858	8 927	−4 069
40–64	10 369	26 282	−15 913
65+	3 913	14 139	−10 226
Total	107 457	146 797	−39 340

Source: 1981 Census

Table 7.3   *Inter-regional migration flow 1983 (thousands)*

Region	Migration to London	Migration from London	Net flow
North	6	4	2
Yorks and Humberside	9	6	3
East Midlands	9	8	1
East Anglia	7	11	−4
South East (excluding London)	72	118	−46
South West	14	18	−4
West Midlands	11	7	4
North West	13	8	5
Wales	6	4	2
Scotland	9	6	3
Northern Ireland	2	1	1

of the South East. It seems that the capital attracts people in from longer distances but dispatches them to adjacent or nearby areas.

London, therefore, presents some attractions to in-migrants. Its size means there are plenty of varied jobs and accommodation available and, perhaps more significantly, at any time there are likely to be large numbers of vacancies in both. This is especially important for white collar workers, for they can develop their careers within the hierarchies of government departments and large private organizations. The size and range of the London job market can also accommodate the joint careers of husband and wife, providing promotion opportunities for both without necessitating migration and the associated job loss for one partner. London is also a major centre of higher education and training, attracting in young people, many of whom stay after completing their studies.

Conversely, London also repels many, who consequently move out. It is expensive in many repects, most notably in housing and journey to work. For many, particularly the low-paid, housing cost is a major deterrent. For others, the sheer size of the capital is intimidating, and access to public open space is not the same as proximity to open countryside.

Migrant characteristics

The general pattern of change has been for the wealthier and more mobile sectors of the population to leave the inner areas for the commuting hinterland. A number of studies have shown how the proportion of upper socio-economic groups in cities has generally declined as decentralization has proceeded, leaving a core population with below average income and disproportionately large numbers of young adults and elderly. Decentralization seems to be less important for manual than white collar workers.

The characteristics of migrants have varied according to whether the outflow is planned, to new or expanded towns, or on a more individual basis. In general, the profile or migrants to new towns is not very different from the Greater London population as a whole. Fewer unskilled manual workers have gone to the new towns, but similarities in socio-economic characteristics are much clearer than dissimilarities. However, if one looks at individual boroughs which provided people for new towns, selectivity is clearer. Compared with areas of Islington from which they moved to Milton Keynes, new town migrants in one study in the early 1970s were more likely to be foremen, skilled manual or self-employed workers, and less likely to be white collar and unskilled manual workers. New town migrants were also more likely to be under 35 and with young families, rather than single. They were also more likely to be renting private, unfurnished accommodation, rather than living in owner occupation, council housing or the private rented furnished sector. Almost three-quarters said they had known someone else living in the new town before moving themselves.

Moves elsewhere tend to be in higher socio-economic groups than those going to new or expanded towns. Nevertheless, in the early 1970s migrants from London were more likely to be in lower status groups and to gain less financially from the move than people leaving other places in England and Wales. There was also a greater tendency for wives to stop working after the move and to start a family.

Motivation

In general, it seems that over half of migrants come to London for employment reasons but most leave to improve their housing situation. This is reflected in the age structure of migration streams (Table 7.2), which shows net gains for London of 17–24 year olds and losses of all other age groups. The size of out-movement among the over 60s gives some indication of the significance of retirement migration. Although it does seem that more unemployed come to London than move away, the overall importance of this group in the pattern of London's labour migration is not great, accounting for only 7 per cent of males and 3 per cent of females over 16 coming to London.

Of greatest significance in movements to London are the recruitment policies of employers, and in particular the role of the capital in the labour transfer policies of large organizations. These policies are a major factor in the turnover of London's population. Data from the Labour Force Survey show that in 1980/81, 65 per cent of employed men and 64 per cent of women moving to London did not change their employer. Comparable figures for those moving away from London were 71 per cent for men and 58 per cent for women. This evidence indicates that the majority of workers moving to and from London did not have to seek a job, but that the move was part of occupational or career development with their existing employer. Although these figures may overstate the total amount of this form of movement, because they include short-distance moves across the GLC boundary, they are consistent with other information. This indicates

that a majority of long distance migration involves people moving between the sites of such multi-locational organizations as government departments, banks, large manufacturers, retailers and nationalized industries.

Survey data for nearly a hundred large organizations in the early 1980s show that there were differences in the characteristics of movers in and out of London. Under 30s were more likely to come to London than move away, with the opposite being true for the over 40s. Particularly important, however, is the association of London with promotion in employment. Of those transferred into London, 59 per cent were promoted, compared with only 31 per cent of those moving away. The geographical pattern of moves within firms bears close resemblance to the inter-regional total migration pattern described earlier. London has gained from transfers originating in other large cities, but has lost to small and medium-sized places in southern England. Corporate policies reinforce and may have an important bearing on the overall geographical pattern.

In view of the large gross movements it is not surprising that studies indicate a restlessness on the part of many Londoners. A survey of over a thousand of them in 1977 found about half thought they would definitely move or would like to move from their present home. Intentions to move were highest among those living in inner London, the under 35s, single people and couples without children. Overall, two-thirds of those in the sample who were considering migration wished to move outwards, and only 4 per cent of those living in the suburbs were contemplating an inward move. Some 46 per cent of those thinking they would move gave improved accommodation as the main reason, a further 30 per cent did not like the area they lived in, and only 13 per cent gave employment change as a reason. The most distinctive feature of labour migration from London is, therefore, the importance of housing. Much movement out of London appears to be part of the life-cycle, associated with the desire of young couples, many of them lower paid (though not the lowest paid), to start and bring up their families in houses they own. The availability of houses for purchase at reasonable prices outside London has become a positive attraction to migrate. In this sense migration from London may be regarded as an attenuated form of ordinary residential migration as people move away from a city which cannot provide the housing they require (see chapter 10).

Conclusion

All the evidence suggests that London's population will decline in the future, albeit at a slowing rate. The relationship between births and deaths will have limited effect on the pace or direction of this trend. Immigration may have some positive effect on local fertility, but in general the high natural increase in 'working-class' London will continue to fall. The critical factor is migration, the engine that drives people through the capital, letting some off, allowing others on. The pace, capacity and selectivity of this will change both the capital's total population and its social structure. It will bring in fresh innovative minds and take them away again. It may leave a residue of the elderly, the infirm, and the less skilled. It will certainly be affected by what happens to the national economy: if depression continues London will continue to gain from migration. Ultimately, however, intriguing questions remain, applying not only to London but to all great cities: how far will the population go down, and will

stable numbers be accompanied by a stable structure?

Further reading

Probably the most useful overall review of London's population is:

Shepherd J and Congdon P (1986) *A New Social Atlas of London: Aspects of Change 1971–1981* Oxford University Press

A very useful series has been produced by the GLC:

Gilje E *et al.* (1983) 'Demographic review of Greater London 1983' *Statistical Series* **20** (contains commentary, maps and statistics)

Greater London Council (1983) '1981 Census data for London' *Statistical Series* **25** (contains statistics at ward level)

Congdon P (1983) 'A map profile for Greater London in 1981' *Statistical Series* **23** (contains maps at ward and borough levels)

On migration from London see:

Deakin N and Ungerson C (1977) *Leaving London: planned mobility and the inner city* Heinemann

Salt J and Flowerdew R T N (1980) 'Labour migration from London' *The London Journal* **6**: 36–50

8   Economic change

Peter Wood

National and local factors in economic change

The economy of London has always been strong. The city's very growth, to dominate a region of 15 million people, is a testimony to this fact. For centuries it has been by far the major centre of political, administrative, cultural and commercial life in Britain, and by the Second World War the size of its own regional markets, and easy access to other markets and to imported materials, enabled it also to become the largest manufacturing centre in the country. While other conurbations were more dominated by specialist industries, London's diverse and adaptable economy gave it a stability which was the envy of other regions of the UK. Why, then, does London now have economic problems? What is the scale of these problems, and are they temporary, or a sign of permanent change? Can Londoners, or central and local governments on their behalf, influence the trends? This chapter will explore these questions.

In seeking causes for change, two important influences need to be recognized as being at work during the past twenty years. The first is very general; the changing character of economic activity in Britain, and indeed in the Western world at large. One aspect of this has been the move towards control by large organizations, often operating on an international scale, controlling a number of sites within the UK. Decisions by manufacturing, office and many service firms about changes in their activities at individual locations have therefore increasingly resulted from comparisons with other places at which they operate. Today investment can more easily be switched away from high cost areas than in the past, when firms in traditional industries were generally smaller, tied more firmly to one region, and less exposed to outside competition.

Another aspect of modern economic activity is the impact of technological change. The pressure to adopt new working techniques and to discard old methods has intensified in recent years both through growing international competition and the increased pace of technical innovation, especially in 'microchip' technology applied to automated production, computing and information exchange. These pressures affect most aspects of production and administration. As a result, although new jobs have been created in some sectors, many traditional activities have reduced their labour needs, and are likely to continue to do so. In evaluating their existing patterns of location, and in seeking new sites, firms have become increasingly aware of the relative ease with which they can adopt these innovations, whether in the factory, warehouse or office.

These general trends in economic organization and other changes associated with them, especially in the demand for labour, affect every part of Britain. Their impacts on particular places, such as different areas of London, depend on a second set of influences arising from the spatial structure of the city itself and its effects on the operation of different economic activities. In the past, London's size and accessibility encouraged firms to exploit its skilled manual and white collar labour force, highly developed transportation facilities, and specialist markets and sources of supplies. High density industrial, port and commercial areas developed, in which the disadvantages of cramped sites and overcrowded working conditions were more than offset by the advantages of being in or near the centre of the metropolis. In recent decades, however, many of these advantages have disappeared. Skilled labour, especially in managerial and technical occupations, has moved to the suburbs and surrounding areas of south-east England, seeking modern housing and pleasant living conditions. The declining use of railways and the rise of road transport for both freight and passenger movement, has improved accessibility to most parts of the South East outside London, while increasing congestion within the city (see chapter 9). As these economic ties to London have loosened, so specialist suppliers and markets have dispersed. Space constraints in the city have become oppressive, as technical change has increasingly favoured modern, spacious factories and larger offices designed to accommodate computer and telecommunications equipment. For many economic functions, the advantages of operating in London have been progressively overturned.

In the late twentieth century, the inconvenience of congestion, long distance commuting and high costs of land and buildings have come to dominate the perceptions held of London and other British conurbations by many economic decision-makers. Now in a better position to choose between alternative sites, they have increasingly favoured investing in locations elsewhere. The evidence for the 1960s and 1970s confirms that many multi-plant manufacturing firms and some office organizations closed or reduced employment in their London establishments. Numerous small firms also closed in the face of declining demand and increased costs, and were replaced by many fewer new enterprises. Factories, offices and warehouses have moved out of London, in some cases encouraged by planners anxious to foster new and expanded towns (see chapter 6). This component of decline, however, has been small compared with the effects of general contraction. In many cases the transfer of new investment has not gone very far, often only to other areas of the South East. Thus, the greater London region has continued to spread outwards, and to dominate the UK economy. Meanwhile, economic problems within the metropolitan area have become more acute.

The problems of London, however, are not simply 'inner city' problems, associated with the decline of old, congested inner areas, and 'counter-urbanization', favouring areas outside. In particular, the collapse of employment in the old port of London has been caused by technological change in one key activity. In the late 1960s and 1970s, working methods in the upper docks failed to adapt to new containerization and roll-on, roll-off methods of rapid cargo handling. At the same time competition grew from smaller east and south coast ports, such as Felixstowe, Harwich and Dover, which did adopt these methods. The number of London dock workers fell from almost 23 000 in 1967 to less than 3 000, mainly at the container port at Tilbury, in 1984. Many other jobs were lost in associated activities such as ship repairing, marine engineering, cargo storage, handling timber and other materials, and food processing. As elsewhere in inner London, large firms closed their East End plants, and small firms also suffered, for example in the clothing trades of Tower Hamlets and Hackney and the furniture industry of Shoreditch. Between 1971 and 1978, 53 000 manufacturing jobs were lost in the five Docklands boroughs, as well as almost 30 000 in the transport industries, a decline of over 30 per cent in each case. Although an inner city element of decline was present, therefore, the experience of Docklands is more like that of coalmining, shipbuilding and steelworking areas elsewhere in Britain than other areas in London, because of the critical role of port decline, and its 'multiplier effect' on much other local manufacturing and service employment.

Another way in which London's economic problems are not purely inner city in their nature is the growing involvement of suburban areas (see chapter 14). Some of these, such as Acton, Ealing, Brent, Haringey or Barking, have already experienced acute economic change, as space and accessibility problems have increased and their physical fabric, predominantly built over fifty years ago, has aged. Also, of course, London is so large that some of its inner areas, especially in central London and in certain sectors (for example around London Airport) remain noticeably more prosperous than elsewhere. Growth in some parts of the city may be able to provide jobs for people affected by decline elsewhere. The problems of 'matching' new opportunities in some areas to the needs of people affected by decline elsewhere are much more complex in London than in the other areas of Britain undergoing inner city decline.

Recent trends in the London economy: the decline of manufacturing

In spite of the changes of the last two decades, the activities which form the economy of London remain enormously diverse. In considering current and future trends, we should distinguish between activities that are likely to decline, as a result of the influences described so far, and those that may prosper, at least as far as the national economy allows. One distinction commonly made is between manufacturing and services. In 1981, manufacturing, which had provided 30 per cent of the jobs in London in 1960, accounted for only 18.5 per cent of the workforce. The share of service employment has correspondingly grown. It is too simple, however, to associate manufacturing with declining employment, and services with stability or growth. While the widespread loss of manufacturing jobs in London is well documented, trends in the services are diverse and poorly understood. Special attention will therefore be given to them later in this chapter.

According to Fothergill and Gudgin (1982), between 1959 and 1975 London lost 37.8 per cent of its manufacturing employment, 586 000 jobs, a decline which had accelerated to an annual rate of 5.1 per cent in the early 1970s. This trend

reflected a national pattern affecting all of the large conurbations in Britain. The unique intensity of London's decline, however, seems to have been related to the effects of its great size on the level of disadvantage suffered by its manufacturing compared with other areas. Table 8.1 (a to c) is derived from the Census of Employment and takes the picture of overall change up to 1981, a year of recession similar to 1975. In the economic upswing between 1975 and 1978, manufacturing decline in London continued, but at less than 3 per cent per year. It increased again to over 5 per cent in the following three years when, in contrast with the earlier period, a marked reduction (4.6 per cent p.a.) was also experienced in the Rest of the South East (ROSE). Steady losses also continued in construction and the utilities (gas, electricity and water). Service activities suffered only a marginal rate of loss in London between 1975 and 1981 in contrast, however, with the vigorous growth taking place in ROSE. Data and classification changes make developments after 1981 difficult to trace.

Table 8.1   *Employment 1981 and changes, 1975–78, 1978–81, 1981–83, by sector*

	Greater London		Rest of South East		Great Britain	
(a) Employment, 1981, '000s (% of total)						
Manufacturing	650	(18.5)	991	(27.3)	5 924	(28.1)
Services	2 650	(75.4)	2 331	(64.1)	13 091	(61.9)
Mining/Construction/Utilities	211	(6.0)	236	(6.5)	1 762	(8.3)
Total (inc. agriculture)	3 513		3 635		21 148	
(b) Changes, 1975–78, '000s (%)						
Manufacturing	−67	(−8.0)	+15	(+1.4)	−217	(−3.0)
Services	−30	(−1.1)	+75	(+3.5)	+332	(+2.7)
Mining/Construction/Utilities	−17	(−7.0)	0	(0.0)	−60	(−3.1)
Total (incl. agriculture)	−114	(−3.0)	+86	(+2.4)	+40	(+0.2)
(c) Changes, 1978–81, '000s (%)						
Manufacturing	−119	(−15.5)	−101	(−9.2)	−1 193	(−16.8)
Services	−32	(−1.2)	+132	(+6.0)	+214	(+1.7)
Mining/Construction/Utilities	−15	(−6.6)	−8	(−3.2)	−145	(−7.6)
Total (incl. agriculture)	−167	(−4.5)	+23	(+0.6)	1 126	(−5.1)
(d) Estimated Changes 1981–83 (September) '000s (%)						
Manufacturing	−60	(−9.2)	−66	(−6.7)	−485	(−8.2)
Services	0	(0)	+12	(+0.5)	+111	(+0.8)

Source: Census of Employment (a–c), Department of Employment Gazette (d)

Table 8.2   *Employment change, 1975–81, GLC area and rest of the South East (principal sectors)*

Industry (In order of absolute loss, 1975–81)	1975 GLC total ('000s)	Changes, 1975–81 London '000s	%	ROSE %
Manufacturing				
Clothing and footwear	56.9	−26	−46	−20
Food, drink and tobacco	90.4	−21	−26	−7
Electrical engineering	136.3	−21	−16	+6
Mechanical engineering	84.7	−17	−20	−10
Metal goods	62.4	−17	−28	+1
Other manufacturing	42.1	−15	−36	−15
Timber and furniture	41.7	−14	−33	−12
Instrument engineering	31.5	−9	−30	−7
Chemicals	54.1	−9	−17	−3
Paper, printing, publishing	126.2	−8	−6	−8
Vehicles	52.4	−7	−14	−18
Services				
Distribution	516.3	−39	−8	+10
Public administration	352.6	−38	−11	−4
Transport and communications	407.4	−33	−8	+5
Construction	186.4	−24	−13	−5
Gas, electricity, water	54.4	−9	−17	+8
Professional and scientific	576.9	−7	−1	+6
Insurance, banking, finance	438.0	+25	+6	+40
Miscellaneous services	419.9	+31	+7	+21

Source: Censuses of Employment

Table 8.1(d) presents estimates, based on Department of Employment data, of changes between 1981 and 1983. Manufacturing employment continued to fall throughout the South East during this period of acute recession, by 4.6 per cent per year in London, to 590 000 and by 3.8 per cent in ROSE to 925 000. Service employment at this time remained virtually static, but had begun to rise again by late 1983.

Table 8.2 demonstrates that, while manufacturing in London generally suffered the largest percentage losses between 1975 and 1981 (with the exceptions of paper, printing and publishing, and vehicles), the service sectors experienced not only gains, but also some large absolute losses (for example in transport, distribution and public administration). The wide industrial spread of the contraction in manufacturing employment is noticeable, afflicting London's clothing, food and drink, engineering, metal goods and timber and furniture activities.

Most rates of loss were more than those experienced in Britain at large, and contrasted with much slower decline or even modest growth in ROSE (for example in electrical engineering). Thus, the 'London factor' was still at work, reducing levels of all types of manufacturing in the city.

The prospects of halting this decline of manufacturing in London, let alone fostering new growth, seem slim in the mid-1980s. Urgent attention has nevertheless been given to this objective in recent years. Most policies for reviving the London economy, as we shall see, have concentrated on manufacturing, in spite of the dominance of service employment. Certain types of traditional manufacturing, with strong market links to London, including printing, clothing, some engineering and related production will need to remain in the city. In many cases, the generally small to medium sized firms in these industries depend for their markets on service functions in London, such as finance, advertising, wholesaling and retailing, and so their prospects will follow the fortunes of these sectors. The same may often apply to new forms of manufacturing, for example in computing and communications equipment, although these may also benefit from the city's nodality as a centre for information and sales contacts farther afield. The particular advantages of London as a 'seedbed' of new small enterprises serving national markets in both traditional and new industries have nevertheless largely disappeared, and their dependence upon the London market, dominated by service activities is now very heavy.

If larger-scale manufacturing, serving national or international markets, is to be retained in London, mainly in suburban areas, the decisions about their sites, made by the remaining multi-plant firms represented in the city, will be critical. Since the late 1970s, these types of establishment have suffered the greatest losses of employment. In some cases, however, the security of employment in large plants can be influenced by planners. Success will depend upon the ability of firms to modernize and expand such plants, in the same way as outside London, for example by zoning vacant land for expansion and improving local and regional road access.

The impact of economic changes on Londoners

These changes in the demand for workers in London represent one side of an equation, the other

Figure 8.1   *Unemployment among economically active persons of working age in the GLC, 1981 (after P. Congdon, 1983)*

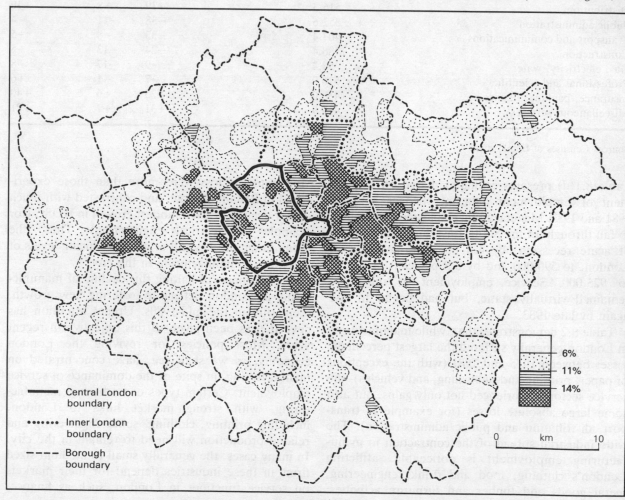

Central London boundary

Inner London boundary

Borough boundary

6%
11%
14%

0   km   10

Table 8.3   *Total employment shortfall in London, 1971–81 (% of 1971 economically active population)*

	Central London	Inner London	Outer London	Greater London
(a) 'Causes'				
(i) Changes in eligible workforce (i.e. age and activity rates)	2.0	−0.8	1.2	−0.3
(ii) Fall in available employment	−22.3	−18.9	−5.1	−10.7
(b) Result				
(iii) Employment shortfall (ii) − (i) or (iv) + (v)	24.3	18.1	6.3	11.0
(c) 'Effects'				
(iv) Net out-migration of workers	21.5	13.6	2.9	7.2
(v) Increased unemployment	2.8	4.5	3.4	3.8
(vi) Change in economically active residents (ii) + (v) or (i) − (iv)	−19.5	−14.4	−1.7	−6.9

Source: GLC Statistical Series No. 31, 1984

side of which is the number of workers available to fill the jobs. If the economic impact on Londoners of declining employment, especially in manufacturing, is to be explored fully, some account must be taken of the 'supply' side of the equation. The 1981 Census allows this to be done, and compared with a decade earlier. The most notable development, of course, which has created the strongest pressures for new economic policies in London, has been the growth of unemployment (Fig. 8.1). Between 1971 and 1981, the rate almost doubled, from 4.6 to 9.0 per cent of the economically active population. In wide areas of inner London, the level in 1981 was over 14 per cent including much of Docklands, inner north London (including Hackney, Islington and parts of Camden), inner south London (including Lambeth, Southwark and north Wandsworth), and north Kensington and south Brent, to the north-west. Generally speaking, unemployment levels were much lower in outer London, averaging only 7 per cent, but they were considerably higher in lower Thameside, to the east, and in parts of Ealing to the west. In spite of these high levels, the unemployment rates in inner London would have been very much worse if the numbers of economically active residents had not

fallen by over 14 per cent (213 000) during the decade (Table 8.3). By far the largest cause of this change was net out-migration, which was especially heavy from central London (21.5 per cent). In outer London, although the proportions of working men and single women declined, the size of the workforce increased (by 1.2 per cent) because of growth in the numbers of married women working. Net out-migration from the suburbs was also quite small (2.9 per cent), so that the loss of jobs (by 5.1 per cent) had a more direct effect on unemployment rates than in inner London. Thus, although levels of unemployment were much higher in inner London, their rate of increase between 1971 and 1981 was faster in outer London.

As might be expected, there was a huge reduction in the numbers of resident manufacturing workers, by 46 per cent in inner London and 55 per cent in central London (Table 8.4). By 1981, 389 000 fewer manufacturing workers lived in London compared with 1971. The decline of service workers was much less, and in fact the number grew by 6 per cent in Outer London, favouring jobs for women. One-third of women's jobs in outer London, however, were part-time, mostly in office-based services, distribution and the catering trades. These trends

Table 8.4   *Changes in residents employed in manufacturing and services, 1971–81, '000s (% of 1971 employed population)*

	Central London	Inner London	Outer London	Greater London
Manufacturing	−27	−160	−232	−389
	(−55)	(−46)	(−36)	(−40)
Services	−61	−96	+66	−30
	(−26)	(−12)	(+6)	(−1.6)

Source: 1981 Census

emphasize the now overwhelming significance of service employment for Londoners. By 1981 only one in six of inner London and one in five of outer London workers were employed in manufacturing. The main concentrations of these (Fig. 8.2) were therefore not in the inner areas of the city, but in the suburbs to the north-east (in Enfield, Waltham Forest and Haringey), to the east (in Barking and Dagenham and Havering), and to the west (in Ealing, Brent, Hounslow and Hillingdon). Services provided jobs for more than 85 per cent of workers living in many areas of inner London as well as those in wide areas of the suburban north-west and south. The predominant types varied widely between these areas, however, with professional, managerial and clerical workers well represented in the suburbs and certain areas of central London, and the lower paid semi-skilled and unskilled more important in inner London.

It follows that unemployment in London is also

Figure 8.2   *Employment in manufacturing in the GLC, 1981 (after P. Congdon, 1983).*

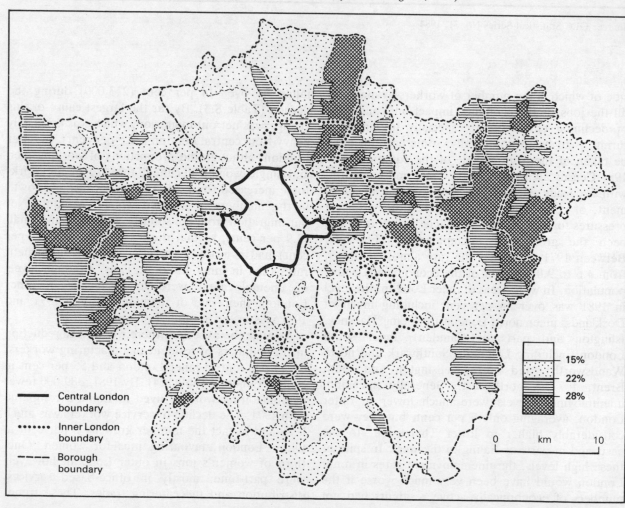

Central London boundary

Inner London boundary

Borough boundary

15%
22%
28%

0   km   10

a problem mainly for service workers. In 1981, 63 per cent of the male and 85 per cent of the female unemployed had last worked in a service industry, particularly in personal services, distribution and catering. Only 16 per cent had been last employed in manufacturing. The unemployment rate in construction was highest (12.5 per cent), but workers in 'other services' were experiencing a level of 11.2 per cent, compared with only 7.1 per cent in manufacturing. Thus, whatever success may be achieved in arresting the decline of manufacturing in London, the fortunes of the service sector are much more fundamental to the economic prospects of both the employed and unemployed of the city.

London's service economy

The dependence of three-quarters of London's jobs upon a wide range of service employment (Table 8.1) is generally regarded as a source of economic strength, especially in a period of rapid manufacturing employment decline. Nevertheless, recent changes show trends which, if they gather momentum, would undermine the role of many services as bastions of employment in the city. The major shift taking place is a dispersion, like that in manufacturing, towards the ROSE. The data to measure this are unfortunately very simple, and allow only a comparison between changes in Greater London as a whole and the ROSE (which includes such diverse areas as south Hampshire, Essex, Berkshire and Kent). Local differences of experience certainly exist both within London and the rest of the region.

In spite of London's established dominance in service employment, with 53 per cent of the region's service jobs in 1981, compared with 40 per cent of its population, some service activities have been following the movement of population out of the city for several decades and are now better represented in the ROSE. These include *consumer-orientated* activities such as retailing, educational, medical and other professional services, personal services, the utilities and motor repair (Fig. 8.3). Of these, between 1975 and 1981, only personal and some professional services showed employment growth in London comparable to that in ROSE, sustained by activities related to business and tourist functions, rather than the consumer services more typical outside the city.

Significantly, ROSE also possessed a higher share of certain *production-related* services, boosted by manufacturing decentralization and transportation developments in recent decades. These include dealing in industrial materials and machinery, road haulage and port activities. In the latter two, the especially rapid collapse of employment in London left ROSE with the dominant share. In addition, construction, serving both consumer and producer needs, declined markedly less rapidly in the ROSE than in London or nationally. Thus, among activities already well represented in ROSE, whether consumer or producer-orientated, growing or declining, relative dispersion from London was still active.

The future of London's service employment probably depends much more, however, upon those business, government and tourist-related activities in which it still possesses a dominant regional and national share (see chapter 13). The *business services* constitute insurance, banking, accountancy, legal and other activities (including, for example, property management and advertising). These continued to grow in London between 1975 and 1981 but at much slower rates than nationally or in ROSE. In fact, the numbers of jobs created in these activities in ROSE were much greater than in London. Some of this rapid growth in ROSE, however, was probably in more consumer-orientated services, and did not challenge London's dominance of national business employment. Nevertheless, there is considerable evidence that business office employment is moving away from the city, in search of lower rents, more pleasant environments, an accessible labour force, and new buildings that can accommodate automated working techniques, linked if necessary to the City of London by modern telecommunications. The effects of technological change, especially on more routine office activities, are likely to continue to limit business employment growth in London and perhaps increasingly to favour ROSE. Although London remains predominant, therefore, considerable uncertainty hangs over the future of employment in its private-sector 'office' functions.

The impact of national cuts in *government* employment between 1975 and 1981 was more severe in London than in Britain at large. Combined with long-established policies of decentralizing jobs in the civil service to other parts of the

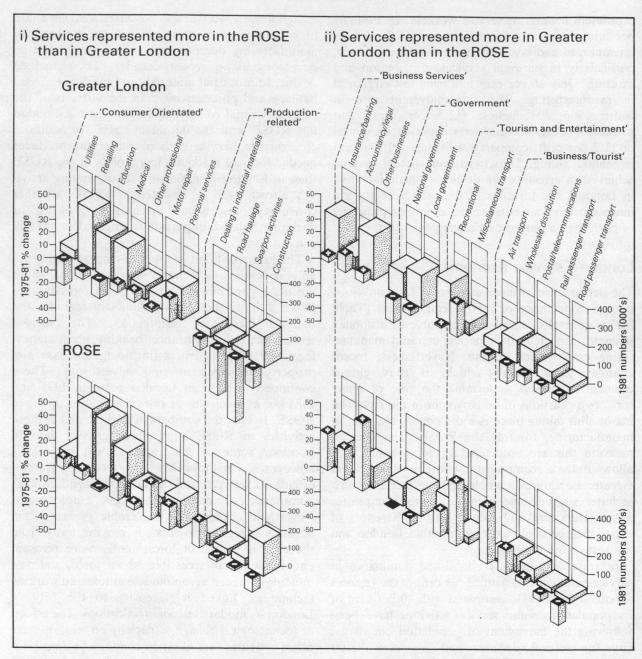

i) Services represented more in the ROSE than in Greater London

ii) Services represented more in Greater London than in the ROSE

Figure 8.3   *Service employment in GLC and the ROSE, 1981, and percentage change, 1975–81.*

country, this trend is likely to continue in the foreseeable future. Employment in local government, on the other hand, was sustained at almost the same level, reflecting the complexity of administration in the capital at a time when educational, housing and many other social problems were intensifying. One important purpose of the local government reorgan-

ization planned for the mid-1980s, however, is to reduce this kind of employment sharply.

Another group of London-dominated activities which is popularly perceived to have shown marked growth in the 1970s is associated with *tourism and entertainment*. Some 'recreational' activities such as restaurants, clubs and sports, in fact grew quite rapidly in London, but employment in others, including public houses and hotels, actually fell between 1975 and 1981. In all of these, employment grew more rapidly and by a much greater number in ROSE. Even in miscellaneous transport services, many of which in London are closely linked to the tourist trade, the rate of growth in ROSE was twice that in London. The employment impacts of tourism in London, as far as they can be detected from these data, have therefore been masked by other shifts, including the decline of inner London's population and growing recreational expenditure by residents throughout the region. The overall effect seems to have been very modest compared with that of decentralization and strong consumer-related growth in ROSE. A similar pattern occurred in the three remaining London-dominated sectors related to business and tourist activities (air transport, wholesale distribution and, to a smaller extent, postal and telecommunication services); namely, a marked drift outwards, in these cases losing jobs in London, with gains in ROSE.

Of these key sectors of London's employment therefore, only local government and the small rail and road passenger transport industries maintained their levels between 1975 and 1981, compared with national trends and the ROSE. None of these offer realistic prospects of growth in the future; a marked reverse is much more likely. Thus, in spite of the importance of services for employment in London, few sectors at present show any sign of convincing employment growth to offset future manufacturing decline. A combination of the relative decentralization of virtually all activities, including those most associated with London's special economic role, technological change, especially in telecommunications and office management, and cuts in government employment, point to a declining level of service employment in the 1980s. These issues are discussed further in chapter 13.

London will nevertheless remain heavily dependent on service jobs and, as well as their quantity, the quality of work they offer may create problems especially for inner Londoners. Much of the growth of service jobs in recent years has been filled by female workers, many low-paid and often part-time, servicing private sector offices, retailing, and seasonal catering, hotels and other tourist activities. Qualified managerial, technical and professional jobs, on the other hand, are increasingly decentral-

izing or being filled by commuters from outer London or beyond. While some relatively skilled or trained manual workers are required in building construction and maintenance, equipment servicing, vehicle driving, security and similar services, the number of these jobs is small compared with the decline of manufacturing and the port, which offered most male employment in the past. There are fears, therefore, that the service economy is offering Londoners increasingly poorly paid and casual or part-time work, compounding the effect of growing unemployment.

Policies for economic revival

Since the 1960s, the problems of declining inner city areas in Britain have attracted growing attention, and increased efforts have been made to reverse the trend of decline by both local and national government. Until the mid-1970s, most emphasis was placed on improving the obvious social, educational, housing and environmental deficiencies of these areas. As the problems persisted, however, and intensified in the post-1973 recession, two important features of urban decline were increasingly recognized. First, it was fundamentally an economic malaise caused, as we have seen, by the national decline in manufacturing employment and the tendency for manufacturing and services to leave cities. Growing unemployment and low incomes underlie many other social ills. Second, only close cooperation between central and local government, and with other agencies where necessary, is likely to reverse the economic decline, if it is possible to do this at all.

These assumptions lay behind the 1978 Inner Urban Areas Act, which set up seven 'partnership' authorities in England, including Hackney/Islington, Lambeth and Docklands in London. In these areas, new government funds were made available, in addition to those already being spent by local authorities. The 'partners' included district and county councils, the Manpower Services Commission, with its responsibilities for training, local health authorities, and various ministries, including especially the Department of the Environment. Although the prime aim was to foster economic regeneration, coordinated policies for housing, transport, educational, environmental, community, recreational and health improvements were also important, as part of the 'total approach'. Other, supposedly less deprived areas also received some aid, as 'programme areas', in London including Brent, Hammersmith and Fulham, Tower Hamlets and Wandsworth.

In all these areas, new powers to encourage economic development were granted to local authorities, subject to Department of the Environment approval. 'Industrial improvement areas' were designated in the partnership boroughs, within which loans for the acquisition and improvement of land were available, as well as loans or grants for environmental improvement and the adaptation of industrial or commercial buildings. Here and elsewhere, the partnership authorities could also make interest-free loans for site preparation and other

infrastructure expenditure, give grants towards the payment of industrial and commercial rents, and help small companies and cooperative enterprises pay the interest on private loans. Seventy-five per cent of the cost of this support was to be paid by central government, within an agreed annual budget. In 1983/84, for example, the provision of partnership funds was £11 millions to Hackney, £10.35 millions to Islington and £13.50 millions to Lambeth, with 32, 38 and 30 per cent respectively going to economic development projects.

Docklands

In spite of this level of expenditure, the partnership schemes have made only a marginal impact on the

Figure 8.4   *Docklands and East London.*

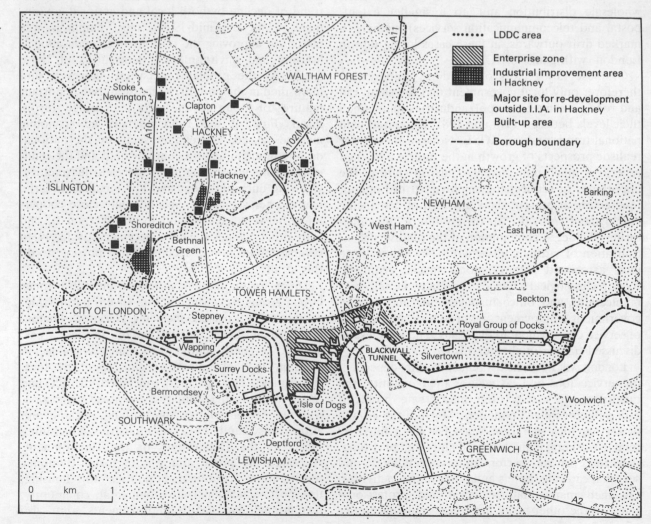

Wapping High Street: Gun Wharf.
The decline of the traditional inner London economy, and especially of its port, was reflected in the empty warehouses
that lined the river in the late 1970s. More recently, many of them, including those shown here, have been renovated
for high-cost residences, but the jobs they once offered have not been replaced.

economic prospects of their areas, mainly, as we
have seen, because general economic decline in
London has continued unabated. Since the election
of a Conservative government in 1979, however, the
schemes have been subject to some important
changes in London. The first of these took the form
of a radical new initiative in Docklands (Fig. 8.4).
A Docklands Joint Committee of representatives
from five London boroughs and the GLC, set up at
the beginning of 1974, had already produced a Strategic Plan in 1976. This, with central government
involvement, had become the partnership authority
in 1978, with the plan as the basis of a development
policy. In 1982, however, the DJC was replaced by
the London Docklands Development Corporation,
a body appointed by the Secretary of State for the
Environment. The LDDC was given complete planning powers for the areas worst affected by the
decline of the port. In effect, the government,
recognizing the scale of the Docklands problem,
imposed its own solution against opposition from
the elected Labour-controlled local boroughs.

This change highlighted different political philo-
sophies about how economic revival may best be
served in Docklands. Before 1979, under the
Labour government, although the need to attract
private investment was recognized, especially in
manufacturing, more emphasis was placed on initial
public spending on council housing, and on transport, social and environmental improvements, to
serve the foreseeable needs of local people. After
this, however, the leading role of outside private
investment became increasingly emphasized. The
LDDC was allocated funds rising to £70 million per
year by 1984/85 to acquire land, especially from the
Port of London Authority, the Gas Corporation
and other large landowners and to implement a
rapid physical transformation of 21 km² of the
derelict port. Priority was given to preparing sites
which would attract new private investment in profitable industries, offices, housing and recreational
activities. Not least among the tasks of the LDCC
was the transformation of the Dockland 'image'
through advertising campaigns, emphasizing its

proximity to the City of London and its potential for high technology industry and services.

Investment in the Docklands areas nearest to the City, in St Katharine Dock and in Wapping, had already been attracted under the DJC, in tourist-related activities, offices and the relocation of a major newspaper firm from Fleet Street. A number of other prime riverside sites near to the City are also being transformed into office and residential complexes. The problem for the LDDC has been to find investment for the much larger and more 'remote' docks on the Isle of Dogs (the West India and Millwall Docks), the Surrey Docks south of the river, and the Royal Group to the east.

In this task, it has been aided by the designation of a large part of the Isle of Dogs as an Enterprise Zone in 1982. In this area, firms were given a ten year period free of local rates, 100 per cent tax allowances on building costs and streamlined planning and other administrative procedures, as well as building grants and loans for site preparation, building costs and rents. Much of the LDDC's effort between 1982 and 1985 was therefore put into transforming the West India and Millwall Docks through land clearance, installation of services, and improving transportation, including the construction of new roads and a light railway to the City of London, to be completed by 1987. Elsewhere, especially in the Surrey Docks, where a huge area of land had been earlier reclaimed for development, and around the Royal Group, progress has been slower, although many speculative development schemes have been proposed. Large-scale private house-building for owner occupation, a new phenomenon in Docklands, has gone ahead at Beckton (see chapter 10), and a proposal to build a 'Short Take-off and Landing' (STOL) airport in the Royal Group to serve the City of London was approved in 1985. The LDDC believes that this could provide a much-needed stimulus to economic regeneration in this area, even though the scheme is opposed by local groups, the Borough of Newham and the GLC (see chapter 19).

The promotion of such huge land development schemes inevitably takes time to make an impact, especially on employment in a period of economic recession. Housing, new infrastructure and recreational facilities are actively under construction, as well as new factories, offices and studios for small and large companies, for example in publishing and television production. In 1985, however, it was still not clear whether significant numbers of permanent jobs would be created, and even less whether they would benefit the residents of the surrounding East End boroughs, rather than in-commuters. Docklands is certainly being transformed, but it is too early to judge the significance of this change for the economy of London or the welfare of Londoners.

Hackney and the Urban Programme

The philosophy of attracting private investment also began to permeate support for projects under the conventional Urban Programme in the early 1980s, in Hackney, Islington (which were made separate programme authorities in 1980) and Lambeth. More emphasis was placed by the Department of the Environment on 'economic' rather than 'social' projects, including the creation of employment, transport improvements, business advisory services and training schemes. The influence of all the inner city programme on private investment, therefore, became more critical to their success. Ideally, relatively modest public expenditure on land improvement, the rehabilitation of old buildings, support to firms in creating or retaining jobs, and transportation and infrastructure improvements, should attract several times as much private capital. This 'levering' of private investment is, of course, fundamental to the Docklands scheme, where the hope is to attract at least five times as much private capital as will be invested by the LDDC.

In a programme authority, such as Hackney, the process is likely to be more difficult (Fig. 8.4). The area is heavily built-up and highly congested. Having lost over 18 000 manufacturing jobs, 40 per cent of the total, between 1973 and 1981, and three major employers, accounting for 3 000 jobs in the early 1980s, the area possessed more than 186 000 m² of vacant factory space in 1984. Most of this, however, was in obsolescent, complex sites, difficult to rehabilitate and provide with modern access and services. The assembly and preparation of sites for employment-related investment is a slow process, and the unattractive image of the area for private investment is difficult to overcome, in spite of its close proximity to the City of London. Such areas, of course, also suffer growing competition for investment from elsewhere in London, especially from the much better-endowed Docklands.

In 1982, a new source of support was made available to partnership areas; the Urban Development Grant. The aim of this scheme was again to encourage large amounts of private capital into job-creating projects through relatively modest government subsidy. In Hackney, insurance companies and pension funds have been encouraged to cooperate in such projects. If successful, they could attract outside finance on a much larger scale than the Urban Programme projects. By 1984, for example, schemes worth £20 million were being negotiated in Hackney.

A further change which affected the pattern of economic promotion in the inner city area in the early 1980s arose from general cuts in the real resources available to local authorities. The Urban Programme was always intended as a 'pump priming' effort, with relatively modest resources used to support innovative ideas for a three year period. If successful, these were intended to be absorbed into spending by local authority 'main programmes'. Even before the 1978 Act, such programmes already included growing expenditure within severe legal and financial limits, on information provision, site preparation, the rehabilitation of old factories, the building of advance factories and support to small firms. This economic promotion effort, however, has to compete with the other commitments of local authorities to housing, education, health, social service and environmental improvement in their areas. The ability of local authorities to sustain independent economic promotion programmes, building on the experience of the Urban Programme, will therefore be severely restricted by any limitations on their resources. In 1983/4, although Hackney received £11 million for partnership projects, it also lost £11.5 million of its rate support grant, because it spent more than government guidelines allowed. Continuing pressures to cut public expenditure in the 1980s are likely to create similar contradictions. The net effect of such changes, apart from limiting the public resources available to inner city regeneration, will be to place more expenditure under the control of the Department of the Environment, through new Urban Programme projects and Urban Development Grants.

This account of economic promotion policies sponsored by central government in association with local authorities does not, of course, encompass a wide range of local efforts to retain or create employment in inner London by voluntary organizations, often with public financial support. Many of these are directed towards encouraging small firms or the training or re-training of the unemployed (see chapter 19). Since 1981, the GLC has also initiated an ambitious economic strategy of its own, particularly emphasizing job saving or creation. The main instrument of this has been the Greater London Enterprise Board, a company set up to help firms, cooperatives and trade union organizations to retain or develop employment opportunities by offering financial help, technical expertise and assisting in land acquisition and preparation. GLEB represents an attempt to use public money directly in the transformation of production to serve community needs. Its so far largely experimental role is, however, likely to come to an end with the abolition of the GLC in 1986 (GLC, 1985).

Conclusion

This chapter has depicted a pessimistic picture of the future of London's economy and of the likely effectiveness of the urban policies designed to reverse its decline since 1978. These policies are arguably too small in scale to have much effect, especially as local authority expenditure is cut, are now critically dependent on the attraction of huge amounts of speculative private investment, and are beset by conflicting political attitudes to their aims and methods. It is also not clear that strategies emphasizing private investment in vacant or derelict land will create jobs, especially the types of jobs needed by the unemployed and poorly paid of inner London. Real success in some areas such as Docklands, also may not be matched elsewhere, or may even worsen the prospects of revival there.

In spite of the detailed arguments about policy, however, the future of London's economy still depends on the broad factors outlined at the beginning of this chapter. All speculation about the future of manufacturing and service employment depends upon assumptions about the growth and international role of the UK economy. Success or failure at this level set the conditions for what happens at the regional scale. Nevertheless, although national trends will affect the rate and pattern of change, Greater London in the late 1980s seems likely to suffer a continuing contraction in

employment; the prospects of reversing the manufacturing decline are slim, and the city's share, and
probably its level of service employment are falling.
The rest of the South East region, however, will
almost certainly increasingly dominate the pattern
of national economic growth.

As we saw in Table 8.3, for the 1970s, the effects
on Londoners of any fall in future labour demand
will depend also on population and economic
activity changes. We are witnessing a long-term
process of population dispersal from Greater
London, which began almost a century ago, and has
been followed by economic activity since the last
war. These changes could be accepted with relative
equanimity, of course, if they were not accompanied
by growing unemployment, declining incomes, and
other associated aspects of deprivation for many
residents of the city. The reduced economic dominance of London might be interpreted in a better
light if the transition to a less dense, less congested,
higher quality living and working environment was
not accompanied by growing social and spatial
divisions of economic opportunity and living standards. In a real sense, therefore, London's economic problems and their spatial patterns, like those
of other British cities, express and are an integral
part of broader divisions and dilemmas in contemporary British society. Only part of the solution is
to be found in London itself; much wider trends
need to be influenced if its economic problems are
to be resolved. This theme will emerge once more
in considering the dilemmas of transport planning
in the next chapter.

Further reading

A basic source of information about recent patterns
of manufacturing change in Britain is:
Fothergill S and Gudgin G (1982) *Unequal Growth:
urban and regional employment change in the UK*
Heinemann

For more details on the causes of urban change and
policy responses to it:
Hall P (ed) (1981) *The Inner City in Context*
Heinemann
Lawless P (1981) *Britain's Inner Cities: problems
and policies* Harper and Row

An interesting account and interpretation of policy
responses to the economic crisis in London is:
Young K and Mills L (1983) *Managing the Post-
industrial City* Heinemann

A review of the nature of industry in London is:
Wood P A (1978) 'Industrial changes in inner
London' in Clout H D (ed) *Changing London*
University Tutorial Press

A valuable insight into the contemporary problems
of Hackney is provided by:
Harrison P (1983) *Inside the Inner City* Penguin

Progress in Docklands can be followed in:
London Docklands Development Corporation
Annual Reports and Accounts (available from
LDDC, West India House, Millwall Dock,
London, E14 9TJ)

A dissenting view has come from the GLC (see also
further reading for chapter 19):
Greater London Council (1982) *The East London
File* GLC

See also:
Greater London Council (1985) *The London Industrial Strategy* GLC

Wider trends in London and the South East are
charted in:
SERPLAN (1984) *Regional Trends in the South
East: The South East Regional Monitor, 1983–84*
(and subsequent editions), South East Regional
Planning Conference, London

9 Transport dilemmas

John Adams

The administration of transport in London is in a state of upheaval. At the time of writing, the control of London's bus and underground system had just been transferred from the GLC to London Regional Transport under the control of the Secretary of State for Transport. Proposals have been published to abolish the GLC and transfer 110 km of metropolitan roads to the national Trunk Road Network, also under the control of the Secretary of State.

Many of the administrative arrangements which would follow the abolition of the GLC had yet to be announced in early 1985, and the abolition proposals themselves were being vigorously resisted by the GLC and many of the London boroughs. This essay will focus on the problems of transport in London which are likely to remain, whatever the outcome of that political conflict.

It will be argued that the disarray which has been such a prominent feature of transport planning in London since the 1960s is caused by a problem which is not being addressed by the principal contestants in the political battle. The underlying cause of London's transport problems is the growth of road traffic *outside* London. As car ownership increases nationwide – and it is the policy of both major political parties that it should increase substantially – those parts of the built environment which pre-date mass car ownership find themselves at a growing disadvantage. Most of London was built to a scale which cannot cope with the levels of car ownership for which the Government is planning, without drastic alteration to its character.

The origins of the problem

The shape and size of London has been strongly influenced by its system of transport. For most of its history it was a compact city, reflecting the capabilities of the prevailing modes of transport. Since the early nineteenth century it has expanded enormously both in population and area.

The geographical pattern of this expansion was largely dictated by the growth of the railway network. This network was highly radial in nature, and was very efficient at channelling large numbers of commuters into the the centre. The centre of London became the peak of accessibility of a large metropolitan region and locations close to the

Traffic Congestion, Fleet Street.
Fleet Street, still the heart of London's newspaper trade, congested with cars, buses and taxis. Major companies are moving out, however, for example to Docklands where traffic problems are less acute.

centre became extremely valuable. As a result, commerce squeezed out residents. This effect was most pronounced in the City, once the most densely populated part of London. In 1801, 129 000 people lived there; by 1961, the number of people working in the City by day was close to 500 000 but there were less than 5 000 residents.

Throughout this period of expansion, longer distance traffic of both people and goods was dominated by the rail system. This system was fed by local road services, horse-drawn in the nineteenth century and progressively motorized during the twentieth century. As a result, London acquired a road system which was, and still is, ill-equipped to cope with long distance traffic (Fig. 9.1).

Even when the road traffic was horse-drawn, the road network was frequently over-burdened and congested. As motorized traffic increased the problem became worse. In the 1920s and 1930s the problem was studied by various government committees, all of which agreed that there was a need to provide London with a hierachical road system, with a primary road network on which traffic seeking local access would be separated from long distance through-traffic.

In 1943 and 1944 the Abercrombie Plans (The County of London Plan and The Greater London Plan) proposed an ambitious and comprehensive solution to London's traffic problems. The plans envisaged a *disciplined* dispersal of people and jobs from over-crowded parts of inner London to new and existing towns beyond the continuously built-up

Figure 9.1   *London's main road network.*

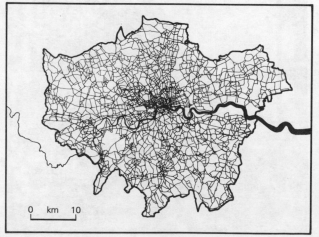

0   km   10

area. They also envisaged the building of a set of high-capacity ring and radial roads to carry longer distance traffic within the expanded metropolitan area.

Abercrombie's transport proposals embodied three important miscalculations. First, he thought that it would be possible to improve the road network and, at the same time, *decrease* traffic. The cause of this miscalculation was his failure to anticipate the enormous increase in car ownership that took place after the war. Abercrombie doubted in 1944 that car ownership levels in England would ever reach the levels then prevailing in the USA. These levels have already been exceeded in England by more than 100 per cent, and current Department of Transport forecasts anticipate a further doubling of the car population before growth stops.

Abercrombie intended a highly disciplined land-use pattern in which most people would live within walking distance of their work. (He lamented that, with the earlier growth of the city, Londoners had become 'a race of straphangers'.) But the intended discipline of his plan was broken before it was established. People took advantage of the increased mobility provided by widespread car ownership and improved roads to expand their residential and employment choices, and traffic increased greatly.

Second, Abercrombie underestimated the resistance that large scale road building would meet. He wrote off large parts of London as follows:

Between [the] main roads, in older parts of London, is found a network of minor streets; in them the services are small, many outworn and not a few have been destroyed or damaged by bombing. Furthermore, these streets are redundant in number, and uneconomically spaced for modern layout either of flats or houses, and enter the main roads at too frequent intervals. To allow this obsolete pattern of streets to govern the new layout would be unwise . . .

While underestimating the attachment that people can have for even the meanest environments, he spared no expense when it came to protecting more favoured parts of London. The map of his road plans shows the motorway running down Gower Street, outside his office window at University College, in a tunnel! (Abercrombie, 1943, pp 49, 52)

Third, Abercrombie underestimated the cost of his proposals. They represented a statement of faith rather than a realistically costed proposal. In answer to the question 'Can we afford it?' he replied, simply, 'Can we afford to do without it?' (Abercrombie, 1944, p 184). The answer to the first questions has clearly been shown to be 'no'. The second question still awaits an answer.

By the 1960s, Abercrombie's first miscalculation had become obvious. Car ownership was growing rapidly and threatening to overwhelm urban roads. Transport planning acquired a sense of urgency and became dominated by strategies for accommodating traffic growth. In 1961, the Ministry of Transport commissioned a study of the long-term problems of traffic in urban areas. This resulted two years later in the Buchanan Report, *Traffic in Towns* (1963). Buchanan observed: 'The motor car is demanding a radically new urban form.' The form that he advocated was one with a three tiered road hierarchy, and 'environmental areas' from which through-traffic would be excluded. In the late 1960s, the enthusiasm for remodelling London to accommodate the car reached its peak with the publication of proposals by the GLC to build a system of urban motorways remarkably similar in pattern to those proposed over twenty years earlier by Abercrombie – and Abercrombie's second and third miscalculations were repeated.

While there was much popular support for the abstract idea of providing more road capacity in London, when the magnitude of the cost, destruction and disruption associated with the proposals became apparent, there was a political reaction. In the 1973 GLC elections the Labour party, which had initiated the proposals less than ten years earlier, campaigned against them, and won.

Since 1973 policies for dealing with London's transport problems have veered with the political winds. Conservative administrations have favoured a resumption of road building, albeit on a lesser scale than that envisaged in the 1960s, while Labour administrations have favoured greater restraints on car use in inner London and larger subsidies for public transport. The picture has been greatly complicated by the overlapping powers of the GLC and the central government in the control of funds for transport in London and by the fact that the responsibility for building and maintaining roads in London is divided rather arbitrarily between the boroughs, the GLC and the government. At the time of writing, a Labour GLC is fighting a Conservative government on three main fronts. It is implementing traffic restraint measures of which the government disapproves, it is resisting government attempts to reduce the amount of subsidy available for public transport, and it is opposing government proposals for a number of major road building schemes in London.

Public transport subsidy and car traffic restraint?

The legal battle between the GLC and the Department of Transport over the level of public transport fares and subsidies was effectively terminated by the removal of control of London Transport from the GLC in 1984. But the political argument continues unabated. The sums of money at issue are very large. In its 1982 Medium Term Plan the GLC advocated a subsidy for public transport in London over a five year period of £1.94 billion. The Department of Transport published guidelines indicating that it should be limited to £1.2 billion.

It was calculated in the Medium Term Plan that, with the £1.2 billion subsidy, fares could be held constant for five years, in real terms. With this level of subsidy it was estimated that over the five year period the number of passenger km carried would decrease by 10 per cent. With the larger subsidy it was calculated that fares could be reduced by 30 per cent and then held constant in real terms for five years. The 30 per cent fare reduction was expected to produce an immediate 10 per cent increase in passenger km, after which the established downward trend was expected to resume. Even with the higher subsidy, the number of passenger km carried was expected to be back at its 1982 level by 1987.

The Medium Term Plan called the continuing decline in public transport and the increasing use of cars 'secular trends'. The need for substantial subsidies to prop up declining public transport is accepted by both the government and the GLC alike with resignation. They differ only with respect to the magnitude of subsidies and rates of decline that they think reasonable.

An international survey of urban public transport subsidies by the Transport and Road Research Laboratory (TRRL) in 1980 found that 'until a decade or so ago subsidization of public transport operations was relatively uncommon, but since then, the practice has been growing in almost all western industrialized countries at such a rate that governments have begun to question whether value for money is being obtained'.

Supporters of increased subsidy for public transport in London present league tables of subsidy levels around the world which show London lagging far behind in the amount of financial support provided to public transport. London Transport published a table showing that London's subsidy, amounting to 25 per cent of operating costs, is the lowest of any major west European city: the median being 50 per cent (Frankfurt), and the highest being 72 per cent (Rotterdam). London Transport also published statistics showing that other countries have succeeded, with the help of generous subsidies, in increasing the use of public transport in recent years. West Germany, Italy, the Netherlands, Finland, Norway, Spain, Switzerland and Japan all achieved modest increases in the number of passenger km carried by public transport between 1966 and 1979. But Table 9.1 places these achievements in the context of changes that have taken place in the use of cars. Despite subsidies which have increased dramatically – to levels which in Britain and a number of other countries appear to be approaching a political breaking point – everywhere dependence on cars has increased, both relatively and absolutely. The TRRL study concluded that subsidies tended to increase the use of public transport by existing users, but that they were ineffective in inducing car travellers to use public transport. At best it appears they can only slow the rates at which car use is increasing.

The distance travelled by car through the road networks of the countries listed in Table 9.1 more than doubled between 1966 and 1979. During this period these networks came under increasing pressure. The pressures were greatest in the oldest, densest parts of the networks. London, especially inner London, exemplifies the problems created by these pressures. 'London has clearly become less and less attractive as a place to live' said the Medium Term Plan. It adduced compelling evidence: the GLC as a whole had lost more than 10 per cent of its population since 1971, inner London more than 18 per cent, and the four innermost boroughs more than 23 per cent.

Geographically selective traffic restraint is likely to encourage the exodus of jobs and people. If traffic restraint measures are implemented only in those parts of the network where pressures are greatest, this will increase their unattractiveness in the eyes of motorists. Augmenting natural restraint (i.e. by congestion) with administrative restraints will encourage the growing number of motorists to seek more hospitable areas in which to live and do business. Given the lack of success of large public transport subsidies in arresting the growth of car traffic, and the perverse effects of inner city traffic restraint measures, it is argued by some that the only alternative is to adapt the city to the car by providing more road capacity.

More road capacity?

The Department of Transport has produced a discussion paper outlining its ideas for the administration of the road network after the abolition of the GLC. They involve giving most of the GLC's metropolitan roads to the London boroughs while identifying about 110 km of road with strategic significance which, it is proposed, should become a part of the national trunk road system administered by the Department of Transport. Also, because some of the Metropolitan Roads to be devolved to the boroughs carry substantial volumes of traffic, and because of the significant impact which traffic measures can have, the department proposes that

Table 9.1 *Percentage of passenger km travelled by private road vehicles*

	1966	1979
Great Britain	71.8	83.2
West Germany	76.5	82.0
Italy	70.5	82.0
Netherlands	75.4	84.4
Finland	66.8	76.7
Norway	68.7	84.8
Spain	54.8	71.8
Switzerland	77.5	85.5
Japan	12.5	43.8
USA*	95.3	98.5

* USA bus and coach travel statistics cover inter-city transportation only

Source: Transport Statistics GB 1967–77 and 1970–80

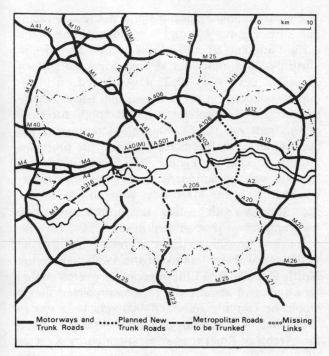

Figure 9.2   *The 'strategic' road network for Greater London.*

'special arrangements' should exist for ensuring 'the free flow' of traffic on these roads; the more important 'principal' roads – about 320–480 km of the 1 320 km of metropolitan roads to be transferred to the boroughs – would be subject to a measure of control by the Secretary of State.

Figure 9.2 illustrates the 'strategic' road network which the Department of Transport envisages for London. Although differing in many details, its pattern is remarkably similar to those of both the Abercrombie plans of the 1940s and the Greater London Development Plans of the 1960s. All but a tiny proportion of the network which the Department of Transport intends to take over consists of roads unsuitable for heavy lorries and large volumes of long distance traffic. They are almost all 'all-purpose roads' providing access to shops, schools and homes, and frequently serving as linear parking lots as well. The fact that Fig. 9.2 designates them as the roads which should carry the main burden of through traffic does not, in itself, make them appropriate for the task.

The department has not, as yet, revealed what it intends to do with these additions to the trunk road network once it acquires them. However, its insis-tence on the importance of ensuring the free flow of traffic suggests that it has it in mind to increase their capacity considerably. This deduction is also consistent with the department's other road building projects in London currently being pursued in parts of the road network already under its control.

In his book *Great Planning Disasters* Peter Hall (1980) derives the following lesson from the failure of the London motorway plans of the 1960s.

> The decision makers . . . should have adopted a more incremental strategy: first developing improved and new stretches of roads in industrial or warehousing areas where opposition was at a minimum; secondly ensuring that generous compensation laws were in operation before any attempts were made to extend the scheme into well-established owner occupied housing (p 274).

In other words, Hall considers the failure of the plan was a tactical failure in implementation, not a failure of planning; the planners should have proceeded by stealth and tackled the easy areas first, before trying to buy off the more difficult areas with generous compensation. There is reason to believe that the department is now following Hall's incremental strategy. Although it has announced no comprehensive urban motorway system for London, it is pursuing a number of individual road building schemes, apparently in isolation, whose large capacities make no sense unless they are ultimately to be incorporated in a comprehensive high capacity network.

In north London a number of Department of Transport road building proposals are currently awaiting the official announcement of the Secretary of State's decision. Schemes for four short sections of the North Circular Road (A406) (see Fig. 9.2), the Archway Road (A1) and the Hackney–M11 Link (parallel to the A106) have been the subject of public inquiries. In each case the traffic estimates, upon which the department justified its proposals at the inquiries, rested upon assumptions about traffic levels in other parts of the network which are untenable unless one assumes road building elsewhere in London on a scale which is not 'officially' contemplated.

The method by which the Department estimates future flows of traffic along roads it proposes to build illuminates a most intractable problem. Because of its history London is still a radial city.

Archway Road Scheme.
View northwards along the Archway Road. To extend the widened road through the terrace of shops and houses would destroy 200 homes.

Figure 9.3   *Patterns of road traffic desires (a) 1962, (b) 1981 (forecast made in 1966).*

The great preponderance of traffic desires are radial in nature. Figures 9.3a and 9.3b illustrate one of the earliest attempts to model these desires. Figure 9.3a illustrates in a somewhat abstract form the pattern of 'traffic desires' in 1962; it was based on information collected in surveys of actual travel behaviour. Figure 9.3 represents the planners' forecasts of this pattern in 1981. Figure 9.4 represents the assignment of the predicted traffic to the proposed motorway system. Figure 9.3b, suggesting that London was in imminent danger of being overwhelmed by a motorized tide, helps to account for the urgency with which the urban motorway programme was propounded in the 1960s.

It is now possible to test the forecasts made in the mid-1960s with the reality of the 1980s. Along the North Circular Road the forecasters overestimated by a factor of about four. (It was predicted that it would be carrying about 170 000 vehicles a day in 1981; in 1984 it was carrying about 40 000.). Along the Archway Road they overestimated by a factor of about six. Along the north-east sector of the outer ring (now the M25) they *underestimated* by a factor of about six.

The forecasting method used in the 1980s is essentially the same as the method used in the 1960s. Greater London is divided into a large number of zones. An estimate of the propensity of each zone to generate and attract trips is made, based upon forecasts of the population, employ-

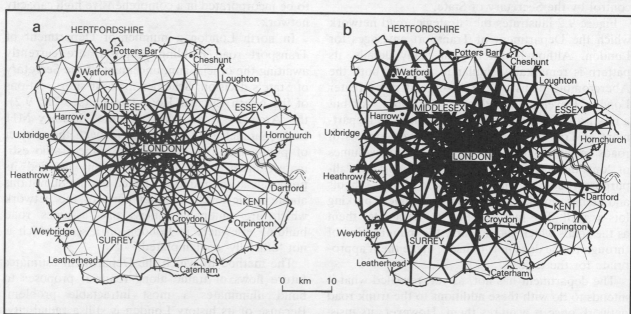

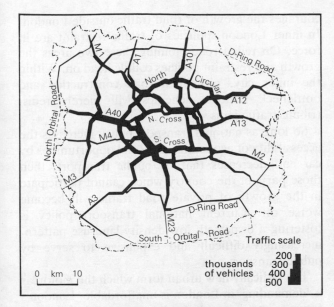

Figure 9.4 *Expected traffic patterns on London's roads 1981 (forecast made in 1966).*

ment and car ownership of each zone. The likelihood of a trip going from one particular zone to another is assumed to be inversely proportional to the time/distance/cost of the trip. The 1960s model overestimated the number of trips into inner London because it was fed with overestimates of population and employment in inner London and underestimates of travel times. Recent modelling exercises repeat these mistakes.

At the Hackney – M11 Link Inquiry, the department fed its model with its standard assumptions about future population, employment and car ownership, and the model responded by attempting to discharge an impossible volume of traffic into inner London. The department calculated that it would require a morning rush 'hour' five hours and ten minutes long for all the in-bound morning rush hour traffic estimated by its model to get past the unavoidable constrictions in the road network. The principal constriction can be seen on Fig. 9.2; it is at the point where the A106 meets the A102 and the 'missing link' in the proposed strategic road network (the North Cross Route in the original Greater London Development Plan).

This problem was unresolved at the inquiry. The department agreed that a five hour and ten minute rush hour was implausible. It simply abandoned the use of its model and declared that its scheme was

justified on the basis of lower levels of traffic. But the model provides a measure of the pressures to which the inner city is being subjected by growing traffic. It shows that the centre of London, the peak of accessibility in Greater London for users of public transport, is seen by motorists as a sink of congestion.

This is seen by the advocates of road building as a compelling argument for more road capacity. But providing road capacity in inner and central London sufficient to permit the free flow of unconstrained numbers of cars is clearly not possible. It can be seen from the maps that greatest demand for more road capacity is found inside the innermost ring of the proposed strategic networks. The road networks represented by Figs. 9.2 and 9.4 contain no provision for this demand. A substantial proportion of the traffic (shown by Fig. 9.4) arriving by the radial roads and circling central London on the motorway box would have sought destinations within the motorway box. There have never been plans to cope with this traffic – and without them the ringway and radial schemes make no sense.

In *Traffic in Towns* the implications of unrestrained car use were studied for a central area bounded by Oxford Street, Tottenham Court Road, Marylebone Road and Great Portland Street. Buchanan conducted an exercise 'to check the consequences if every person should seek to go to work by car, every shopper use a car, and the residents have all they desired in the way of cars and parking spaces' (p 130). He estimated that the space required for parking would be 'nearly as extensive as the whole study area itself' (p 136). This led to the conclusion that complete redevelopment of the area would be required, with cars parked underground, the ground level reserved for traffic, and a pedestrian deck to provide access to businesses, shops and homes. He did not pursue the scheme in any further detail because his calculations showed that 'the area, even when redeveloped completely, would still have to depend very largely upon public transport to bring in the working population and shoppers' (p 141). He concluded that the ultimate limit to the amount of traffic the area could accommodate was dictated not so much by its own capacity as by the capacity of the links it would be feasible to provide with adjoining areas.

How then are the traffic pressures to be resolved? They are currently being resolved by a deflection of traffic outward from the centre. There are large differences in the rates of traffic growth in and around London. During the 1970s road traffic nationally grew by 40 per cent. Traffic across the outer boundary of the GLC grew by 28 per cent. Traffic across London's inner area cordon grew by only 6 per cent.

Traffic is purposeful. It represents journeys to *desired ends* – jobs, shops, homes, friends, etc. The discrepancies between the flows to inner London predicted by the planners in the 1960s and the actual flows in the 1980s provides a measure of the pressures at work squeezing 'desired ends' out of inner London and into the outer ring served by the M25.

A solution advocated by some is that these pressures should be allowed to run their course; if land-use densities in inner London are too high to accommodate the officially forecast levels of car ownership, then they should be encouraged to decline until they can. Outward migration, according to this view, is seen as creating valuable space and development opportunities in the inner city. There is, unfortunately, a dearth of evidence that such a policy can succeed. The pressures that are currently reducing employment and residential densities in the inner city are doing so because the inner city is seen, by those who decide to leave, as the exact opposite of an area of opportunity. In the USA, where car ownership levels are about thirty years ahead of Britain's, the dispersal to the suburbs has not created opportunities in the inner cities which significant numbers of people have rushed in to exploit. Rather it has created areas of physical blight, dereliction and abandonment – areas of acute social, racial and economic stress.

A national problem

Road building in London is counterproductive. More orbital road capacity will increase the mutual accessibility of outer areas to each other and thereby increase the relative inaccessibility of the inner city; it is likely to have the same effect that it has had in eastern North America – to drain the life out of the inner city. More radial capacity will entice more traffic into the inner city and make a bad situation worse. National transport policy en-

courages the growth of road traffic outside London. In inner London, policies of traffic restraint are in force. On radial roads joining these two areas the growth and restraint policies collide head on. Within the inner city, piecemeal road construction and bottleneck removal schemes will merely redistribute traffic jams.

So long as national transport policy increases the accessibility of economic and social opportunities by car and decreases that by public transport, then those parts of the country which cannot participate in the growth of private road traffic will become worse off. Current national transport policy is fostering a dispersed, low-density land-use pattern, increasingly difficult and expensive to serve by public transport.

The radically new urban form which the motorcar is 'demanding' in London is unaffordable. London's future prosperity depends on a revival of an attractive and efficient public transport system. So long as national transport policy continues to entice people into cars and out of London, such a revival is unlikely.

Further reading

The planning context is presented in:

Abercrombie P (1943) *County of London Plan* Macmillan

Abercrombie P (1945) *Greater London Plan* HMSO

The problems of urban public transport, with stress on London, are examined in:

Bly P H, Webster F V and Pounds S (1980) *Subsidization of Urban Public Transport*, SR541 Transport and Road Research Laboratory, Crowthorne, Berks

Buchanan C (1963) *Traffic in Towns* HMSO

Greater London Council (1982) *Transport in London: The Medium Term Plan and Transport Policies and Programme 1983–85* GLC

Hall P (1980) *Great Planning Disasters* Weidenfeld and Nicholson

A wider overview is contained in:

Adams J (1981) *Transport Planning: vision and practice* Routledge and Kegan Paul

10 Housing problems

Richard Dennis

Prologue

By 1981, the number of dwellings in Greater London exceeded 2.75 million but the census recorded only 2.51 million households, an apparently comfortable housing surplus. Hence comes the argument that the principal remaining housing problems are those of distribution and access, to be overcome by reducing the number of houses that stand empty for long periods and by facilitating homeownership among lower income groups. In contrast to this analysis, this chapter argues that:

(i) there is a continuing absolute shortage of satisfactory housing;
(ii) while investment remains at its current low level housing problems can only intensify, as inadequately maintained dwellings fall into disrepair, and as popular aspirations for housing outstrip rates of housebuilding and renovation;
(iii) there is a particular need for *rented* accommodation in London;
(iv) current policy benefits those who can afford to buy, especially those who occupy council *houses* in outer London, at the expense of those who must rent, including those who are trapped in inner-city council *flats* which they would not want to buy even if they could afford to do so;
(v) problems of housing stress cannot be solved *in situ* in inner London; they need the co-operation of local authorities in outer London and beyond, but since suburban councils are unlikely to volunteer either land or resources, a strategic housing authority, co-ordinating policy and programmes throughout the London region, is an *essential* element in the future management of London.

Housing supply

In reality, there are far fewer than 2.75 million dwellings available and fit for habitation. To start with, some dwellings are the second homes of householders with first homes elsewhere. The *pieds à terre* of politicians in Westminster, businessmen in the Barbican and some academics in Bloomsbury fall into the category of second homes.

Secondly, about 130 000 dwellings are empty (4.8 per cent of the housing stock). Far from reflecting a lack of demand, two-thirds of these dwellings are awaiting demolition or renovation. Local councils have been criticized for keeping large numbers of properties vacant for long periods while simultaneously accommodating homeless families in expensive, inadequate and unsafe bed and breakfast hotels. But they have little alternative as long as central government allows *recurrent* spending in fulfilment of statutory obligations towards the homeless, while banning *capital* expenditure on house building, compulsory purchase of dwellings kept vacant by private landlords, and improvement of substandard dwellings which would provide permanent relief. Moreover, most empty dwellings are privately owned. Some houses need to be empty to facilitate residential mobility but many are deliberately kept empty by landlords hoping to sell their properties to middle-class owner-occupiers.

Thirdly, an increasing proportion of London's housing needs major repairs. Certainly, few dwellings now lack basic amenities. In 1971, 9.1 per cent of London households had no fixed bath and 8.3 per cent had no indoor toilet, while more than another 10 per cent had to share these facilities with other households. By 1981, the bath-less or toilet-less were down to just over 2 per cent with another 3.5 per cent sharing. But conditions are still bad in certain types of housing. Among tenants of private, unfurnished accommodation, 9.4 per cent still lacked access to a fixed bath and 7.8 per cent to an inside toilet, while among tenants of furnished accommodation over 30 per cent had to share basic amenities with other households. There are also geographical concentrations of poor housing. Yet these census indices are the crudest of measures: what about the provision of central heating, double glazing, insulation, freezers and the other amenities expected by families in 'comfortable Britain' in the 1980s?

Meanwhile, the *quality* of housing is deteriorating, as the rate at which unfit dwellings are demolished or improved, and new dwellings are built, falls short of the rate at which hitherto satisfactory dwellings fall into disrepair. The Greater London House Condition Survey of 1979 found that almost a quarter of London's housing was unsatisfactory: 9.2 per cent was statutorily unfit, another 5.4 per cent was fit but lacked at least one basic amenity, and 9.8 per cent was fit but required repairs costing at least £3000 at 1979 prices. Conditions were worst in privately rented dwellings but disrepair is also a growing problem for suburban owner-occupiers (see chapter 14). The problem is exacerbated because building standards have declined over time: Victorian terraces, inter-war semis and shoddily built 1950s council houses all need renovation at the same time.

Need

It is also arguable that the real need for housing exceeds the 2.51 million households enumerated in the 1981 census. The National Dwellings and Households Survey (NDHS) of 1978 estimated that London had 45 000 'concealed households', comprising a married couple or a single parent with children, counted as belonging to somebody else's household. While some of this sharing may be voluntary, as where a middle-aged couple look after elderly parents, much is forced, the consequence of young people's inability to obtain housing of their own.

One indication of unmet demand is the length of waiting lists for council housing. In 1972 there were 208 000 applicants on borough waiting lists; in 1983, 241 000. In most inner boroughs there are more than 100 applicants per 1 000 resident families; by contrast, in Harrow, Kingston and Sutton there are fewer than 35 per 1 000.

Another measure of need is the extent of homelessness. In 1978, 14 430 households were accepted as homeless under the Homeless Persons Act (1977); in 1983, 24 050 were accepted. The rate varies from over 20 per 1 000 resident households each year in Brent and Islington to only 2 per 1 000 in Havering. Some boroughs, including those with mainline railway termini, attract homeless families from beyond their own boundaries. Some interpret the legislation more strictly than others and accept the claims of a smaller proportion of applicants: how do you define who is 'intentionally homeless' and technically ineligible for rehousing? But since most single people and childless couples are excluded from the provisions of the Act, there is no doubt that official statistics underestimate the real extent of homelessness.

There are also approximately 30 000 squatters in London, recent increases reflecting growing numbers of unemployed single people, effectively excluded from becoming private tenants or getting mortgages, and the quantity of empty, unlettable council flats, which local authorities cannot afford to renovate.

The housing shortage

Table 10.1 presents a balance sheet of housing in London, indicating a shortfall of about 600 000 *satisfactory* dwellings in 1981. Yet the real shortage is worse than this, since even dwellings that have adequate amenities and are in good repair may be located in the wrong area, or be the wrong size or tenure to satisfy need.

Location

Some boroughs have a crude surplus of dwellings over households but others have a shortage. The NDHS found that, even before allowance was made for concealed households or vacant dwellings, households outnumbered dwellings in Brent, Ealing, Hammersmith, Haringey, Lambeth, Richmond and Wandsworth. Few households in multiple occupancy in these areas could either afford to live or find jobs in areas of housing surplus.

Size and situation

In the East End many dwellings, especially council flats, are in high-rise blocks, clearly unsuitable for elderly people and families with children. In Tower

Table 10.1 *Housing supply and demand in Greater London, 1981*

	Greater London	Inner London	Outer London
Estimated dwelling stock	2 758	1 119	1 639
– vacant and second homes	111	68	43
Available dwelling stock	2 647	1 051	1 596
– unfit dwellings (1979)	241	140	101
– dwellings fit but lacking amenities	140	73	67
– dwellings fit but requiring repairs costing more than £3 000 (1979)	255	90	165
Satisfactory dwelling stock*	2 011	748	1 263
Estimated demand for dwellings	2 647	1 057	1 590

All figures in thousands

* This row *slightly* underestimates the satisfactory dwelling stock since dwellings that were both unsatisfactory and vacant have been subtracted twice.

Sources: GLC Housing Strategy and Investment Programme 1982–83 (GLC, 1981), Greater London House Condition Survey (GLC, 1981)

Hamlets, almost one in five households lives at least five storeys above ground level. When the local authority sector was still expanding, and before council house sales removed many of the most attractive suburban houses from the system, inner-city tenants could reasonably expect transfers after a few years to more pleasant surroundings. Now that the likelihood of such moves has diminished, prospective council tenants may reject offers of unattractive accommodation for fear of being trapped there permanently. Hence the apparent paradox of large numbers of 'hard to let' dwellings in boroughs with the most homeless, overcrowded and involuntarily sharing households, and the longest waiting lists. In 1981 nine boroughs claimed that at least one-sixth of their council housing, usually in unmodernized, pre-war or high-rise, post-war blocks, was 'difficult to let'. Many councils now let such flats to single sharers, groups of students and childless couples.

In suburbia a more common problem is under-occupation, associated with a shortage of one-bedroom flats. The number of elderly, one or two-person households is increasing, but many still occupy three-bedroom houses. Those in council houses are unlikely to surrender their tenancies to young families unless suitable sheltered accommodation is available in the same neighbourhood, close to friends. High divorce and separation rates, and

the expectations of young, single adults to set up homes of their own, add to the demand for small dwellings.

Tenure

There are three principal forms of housing tenure: renting (furnished or unfurnished) from a private landlord; renting from a local authority; and owner-occupation (either outright or with the aid of a mortgage). In the nineteenth century almost everybody rented from a private landlord, but since World War I few private dwellings have been built for renting, apart from some blocks of luxury 'mansion flats' in the 1930s. As the financial position of landlords has deteriorated, many have sold their dwellings to sitting tenants, or on the open market once they had obtained vacant possession, or to local councils, often under the pressure of compulsory purchase orders. Their properties were also prime targets for slum clearance. Some new rented dwellings have been built by housing associations, subsidized by the government-backed Housing Corporation to act as socially responsible but nominally private landlords. Overall, the number of private tenants in London has declined from about 90 per cent of all households before World War I, to 20 per cent in 1981, still substantially higher than the national rate of 13 per cent (Table 10.2). Many more *new* households (for example young singles,

Table 10.2   *Housing tenure in Greater London, 1961–81*

Percentage households in each tenure

	Owner-occupiers	Renting from local authority	Renting private unfurnished*	Renting private furnished
Inner London				
1961	17	20	50	14
1971	20	30	33	16
1981	27	43	20	10
Outer London				
1961	53	17	25	5
1971	56	21	17	7
1981	62	23	11	4
Greater London				
1961	37	18	37	9
1971	40	25	24	11
1981	49	31	14	6

* including housing associations

Source: Census

newly married couples, and persons newly arrived in London) rent privately, at least until they have saved deposits to become owner-occupiers or fulfilled residence requirements to qualify for council housing.

Most people today express a preference for owner-occupation; yet that response is only rational in the light of *artificial* market conditions created by the policies of successive governments. Victorian middle-class families neither owned, nor wanted to own their homes. Ownership inhibits residential mobility, if only because it is so expensive and complicated to buy and sell houses; it imposes responsibilities of repair on occupiers who may be far from expert; arguably, it diverts private capital away from industrial investment. Nor – as long as it depends on tax relief and hidden subsidies – does it reduce public spending. From a political perspective, the principal attraction of owner-occupation is that it encourages personal responsibility and social stability. Homeownership makes conservatives of us

all, concerned to maintain the value of our property by maintaining the quality of its environment.

It is ironic that owner-occupation was promoted after 1979 by a Conservative government committed to abolishing inflation since home ownership is most advantageous to individual households in times of high inflation when rents rise faster than mortgage payments. Moreover, at times when there are substantial regional variations in employment opportunities, owner-occupancy can inhibit labour mobility: what are the economics of selling a house in an area of high unemployment and low demand, and buying one in an area of relatively low unemployment and buoyant demand?

The costs of owner-occupation are substantially higher in London than the rest of the UK. In early 1984 the average price of houses purchased with a mortgage from the Nationwide Building Society was £39 060 in Greater London, £29 690 in the UK as a whole; and prices were rising more quickly in London than elsewhere. However possible and desirable owner-occupation may be for the prosperous majority, there is no prospect of universal homeownership.

By 1981, nearly one-third of London dwellings were owned by local authorities (Table 10.2). But, with the passage of the 1980 Housing Act, which gave council tenants an automatic right to buy their homes, policy now concentrates on encouraging owner-occupation among lower-income groups. In the Act's first year of operation, buyers were typically household heads aged 40–50, who had been tenants for 15–20 years, and qualified for discounts of over 40 per cent on the free-market value of their homes. However beneficial the policy for those who become owners of suburban houses (and, in London, fewer than 5 per cent of homes sold were flats), it inevitably reduces the variety and average quality of remaining council-owned stock, particularly when combined with a virtual freeze on new building. Meanwhile, local authority rents have increased, so that government subsidies to homeowners now exceed those to tenants.

Historically, both the GLC and individual boroughs built and managed council housing in London. In 1980 the GLC owned 234 000 dwellings and the boroughs about 550 000. Although Conservative councils, including the GLC before 1973 and after 1977, offered houses for sale to sitting tenants, only 30 000 were sold in the decade

Table 10.3 *House building in Greater London, 1971–83*

	GLC	Percentage of all starts made by: Boroughs	Housing Associations	Private Builders	Total number of dwellings started per annum ('000s)
1971–3	18	45	7	30	31.8
1974–7	23	49	10	19	27.6
1978	16	51	9	24	19.6
1979	8	49	11	31	15.7
1980	7	43	12	38	7.6
1981	2	21	14	63	9.1
1982	2	27	14	57	12.9
1983	10	19	14	57	12.7

Source: Local Housing Statistics

to 1979. In the same period the boroughs and the GLC together built an average of 17 800 dwellings per annum (Table 10.3).

But between 1980 and 1983 the average fell to only 3 300 per annum and the GLC, Conservative-controlled from 1977 to 1981, phased out its day-to-day housing activities. Existing GLC houses were transferred to the boroughs in which they were situated. By 1984 the GLC retained responsibility for only about 30 000 dwellings, mostly older 'hard to let' flats, and for new building at Thamesmead. The Conservatives argued that the GLC duplicated borough housing functions and that estates were best managed from local offices. But this argument ignores both the continuing need for *new* council housing and the redistributive role of the GLC, building throughout and even outside Greater London (for example in expanded towns such as Basingstoke), but drawing tenants mainly from the waiting lists of boroughs with greatest need. In this way, families from stress areas in inner London could move into more attractive homes in suburban or outer metropolitan areas. For example, in 1977–78, inner boroughs 'exported' a net total of 4 804 households, 2 098 to outer London, 2 706 to GLC estates outside London.

The GLC had also negotiated with suburban boroughs where, in return for an agreement not to build, it was allocated a proportion of vacancies in borough-owned dwellings. As outer boroughs sold their council houses, however, and as they ceased building new dwellings, so the number of vacancies for GLC nominees declined. In the 1970s this was a local irritation; with the demise of GLC housing, and the Conservative boroughs' antipathy to council housing, it is now a major barrier to mobility.

In theory, the statutory Greater London Mobility Scheme and the voluntary Inter-Borough Nomination Scheme continue to facilitate London-wide mobility. In practice, bureaucratic delays, the reduction in the total number of vacancies, and the refusal of several boroughs to participate in the voluntary scheme, all conspire to reduce opportunities for households from stress areas.

While outer boroughs lack the motivation to help inner Londoners, Labour-controlled inner London councils have the will but lack the finance to promote major housing programmes. Their activities are limited by the scarcity and high price of suitable sites, by public expenditure cuts and, latterly, by rate-capping. Somewhat disingenuously, central government has allowed local authorities to use income from council house sales to supplement expenditure on new construction and renovation of surviving council housing. This might work in cities where all public housing is controlled by one authority, where receipts from sales of suburban cottages could help pay for improvements in inner-city flats, but in London, sales have been concentrated in places like Barking, Croydon, Havering and Bromley, while areas in need of additional finance have sold far fewer dwellings (Fig. 10.1). The only exception, Wandsworth, where a massive sales drive disposed of 10 per cent of public housing (3 873 dwellings) between 1979 and 1983, does not vindicate the government's argument: public

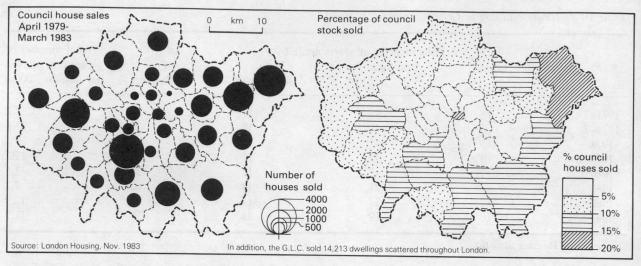

Figure 10.1   *Council house sales in Greater London, 1979–83.*

housing starts in Wandsworth for 1981–3 numbered 0, 81 and 0. Moreover, because only part of the receipts can be used and because sale prices are reduced by generous discounts, boroughs must sell about ten old houses to pay for one new dwelling.

This mismatch between housing supply and demand is not only in quantity and quality, but also in tenure. While current supply policies concentrate on homeownership, in London there is a continuing demand for all forms of renting. This derives from recent arrivals from overseas or from other parts of Britain, from short-stay visitors, students, tourists and visiting businessmen, from low-income households who cannot afford to buy, and from young single people who expect to be mobile in both jobs and housing during their first years of independence from parents.

The geography of housing stress

Figure 10.2 plots the average rank of each borough on eleven different indices which together provide an index of housing stress. The map shows *relative* levels of stress at the scale of inter-borough variation. It does not demonstrate how serious the inequalities are; and *local* pockets of very good or very bad housing are ignored. Nor is account taken of social indicators – unemployment, the elderly, the car-less, ethnic minorities – which may compound problems of bad housing.

The pattern is unsurprising, but no less disturbing. Problems are concentrated in inner

London, especially where ageing unmodernized, hard to let council flats are combined with a high level of private renting, and where there are high levels of homelessness, overcrowding, multiple occupancy, inadequate amenities and disrepair. Boroughs with very high proportions of council housing (for example Tower Hamlets) may have high levels of unmet need, but at least those who are housed are less likely to suffer overcrowding or lack amenities. Few boroughs boast rankings in the middle of the scale. Only five; Lewisham, Ealing, Waltham Forest, Greenwich and Hounslow; occupy the middle ground. In housing, London is geographically as well as socially 'two nations'.

Figure 10.2   *Housing stress in Greater London.*

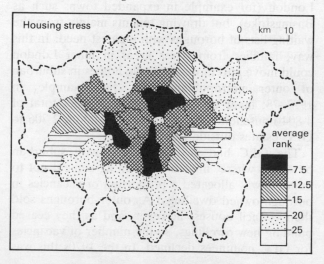

What is being done?

Extending homeownership is no substitute for improving existing homes and building new ones. Some examples will demonstrate the inadequacy of even those improvement and new building programmes that have gone ahead.

Improvement

Improvement is most necessary in the privately rented sector, but the take-up of government grants is greatest among young, middle-class owner-occupiers. Elderly householders cannot afford their share of the cost or may be unaware of the availability of grants. Private landlords will not invest in repairs or modernization unless they can re-let property at higher rents or sell it into owner-occupation.

Under legislation of 1969 and 1974, local authorities can designate General Improvement Areas (GIAs) and Housing Action Areas (HAAs). In the former, householders can claim grants to provide basic amenities in structurally sound dwellings that have a life expectancy of at least thirty years, while additional sums are available for tree-planting, children's playgrounds, parking facilities and schemes to exclude through traffic. In HAAs, designation depends on social and tenurial criteria, as well as the physical condition of housing. GIAs are usually areas of owner-occupation. HAAs begin with a predominance of privately rented dwellings which are then compulsorily purchased by the council or acquired by a housing association.

Louvaine HAA, 400 properties in eight roads in Battersea, was one of the first to be designated, early in 1975, at the instigation of local people who established a Residents' Association when they heard rumours that their homes were scheduled for demolition. They persuaded the council that rehabilitation was feasible. By 1978, Wandsworth Council's share of property in the HAA had increased from 8 to 31 per cent, while the proportion owned by private landlords declined from 53 to 27 per cent. Council and residents eventually agreed that improved dwellings should be allocated to local people, rather than to whoever topped the borough-wide waiting list. The integrity of the local community was preserved, but only by disregarding the more urgent needs of outsiders. In 1978 Wandsworth Council changed from Labour to Conserva-

tive control. Improved properties were now sold to first-time buyers from the Council's lists, unimproved properties to 'homesteaders' who promised to renovate them with grant aid. In neither case were the beneficiaries likely to be either local residents or those in the greatest need.

Parfett Street HAA, Whitechapel, comprising about 480 properties, all dating from the 1890s and most occupied at very high densities by Bengalis, was designated in 1983. Roughly half the dwellings have been purchased by a housing trust; the remainder are owned by a Bengali housing cooperative and various private landlords. The intention is that the Bengali population should remain *in situ* while improvement is undertaken around them.

Parfett Street is unusual in that *all* the property needs improvement. But area improvement schemes are often criticized for providing aid to some dwellings that do not need it and, by concentrating resources geographically, denying aid to isolated poor dwellings. Most *areas* of poor housing have now been tackled, by either slum clearance in the 1960s or designation as GIAs or HAAs in the 1970s. Three-quarters of remaining unfit properties in London are scattered as single units. The Parfett Street scheme is helping existing residents, but in many improvement programmes, especially in GIAs, the physical fabric is overhauled, while the original tenants do *not* benefit. They are 'decanted' into other poor quality, hard to let accommodation, or cannot afford the rents of revitalized properties. As emphasis shifts to the sale of modernized dwellings, so improvement inevitably means gentrification.

New construction

One of the few extensive areas of new house building is on sites released by the London Docklands Development Corporation (LDDC) on both sides of the Thames, especially around the Royal Docks (in Newham) and the Surrey Commercial Docks (in Southwark). But even this apparently bright spot has its critics.

During the 1970s, as industrial and commercial premises in Docklands fell vacant, local authorities acquired derelict land which they hoped to use for council housing for local people. All the riverside boroughs had long waiting lists and large numbers of families in unsatisfactory high-rise accommodation, awaiting transfers to a scarce supply of terraced and semi-detached houses. The London Docklands Strategic Plan (1976) proposed that the sites should 'cater for a cross section of the population of Dockland boroughs as a whole'; about a quarter of new housing should be reserved for the elderly, and two-thirds should be rented, owned by either local authorities or housing associations.

In 1981 the government established the LDDC with development rights similar to those already exercized by new town corporations on greenfield sites (see also chapters 8 and 19). Council-owned land was transferred to the LDDC, whose housing plans proved very different from those of the boroughs. The LDDC saw Docklands as a *national* and not a local resource, and proposed a 'more balanced' community in terms of class, income and housing. In practice, this means a heavy emphasis on houses for first-time buyers (costing £25–45 000 at 1983 prices), with more expensive housing in converted Victorian warehouses overlooking the Thames. Council housing is not excluded but little seems likely to be built since the boroughs, whose land was appropriated, have been antagonistic towards the LDDC.

In order to provide houses that low-income households could afford, low building standards have been permitted: houses lacking central heating, garages, and predominantly one and two-bedroom 'starter homes', adequate for childless couples but unsuitable once children are born. Consequently, there is little prospect of Docklands providing the 'stable community' claimed by developers. Families unable to afford more spacious homes in Docklands will be obliged to move farther out into Essex.

This scenario is already evident from a survey of the first 118 households who moved into owner-occupied housing at Beckton in 1982. One third had previously been council tenants, but only half of them had come from elsewhere in Newham, where the estate is situated. Almost 60 per cent were 2-person households, almost 90 per cent of adults worked full-time; a far from balanced population. Two-thirds expected to stay for less than five years and most wanted to move away from Docklands. This is typical of new estates everywhere but gives the lie to bold claims about the creation of new 'communities'.

The LDDC claims that its new houses are available at prices 'within reach of existing local resi-dents on average London incomes', but most East Londoners have below average incomes. Of those currently in council housing or on waiting lists, only about one in five could afford a 'starter home' in Beckton. Moreover, most are families with children, who would be overcrowded in the type of house they could afford to buy.

Geographical and social implications

The ways in which dwellings have been built and managed help to explain the distribution of social classes, household types and ethnic groups in London. Different types and ages of dwelling, each restricted to particular localities, are associated with different types of resident. The precise associations change over time, but the principle remains the same. For example, young single people, once associated with privately rented housing in inner west London, now occupy hard to let council housing or squat, usually in property the local authority has emptied but cannot afford to improve. They are now more likely to live in the East End. The extension of owner-occupation means that other, more securely employed, young singles and sharers can obtain mortgages to buy flats in suburbia, often on sites previously occupied by large Victorian or Edwardian villas.

While owner-occupation is now open to a wider social spectrum, there are continuing geographical differences between types of owner-occupier. Few purchasers of council houses in Watling (Edgware) stand much chance of trading up into the leafy lanes of Mill Hill, only 2 km away but conveniently separated by the M1 and a main railway line.

For the poor, the expansion of homeownership provides no opportunities, only a condemnation to continued occupation of bad housing in the inner city. In the USA, inner cities have faced bankruptcy while independent suburbs need ask little in the way of local taxes from their middle-class residents. Federal housing, the US pale equivalent of council housing, is little more than welfare housing for problem families, the unemployable and those in receipt of social security. Do we want the same in London, with potentially the same consequences for race relations, class conflict and civil disorder?

Like their American counterparts, local authorities in outer London have never volunteered assistance to the inner city. In 1980, when the GLC surrendered its day-to-day functions of housing management, *all* the Conservative-controlled outer London boroughs thought that it should also give up its strategic role and that its allocation of government funds should simply be divided among the boroughs. Effectively, they wished to abdicate responsibility for inner London's housing problems. Equally isolationist attitudes were evident in the successful opposition of outer suburban authorities such as Epsom and Ewell to being included in the newly created GLC in 1964; and in the unsuccessful resistance of Home Counties authorities in the 1920s to the building of 'out-county' estates (for example Becontree, St Helier and Watling) which they feared would reduce property values and lead to an influx of Labour voters.

In the 1880s rich West End vestries had opposed the creation of the LCC, which they perceived (rightly) as involving a transfer of rate income from West End to East End. No sooner was the LCC founded than there were demands for abolition. The fundamental housing problem in the 1880s, as now, was the shortage of good quality housing for the poor. Private builders ignored them, while philanthropic initiatives (like the Peabody Trust) proved worthy but inadequate, helping only the respectable working class. Faith rested in a process of 'levelling up', whereby the poor would move into houses vacated by the regularly employed who moved to suburban terraces or Peabody flats. The same arguments are applied in our current rediscovery of 'Victorian values': concentrate on private-sector initiatives for marginal owner-occupiers and trust to providence that the poor will benefit somehow.

Fortunately, Victorian and Edwardian Londoners persevered with the LCC, which initiated the construction of such high quality council housing that many of its turn-of-the-century estates, both inner-city flats and suburban cottages, are still popular and attractive living environments in the 1980s.

All too often, housing policy has purely political ends. Selling council houses wins votes, so council houses are sold, regardless of the social consequences. Housing problems take time to develop, longer than the life of most governments, so housing programmes are sitting targets for public expenditure cuts. But London requires a housing policy based on need, not on political expediency.

House building, maintenance and improvement deserve a much higher priority, and policy should be sensitive to *local* conditions. London is an entity, meriting a strategic regional housing authority, covering the entire metropolitan area, not just Greater London, with powers to levy rates, receive government finance and promote building, for sale *and* to rent.

Further reading

One result of local government cuts is that statistical returns published quarterly in *Local Housing Statistics* (HMSO, London) contain increasing numbers of gaps, incomplete data and estimates. More complete, but one-off sources include the 1981 census and the *Greater London House Condition Survey* (1981), Greater London Council.

Two useful research reports, both published by SHAC (The London Housing Aid Centre) are:
Conway J (1984) *Capital Decay: an analysis of London's housing* SHAC Report no 7
Lansley S, Randall G and Raynsford N (1981) *The London Report: prospects and policies for housing* SHAC Report no 3
SHAC is also responsible for publishing a monthly journal, *London Housing*, while items of national importance appear in the bi-monthly, *Roof*, published by Shelter.

A straightforward introduction to national housing policy is contained in:
Short J (1982) *Housing in Britain: the post-war experience* Methuen

On the history of council housing in London see:
Dunleavy P (1981) *The Politics of Mass Housing in Britain 1945–1975* Clarendon Press, Oxford (includes a case study of Newham)
Young K and Garside P (1982) *Metropolitan London: politics and urban change 1837–1981* Arnold

Two local studies which add flesh and human interest to the bare bones presented here are:
Harrison P (1983) *Inside the Inner City* Penguin
Wallman S *et al* (1982) *Living in South London: perspectives on Battersea 1871–1981* Gower, Farnborough (esp. chapter 4)

11   Air pollution control

Clive Agnew (with Ron Cooke)

Introduction

Atmospheric pollution, which now affects most of the world's major cities is an unfortunate and seemingly inevitable consequence of the concentration of people, buildings and vehicles. The GLC (1983) reports, however, that there have been improvements in the quality of London's air since the notorious smog of 1952 and that today it no longer suffers the conditions that brought about the Victorian nickname of 'The Smoke'. Today few of London's inhabitants probably realize that the term 'smog' was first coined around the turn of the century to describe the combination of fog and smoke so frequently found in London. Conditions so graphically described in the novels of Charles Dickens, as the following extract from *Little Dorrit* (1857) shows:

> It was a Sunday evening in London, gloomy, close and stale . . . Melancholy streets in a penitential garb of soot . . . Miles of close wells and pits of houses, where the inhabitants gasped for air . . . In the city it [the rain] developed only foul stale smells, and was a sickly, lukewarm, dirt-stained, wretched addition to the gutters.

Concern over air pollution extends far beyond the nineteenth century, with the earliest recorded comment on the noxious effects of coal smoke reaching as far back as those of King Henry III's wife, Eleanor, in 1257. Such complaints were not considered serious until the seventeenth century when the effects had become more noticeable. King James I complained about the soiling of St Paul's in 1620; John Evelyn in *Fumifugium* (1661) noted the decreased visibility, increased corrosion and reduced plant vigour in London; and by the middle of the seventeenth century there was a growing appreciation that air pollution was a cause of London's rising mortality rates. The naturalist Gilbert White noted in 1784 the development of dark plumes over London and by the nineteenth century blame for causing such conditions was being directed at factory owners and industrialists (Fig. 11.1). But the domestic consumer also adopted coal as an alternative to wood and some of the worst smogs have occurred during still autumn Sundays when most workers were at home. The nineteenth century brought the development of London's railways and a greater influx of both

Figure 11.1   *Smoke Nuisance Bill. This cartoon appeared in Punch (1853), caricaturing a meeting held in London to protest against the Bill. Arguments put forward in favour of smoke included its curative properties and its antiseptic qualities, while sulphurous gases were believed to act as a tonic!*

Table 11.1　*Pollutant emissions following combustion of fossil fuels in London, 1978*

		(Thousand tonnes per annum)				
Source	CO	SO_2	NO_x	Smoke	Hydrocarbons	Lead
Vehicles	920	5.3	53	6.5	47	0.8
Domestic	25.1	9.6	5.1	6.1	2.0	–
Commercial and industrial	2.6	90.8	22.6	1.8	0.7	–
Total	950	105	81	14	50	0.8

Source: GLC, 1983

Particulate matter encompasses all airborne material whereas the word 'smoke' should only apply to fine particles of carbon and tar. Unfortunately this convention has not been strictly adhered to in the past so the term has been used in its most liberal form.

people and fossil fuels. As dense suburban housing spread, so domestic and industrial smoke mingled, the former possibly having a more deleterious effect because of its low level of emission.

The twentieth century has seen a marked change in the atmosphere of London. On the one hand, smoke – so apparent during the nineteenth century and a familiar ingredient of London's smogs into the 1950s – has declined. Peak smoke concentrations in London (Fig. 11.2) are now comparable to, if not at lower levels than, other major English cities. On the other hand, new pollutants have come to the

fore (Table 11.1), less visible than smoke but of equal if not greater toxicity.

Vehicles account for carbon monoxide, one of the major air contaminants of London, and for the high levels of hydrocarbons and nitrogen oxides. Peak concentrations of sulphur dioxide (Fig. 11.3) can exceed the EEC guideline value of 250 $\mu g/m^3$, the main sources today being the combustion of oil in commercial and industrial premises. Despite several acts of Parliament and various measures of control, London continues to suffer from occasional high atmospheric pollution levels.

Figure 11.2　*Peak concentrations of smoke for four major English cities observed in commercial areas in smokeless zones (after data from the Warren springs Laboratory).*

Figure 11.3　*Peak concentrations of sulphur dioxide for four major English cities observed in commercial areas in smokeless zones (after data from the Warren Springs Laboratory).*

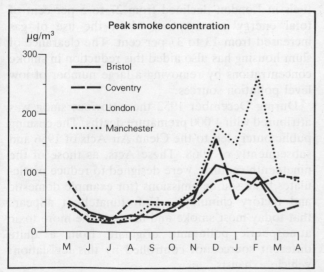

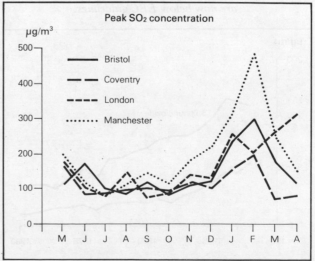

London's atmospheric pollutants

London's air pollutants are particulate matter, sulphur dioxide, carbon monoxide, oxides of nitrogen, photo-chemical smog and lead. Whether or not these waste products of combustion become a nuisance or endanger health is a function of their nature, origin, concentration and diffusion. It is therefore worth considering these characteristics before discussing their effects and subsequent measures to control them.

Particulate matter

Until the second half of the twentieth century coal was the major source of atmospheric particulate matter, and the history of air pollution up to the 1950s mirrors the use of coal in London. Coal was first introduced to London during the thirteenth century, brought from Newcastle as ballast in returning boats and by 1620 it had become an important trade. Wood was preferred for many years because of the fumes given off by the coal, which had a sulphur content twice that of today's supplies. Coal was at first used primarily in smelting and lime burning where the advantage of its higher temperatures offset the disadvantage of obnoxious

Table 11.2   *Energy use in London (peta-joules)*

Source	1965	1978
Gas	66	200
Motor Fuels	92	129
Liquid fuels	148	114
Electricity	59	75
Solid fuels	138	28
Total	503	546

Source: GLC, 1983

fumes. But by the end of the fifteenth century the shortage and consequent rising cost of wood had forced coal into the home. By the middle of the nineteenth century it was generally recognized that smoke had affected the climate, reducing visibility and sunshine levels whilst also posing a serious health hazard. Recognition of the serious nature of this problem resulted in the passage of the Smoke Abatement Act (1853–56) and the Sanitation Act (1866) aimed at curbing coal based emissions.

During the twentieth century (Fig. 11.4) smoke concentrations have generally declined. It is not clear if this reduction is due to legislation or, as seems more likely, if it has been caused by fundamental shifts in energy use. During the twentieth century domestic and industrial heating has changed substantially from coal to gas and oil, and the railways are now powered by diesel and electricity. As Table 11.2 shows, from 1965 to 1978 the use of solid fuels in London declined from 27 to 5 per cent of total energy consumption whilst the use of gas increased from 13 to 37 per cent. The clearance of slum housing has also aided this reduction in smoke concentrations by removing a large number of low level pollution sources.

During December 1952 the notorious smog was attributed with 4 000 premature deaths. The ensuing public outcry led to the Clean Air Acts of 1956 and subsequently of 1968. These Acts, as those of the nineteenth century, were designed to reduce particulates from source emissions (for example domestic and factory chimneys). Unfortunately it appears that today most smoke and many of the more toxic atmospheric pollutants originate from a quite different source not controlled by this legislation: vehicle exhausts.

Figure 11.4   *Smoke and sulphur dioxide concentrations in inner London, showing a marked decrease following the Clean Air Acts of 1956 and 1968 (after data from the Greater London Council). Average concentrations are now below EEC guidelines.*

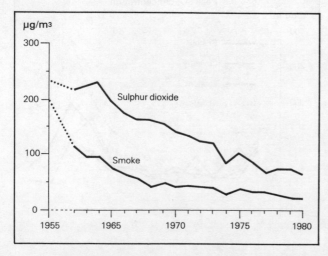

Sulphur dioxide

Sulphur dioxide is liberated during the combustion of fossil fuels and it has been evident in London since the seventeenth century. Concern over sulphur dioxide concentrations is due to its pungent smell, and association with chronic bronchitis. There has been an increase in UK emissions from 4.4 to 5.7 million tonnes between 1950 and 1969 (Chandler, 1976) in spite of the implementation of the Clean Air Acts. This was primarily due to rising fuel consumption and the higher amounts of sulphur found in oil than in coal. Table 11.3 indicates that 65 per cent of sulphur dioxide now comes from fuel oil whereas solid fuels only supply 17 per cent. It is not suprising, therefore, to find that industrial and commercial premises provide 59 per cent of SO_2 emissions and electricity generation supplies a further 31 per cent. Fortunately for London these sources have dispersed during the twentieth century and SO_2 concentrations have been declining recently (Fig. 11.4) following rises in oil prices. Despite this improvement, guideline standards for peak concentrations are still occasionally exceeded in London.

Table 11.3 *Sources of sulphur dioxide in London during 1975/6*

Source	Amount (1 000 tonnes per annum)	Sulphur content (%)
Fuel oil	116	2.4
Solid fuel	30	1.3
Diesel oil	19	0.75
Industrial processes	6	–
Derv	3	0.35
Motor spirit	2	0.1
Total	179	

Source: GLC, 1983

Carbon monoxide

This odourless, tasteless, colourless and poisonous gas, is now principally produced from petrol engines. In terms of the amount produced it is the commonest man-made air pollutant in London and concentrations have increased with the rise of traffic. Regular records of carbon monoxide in London have not been kept, but kerbside concentrations of 10–21 mg/m³ appear common and concentrations can reach 60 mg/m³. The World Health Organization (WHO) recommends that concentrations should not exceed 10 mg/m³ (8 hourly mean) or 40 mg/m³ (1 hourly mean). Carbon monoxide is viewed as a hazard because it is taken up by the blood in preference to oxygen causing oxygen starvation but there is doubt as to whether the above levels would cause any damage to health. It is widely held that a 2 per cent saturation of the blood by carbon monoxide would impair perception and performance. Exposure to air concentrations found in London rarely produces more than 3 per cent saturation in non-smokers while smokers experience up to 17 per cent. Yet clinical trials have shown levels of 10 per cent saturation to have no significant short term effects. It is probable that normally CO levels do not attain dangerous concentrations in the streets of London and that problems are mainly confined to tunnels and underground car parks where this heavy gas can collect. But a report by the Royal Commission on Pollution (1984) expresses concern for the levels of CO found in homes following the installation of double glazing and reductions in ventilation. Concentrations of 18 mg/m³ (24 hourly) and 184 mg/m³ (15 minute) have been recorded in a London domestic kitchen.

Nitrogen oxides

The levels of nitrogen oxides have remained fairly constant for the UK as a whole between 1971 and 1981 with 41 per cent from power stations, 36 per cent from commercial premises, 19 per cent from vehicles and 5 per cent from domestic emissions. In the City of London (Table 11.1) vehicular emissions account for a far larger proportion. Nitrogen dioxide levels of 50 000 µg/m³ would prove fatal and the WHO recommends that hourly mean concentrations should remain below 190–320 µg/m³. Mean hourly levels of 70 µg/m³ are found in the streets of London, seemingly posing little threat and the WHO guidelines are only occasionally exceeded. Little is known, however, about the long-term effects of low concentrations although there is some inconclusive evidence of a link with respiratory illness. As with carbon monoxide there is also awareness of the high concentrations found in some domestic kitchens, higher levels being recorded in homes reliant on gas rather than electricity.

Photo-chemical smog

Vehicles also emit hydrocarbons. Some of these are considered harmless (for example methane), whereas benzine and polycyclic aromatic hydrocarbons known as carcinogens are dangerous to health. The action of sunlight on this mix of vehicle emissions can produce toxic secondary pollutants (for example ozone, aldehydes and various aerosols), known as photo-chemical smog. London may have eradicated its 'pea-souper' smogs but they are being replaced by photo-chemical smogs during certain climatological conditions in the summer similar to those found in Los Angeles. High levels of ozone occur during hot periods with high sunshine levels, the ensuing reactions resulting in reduced visibilities. Ozone concentrations of 300 $\mu g/m^3$ can impair breathing, especially for people physically exerting themselves. Records have only been kept since 1972, but peak amounts occasionally exceed the GLC guideline of 160 $\mu g/m^3$. Despite a general decline in ozone concentrations since 1972, this figure has been exceeded in 1974, 1975, 1976 and 1979 in central London (GLC, 1983).

Lead

Lead is added to petrol to produce quieter engines. Most adults derive up to 20 per cent of blood lead content from petrol combustion and nearly all atmospheric lead is from vehicle emissions. High concentrations of lead are toxic, causing a variety of ailments including anaemia, renal damage and reduced muscle coordination. Of equal concern is the uncertain effect, especially to children, of exposure to low concentrations. An EEC directive (82/844/EEC) recommends that atmospheric annual mean concentrations of lead should be less than 2 $\mu g/m^3$ by 1987. Concentrations in London are generally below this value but it is occasionally exceeded where traffic is heavy and pollutants fail to disperse (for example Blackwall Tunnel). Government concern over atmospheric lead concentrations began to be voiced in the early 1970s resulting in legislation controlling the lead content of petrol. In 1971 a level of 0.84 g/l was stipulated,

falling to 0.4 g/l by 1982. Unfortunately the rate of emissions only declined by 5 per cent during this period because petrol consumption increased by 29 per cent. Although it is planned that the lead content of petrol should fall to 0.15 g/l by the end of 1985, the Royal Commission on Environmental Pollution (1983) recommended that all petrol should be unleaded by the 1990s.

Effects of pollutants

The previous section introduced the sources of London's atmospheric contaminants and their potential health hazards. The degree and extent of any damage caused depends upon the nature and concentration of pollutants, the latter being controlled by the rate of emission and the prevailing meteorological conditions. London's weather controls the concentration of pollutants by influencing rates of dispersion, but conversely these contaminants also affect the prevailing weather by changing the composition of the atmosphere.

Dispersion of pollutants

The capacity of the air to disperse pollutants depends upon the amount of mixing taking place (which is a function of windspeed). High windspeeds may be reduced by frictional drag over cities where buildings are packed closely together. Fumes from domestic fires and other low level sources are then unable to escape and so accumulate at street level. The amount of atmospheric mixing is governed also by the rate at which the buoyancy of air is lost. Most effluent gases, being the products of combustion, are hot. They will therefore rise until cooled by contact with ambient air or through adiabatic expansion. In unstable conditions where the environmental lapse rate is greater than the dry adiabatic lapse rate, pollutants will continue to rise and disperse. The vertical motion of pollutants will be dampened, however, by stable conditions, especially if an inversion develops where temperatures increase with height (Fig. 11.5).

Low-level inversions tend to form overnight during periods of clear skies and light winds when there is a rapid cooling of the urban surface. Such inversions are more common in rural areas because night-time inversions in the metropolis are restricted by anthropogenic (i.e. man-made) heat emissions,

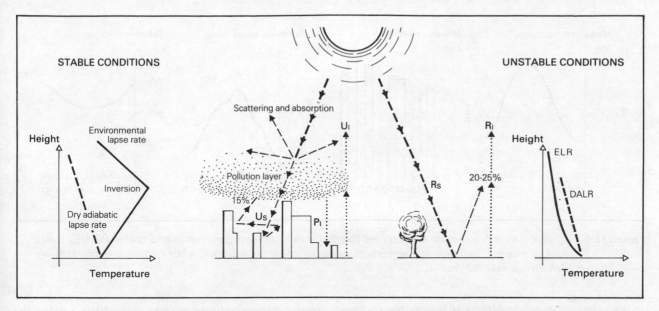

Figure 11.5 *Possible temperature and radiation variations in the atmosphere over London and its rural environs. The solar radiation (Rs) received in the rural area heats the lower atmospheric layers leading to unstable conditions and ascent of air. Less solar radiation is received in the urban zone (Us) because of adsorption and scattering of pollutants aiding the development of an inversion. Net longwave radiation for urban (U1) and rural (R1) areas is approximately the same, despite emissions from the pollutants aloft (P1).*

the mixing of air by traffic and convective circulation, together with the release of heat absorbed by buildings and the atmosphere itself. Elevated inversions tend to be more widespread. They can form at frontal surfaces, separating cold and warm air, by the intrusion of a layer of cooler air under the rising mass of warmed urban air or by the subsidence of air in an anticyclone which warms adiabatically and results in a warmed layer coming to rest above the original cool, stagnant air mass.

Inversions act as a 'lid' on the urban atmosphere trapping any pollutants and resulting in higher concentrations. This was the cause of London's 1952 smog when an anticyclone spread from the north-west and became stationary over the Thames valley, filling it with cold air and establishing a durable inversion. Chandler (1965) reported that anti-cyclones account for nearly a quarter of all air mass types over London, being most frequent during March, April, June and September. Air in frontal zones was observed 13 to 18 times each month throughout the year with a slight increase in frequency during winter. The monthly climatic averages shown in Fig. 11.6 mask these atmospheric fluctuations caused by the highly mobile nature of

air over the UK. Inversions over London can occur throughout the year due to the high frequency of fronts and anti-cyclones but inversions are often ephemeral and poorly developed. High pollution episodes require stable conditions enabling pollutants to concentrate over several days. The weather of south-east England is so variable that intense inversions together with high pollutant emissions only occur infrequently.

Effects of pollutants on climate

It is difficult to describe the effect of London's air pollutants on its climate because of the variability of the weather and the results of other human influences. Chandler (1965) noted that the character of the urban fabric reduced the frequency of high windspeeds in London compared with its rural environs whereas convective circulation increased the occurrence of light breezes. Emissions of heat and changes in the radiation balance can produce a 'heat island' effect (Lyall 1977), and cause unstable conditions leading among other things to a higher frequency of thunderstorms. Although the overall effect of air pollution cannot be easily distinguished

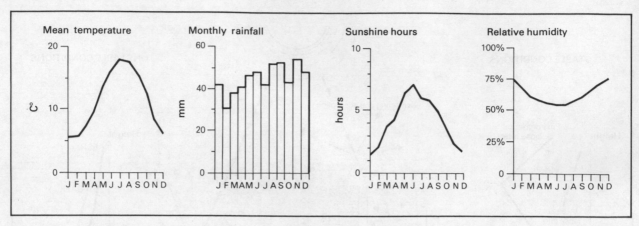

Figure 11.6   *London's monthly climatic averages are largely the same as those for other inland sites in the UK, with a marked seasonal variation in temperature, humidity and solar radiation, while rainfall remains relatively high throughout the year.*

from other man-made effects it is possible to identify alterations of rainfall, the radiation balance and visibility attributable to pollution.

Condensation of water vapour, leading to cloud formation and ultimately rain, requires the presence of condensation nuclei. Some pollutants provide such nuclei and thereby may assist in the development of fog and cloud. Atkinson (1979) observed the passage of several storms over London and concluded that the higher intensity downpours in urban areas compared with rural environs is likely to be due to the frictional effect of the city together with heat emissions causing greater atmospheric instability. Rainfall acidity can be directly related to pollutant emissions, especially SO_2. The highest acidity levels in the UK occur in the south-east. London's acidity trends are not clear although there is some indication of a reduction during summer periods (GLC 1983).

Atmospheric pollutants absorb and scatter solar radiation resulting in reduced amounts being received by London and a marked filtering out of ultra-violet wavelengths. However, the net radiation budget is little affected because less solar radiation is reflected by the urban surface as a whole compared to the rural environs and a larger amount of the heat emitted (terrestrial radiation) is absorbed by the atmosphere.

The recent decrease in smoke and sulphur dioxide concentrations has improved winter visibilities and reduced the frequency of fogs. This has been partly offset by an increase in photo-chemical

smogs during summer months since 1930, related to increases in vehicular emissions. But recent work has shown that this decline in summer visibilities was probably reversed after 1973, as a result of falling oil consumption.

Plants

Pollutant gases can gain entry to plants during photosynthesis via their stomata. It is often difficult to distinguish between natural effects, such as nutrient supply and water availability, and the effects of atmospheric pollutants, but there is sufficient evidence to conclude that sulphur dioxide, nitrogen dioxide and ozone can cause serious damage to vegetation. Lichens have been used to examine the effects of London's atmosphere on vegetation, with the conclusion that while smoke had little effect, London's SO_2 concentrations had severely reduced the populations of certain species in the capital. Recently there has been a reversal of this trend. Despite some lichens being particularly sensitive to air pollution, sites in north-west London have been recolonized, probably due to falling SO_2 concentration (see also chapter 17).

Weathering of buildings

Various gaseous pollutants in urban areas, especially CO_2, SO_2 and NO_2, may accelerate the decomposition of building materials. This degradation is particularly important for natural building stones in

Stone erosion on the parapet of St Paul's.
The extent of the weathering is revealed by the exposure of lead plugs which were originally flush with the surface.

ancient monuments, where costly remedial work may become necessary. Limestones, for example, may be dissolved both in rainwater made acid by the gases (solution), and by direct reaction with SO_2 in its gaseous state (sulphation). Both of these types of change may disfigure the stone surface. They may also create secondary salts, such as gypsum, which can contribute to stone degradation by causing such features as blistering. In London, as in other major cities, many building stones suffer from these processes. At St Paul's cathedral, for example, the Portland stone balustrade has been lowered over its exposed surface by an average of 0.078 mm per year since it was completed in 1718. In addition to building stone destruction, many buildings are soiled by smoke and other particulate pollutants, although the reduction of smoke in recent years has allowed the grime to be removed from many buildings which should now remain clean for some time. Other weathering problems associated with air pollution include a disfiguring bloom on painted surfaces exposed to NO_2 and the corrosion of metal by acid rain. Work is continuing at the Building Research Establishment and the Department of Geography at University College London, exploring in detail some aspects of the spatial and temporal variability of building stone weathering in London.

Control of air pollution

Concern over the quality of air in London can be traced back to the introduction of coal in the thirteenth century, but it has proved difficult to assess the full impact of the various pollutants because of the complexity of the interactions of climate, health, living conditions and source of contamination. It is evident that London's atmosphere has been modified by human activities causing higher temperatures, reduced visibilites and an increase in the frequency of thunderstorms. Such urban climatic effects are ephemeral and dependent upon certain meteorological conditions, resulting in relatively few occasions when there are significant differences between London and its rural environs. Today, the same observation applies to the occurrence of high pollution episodes in London, the concentration of pollutants being strongly influenced by the prevailing weather as well as the source and rate of emission. In the past, atmospheric pollutants, particularly smoke, were more apparent and persistent resulting in a series of acts of Parliament culminating in the Clean Air Acts of 1956 and 1968, with over 93 per cent of premises subject to control. In addition, the 1972 Various Powers Act introduced a limit of 1 per cent for the sulphur content of fuel used within the City of London.

The Department of the Environment has overall responsibility for pollution control but it is local authorities that implement the air pollution control powers in conjunction with the Alkali Inspectorate. The setting of air quality standards is difficult both because the precise effect of many pollutants is indirect and poorly understood and many different agencies and political pressures are involved. The GLC identified seventeen different public bodies in London with responsibilities for air pollution control measures. This, together with the variety of sources (Table 11.1) and concentrations of pollutants makes effective control difficult. At present, the only air quality standards in force in the UK are for smoke, sulphur dioxide and lead, although controls on nitrogen dioxide levels are being discussed. Control of vehicular emissions is based upon vehicle design and the contaminants present in the fuel. EEC regulations stipulate acceptable lead and sulphur levels for petrol but until recently there were no corresponding measures for diesel.

Surprisingly, the general public have little opportunity to pursue pollution control through the courts. Individuals may only sue in a civil court if they can prove a 'legal interest', i.e. ownership of the polluted environment, while in many cases only the control authority has the power to prosecute in criminal law. Whatever the circumstances the decision on whether or not to enact the various control measures rests largely upon the evidence supplied by the monitoring of pollutant levels.

Rainfall acidity and dust fallout started to be measured from 1917; regular monitoring of SO_2 and smoke levels by the LCC began in 1946. However, the need for more comprehensive observations, especially of vehicular emissions, was not recognised until the 1970s. This late recognition arises partly from the slowness to appreciate the importance of vehicular emissions and partly from the difficulties of monitoring the enormous range of pollutants emitted. Most attempts at control have focused on the more easily monitored stationary sources yielding smoke and SO_2. At present such monitoring is undertaken by the GLC but it is uncertain who will retain responsibility for these observations when the GLC is abolished.

In common with many other British cities London still has an atmospheric pollution problem, but much has been achieved to clean London's air and in 1976 it was the GLC's aim to ensure that 'there is no overall deterioration in the quality of London's air and, wherever possible, to seek action to reduce the existing levels of air pollution'.

This task has been aided during the last 30 years by changes in fuel consumption and a dispersion of industry. In the future, control will be more difficult as vehicles contribute an increasing proportion of atmospheric pollutants and the next series of measures will probably be directed towards the control of vehicular emissions, through traffic management measures and exhaust emission control.

Further reading

Atkinson B W (1979) 'Urban influence on precipitation in London' in G E Hollis (ed) *Man's Impact on the Hydrological Cycle in the UK* Geo Books, Norwich

Chandler T J (1965) *The Climate of London* Hutchinson

Chandler T J (1976) 'The climate of towns' in Chandler T J and Gregory S (eds) *The Climate of the British Isles* Longman

Greater London Council (1983) *Thirty Years On: a review of air pollution in London* GLC

Lawther P (1976) 'Twenty years of clean air research' *New Scientist* 9: 584–5

Lyall I (1977) 'The London heat island in June–July 1976' *Weather*, **32**: 296–302

Oke T (1978) *Boundary Layer Climates* Methuen

Royal Commission on Environment Pollution (1983) *Ninth Report: Lead in the Environment* HMSO

Royal Commission on Environmental Pollution (1984) *Tenth Report: Tackling pollution, experience and prospects* HMSO

Spedding D J (1974) *Air Pollution* Clarendon Press Oxford

Open University (1975) *Environmental Control and Public Health, Units 13–14, Air Pollution* Open University, Milton Keynes

12   Water management

Ted Hollis

Introduction

London makes heavy and diverse demands on water in the Thames basin. On average the volume of water supplied, and the consequent volume of sewage treated, is about half of the flow in the Thames at Teddington, but during the summer the man-made water system handles twice the volume of the natural river flow. Nine million tons of sewage sludge must be disposed of each year, 35 500 km of water mains and 40 000 km of sewers must be maintained and 20 000 craft cruise on the freshwater Thames. Careful management of the whole of the Thames catchment is necessary to meet London's demands because the city is located at the bottom of a heavily populated catchment in the driest and warmest part of Britain, with a major estuary at its heart. It is, therefore, a notable feat of river basin management that London is supplied with 70 per cent of its water from the Thames, that the Thames estuary has been transformed from a putrid state to a salmon river and that the Thames Barrier will protect London from the growing threat of tidal flooding well into the twenty-first century.

London's achievements in water management (Fig. 12.1) result from three historical circumstances. The first is the development of institutions, ranging from the New River Company of 1619 and the Thames Conservancy in the 1860s, to the Metropolitan Water Board in 1903. Second, a rich legacy has been left by centuries of investment in capital works such as Bazalgette's sewer system in the 1850s and the Thames valley and Lea valley reservoirs of the Metropolitan Water Board. Finally, crises, such as cholera in 1854 and the coastal flooding of 1953, have stimulated developments. This chapter identifies four areas of change

in the 1980s that have developed from changes in the 1970s. First, political changes stem from the government's approach to public spending and public enterprises, EEC policies, and the GLC's imminent demise. Second, social trends in population and the demand for water continue to require policy responses. Third, technological developments can both combat the ageing infrastructure and facilitate increased efficiency with reduced manpower. Finally, physical changes in the environment result largely from man's actions, the exception being the rising sea level relative to the land.

Political changes

Until 1974, water management in the Thames basin was fragmented amongst 200 local authorities and bodies each normally responsible for one function. The 1973 Water Act produced ten Regional Water Authorities in England and Wales with responsibility for all aspects of water. As regards London, Thames Water Authority was created but the Act left seven Water Companies as agents of Thames Water and the GLC retained land drainage and the Thames Tidal Defences. The Water Authorities, including Thames Water, had a majority of local authority representatives and functioned as local authorities. Thames Water was multifunctional but its operations were organized around the pre-existing single function bodies such as the Metropolitan Water Division (Board) and the Lea Division (Conservancy).

Developments 1974–1979

The 1975–6 drought brought no major interruptions to supply in London. Thames Water's unitary control of water and ability to transfer resources

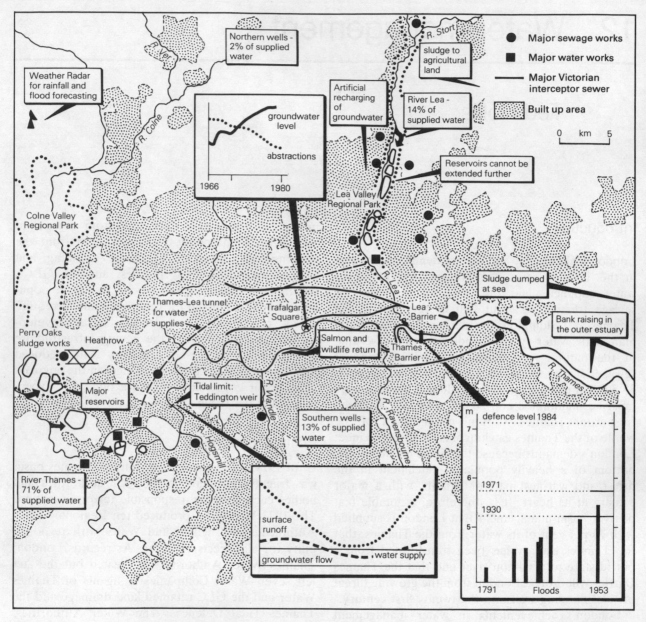

Figure 12.1   *London's water management.*

around the basin were largely responsible for this success. The 1976 Drought Act was passed during August because no appropriate legislation had been enacted during earlier droughts. It has had enduring value, with drought orders being made in the west of the country during the summer drought of 1984.

The reorganization of the water industry in 1974, its separation from local authority finances, and a court ruling that properties without sewers should be exempt from sewerage charges brought substantial bills for householders. These were regarded, wrongly, as new charges but their rapid escalation in the mid-1970s was a cause of considerable disquiet. Partly in response to this, the Labour Government passed the Water Charges Equalization Act which increased Londoners' water charges in order to subsidize rural consumers in other authorities. Charging by quantity of service

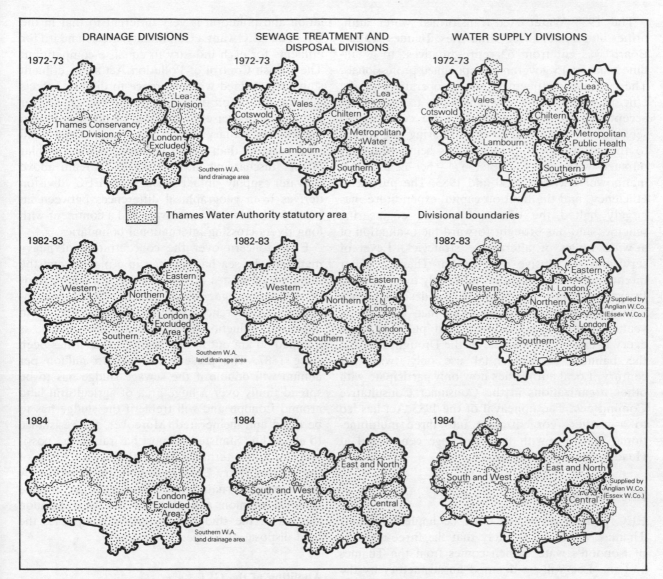

Figure 12.2   *The changing structure of water management in the London region.*

provided rather than through bills based on rateable value has also developed with, for example, the optional use of water meters by householders. Most significantly, developments in the water industry since 1974 have taken place against the background of the deep economic recession following the 1973–4 oil crisis.

Developments 1979–1984

The new 1979 Conservative Government imposed cash limits, directives on the allocation of reserves, instructions on capital investment, manpower economies and the disposal of surplus property on Water Authorities. The Lords' Select Committee on Science and Technology has also identified a number of issues requiring attention, including the need for better leakage control and the management of demand rather than increasing supplies of water indefinitely. Thames Water was reorganized in 1982 into six multifunctional divisions (Fig. 12.2) because of dissatisfaction with the largely single-function divisions which had retained established attitudes and practices.

The 1983 Water Act transformed water authorities into 'nationalized' industries. Thames Water's Board was cut from 62 representatives, to a full-time team of 15 government appointed professionals. Their primary objectives are to operate with the efficiency of a well-run business and to provide an acceptable quality of service, while continuously seeking to reduce real costs and having due regard to the environment. Efficiency is being ruthlessly pursued with, for example, a 14 per cent cut in manpower between 1980 and 1983. The pursuit of efficiency, and the limit on capital expenditure, has largely halted the emphasis on big engineering schemes and has brought forward the evaluation of a wide range of alternative strategies. Level of service is an elusive concept but Thames Water intends to achieve its goals uniformly over its area. In water supply, for example, the desired service includes hosepipe bans no more than once in six years, voluntary restrictions, and publicity once every twenty years and use of the Drought Act and the banning of inessential use only twice per century. Local authorities now only participate with other organizations in the Consumer Consultative Committees. The upheaval of the 1983 Act has led to a further reorganization into three multifunctional divisions with land drainage centralized at Headquarters (Fig. 12.2).

EEC directives

EEC policies on water must be implemented by Thames Water. It is likely that the three-quarters of London's water which comes from the Thames and the Lea will be deemed unsatisfactory by the EEC because of trace organic compounds resulting from the re-use of water as it flows down to London. Activated carbon filters could be installed at water works but costs, and charges, would rise. Evidence of the adverse effects of water re-use are limited. Indeed, an investigation into mortality in London boroughs since 1926 showed an apparent relation between the amount of re-used water consumed and gastro-intestinal cancers, but this disappeared when socio-economic differences between the boroughs were taken into account.

Over 65 per cent of Thames Water's watercourses are unpolluted on Department of Environment criteria and only 37 km (1 per cent) are grossly polluted. However, EEC thinking on effluent regulation and pollution is very different to that in the UK. The EEC want a Community-wide standard for effluents for each industry to equalise competition. The British Control of Pollution Act seeks effluent standards defined with reference to dilution effects and the utilization of specific watercourses. So, for instance, a poorer effluent could be discharged into the Thames estuary with its huge volume and rapid tidal currents than would be licenced for a similar factory discharging into a Cotswold stream above a water supply intake. The UK–EEC division derives from geographical differences between an island with a lot of short rivers and a continent with long rivers crossing international boundaries.

EEC concern over the concentration of heavy metals in the sea has resulted in a plan to end the dumping of wastes at sea. London's 5 million tons of sewage sludge, which includes small concentrations of mercury, silver, cadmium, etc. from industrial effluents discharged to the sewers, is dumped 80 km out in the North Sea, as it has been since 1887. The present cost of £15 million per annum will double if the sewage sludge has to be spread thinly over a huge area of agricultural land around London and will treble if the sludge has to be dried and incinerated. Moreover, the resistance to expanding Stansted Airport has raised the possibility of a fifth terminal at Heathrow on the site of the existing Perry Oaks sludge treatment works. A move to an alternative sludge works site, acceptable to local opinion and close to the west London sources of the sludge, will further complicate the land disposal of sludge.

Abolition of the GLC

The government intends to abolish the GLC in 1986, with Thames Water assuming responsibility for land drainage, tidal defences and the Thames Barrier. Such a change would remove an anomaly of the 1974 reorganization and bring the tidal and freshwater Thames, and the rivers and sewers of London under one authority for the first time. Thames Water has welcomed the proposals but has cautioned over the transfer of staff and liabilities because the GLC employs a very large staff compared to the land drainage personnel of the rest of the Thames basin.

It used to be said that the water industry was 'out of sight and out of mind' and that there were 'no votes in sewage'. Recent droughts, changes in water charges and political developments have certainly brought water into view but there are now literally no votes in sewage by statute, since local authority elected representatives have been superceded by efficiency-conscious, business-oriented professionals appointed by the government!

Social changes

Growth in the demand for water

Per capita water consumption has risen 23 per cent since 1977 because of improved standards of living and increasing leakage from the water mains. Continued growth in demand is expected to raise consumption by a further 100 litres to 450 litres per head per day in 2011. The population of the Thames Water area is forecast to grow by 5 per cent by 2011 with the metropolitan population declining by 1 per cent and the non-metropolitan zone growing by 11 per cent. The largest increase, of 22 per cent, will be in the Western Division incorporating Swindon, Oxford, Banbury and Aylesbury. The continued decline in household size will increase the number of households by 7 per cent by 1991, with an 18 per cent rise in the non-metropolitan areas. This will bring a rise in the number of connections to water services and a proportionate rise in the demand for water and sewage services. The regional implications of these social changes are shown in Table 12.1.

Table 12.1 *Total water demand 1981–2011 (Ml/day)*

Division	Actual 1983	Projected 2011	Percentage Increase	Absolute Increase
Western	253	414	64	161
Southern	603	911	51	308
Northern	480	676	41	196
Eastern	517	696	34	179
North London	954	1280	34	326
South London	820	1104	22	284

The most immediate water shortages will occur in London. The proposed abolition of the statutory minimum flow of 773 Ml/day over Teddington Weir will allow the maximum filling of the reservoirs in droughts. It is desirable to allow maximum flexibility in river management because pollution in the Thames estuary and the demand for water have changed dramatically since the minimum flow was defined in 1911. A conventional reservoir to provide an equivalent volume of supply would cost £40 million and take 20 years to realize. There will also be an extension of the artificial recharge scheme for groundwater in the Lea valley. This stores surplus drinking water in the aquifers in the winter months and allows its withdrawal the following summer. A further short-term measure involves using the Lea Flood Barrier, defunct since the completion of the Thames Barrier, to improve the quality of water in the lower Lea to allow abstraction during drought periods. Another significant development is the London water ring main concept which will link all of London's water works. This will assist their operational efficiency, offset local supply shortages and allow the networking of water sources and demands throughout London.

The growth in demand at the western end of the catchment poses special problems because water will have to be moved uphill at extra cost. A link is planned from the Farmoor reservoir near Oxford up to Swindon and a major new well at Goring will provide water for an area as far west as Wantage once planning permission has been obtained.

Recreation and conservation

Water Authorities must use their water bodies and associated lands for recreation. Before 1974, Londoners were denied access to large reservoirs on public health grounds, but today 31 reservoirs in London are used for fishing, bird watching, sailing and picnicing. Sub-aqua clubs use the King George reservoir near Chingford and water skiing is under consideration.

Growing public interest in nature conservation, exemplified by the growing membership of the Royal Society for the Protection of Birds from 139 000 in 1973 to 370 000 in 1984, is also affecting water management. The 1973 Water Act required water authorities to 'have regard to' nature but the Wildlife and Countryside Act 1981 required water authorities to 'enhance' the conservation of natural features. Procedures now exist for consultation with conservation groups and Thames Water's engineers have been issued with guidelines on engineering and the environment. Drainage works have attracted particular criticism on ecological grounds and the 'improvement' of the lower River Stort by dredging and channel straightening has been shelved as a result. The formal representation of a range of conservation bodies on the newly consitituted Regional Recreation and Conservation Consultative Committee is another step towards a more sensitive approach to the environment.

The River Ver, a chalkland bourn north of St Albans, once flowed strongly down the dip slope of the Chilterns where living memory describes children swimming in the river each summer. Post-war housing developments increased the demand for water and brought a series of wells. The licensed abstraction was set at the calculated recharge of the aquifer, namely 22.73 Ml/day. Abstractions grew to 18.6 Ml/day by 1979 and large sections of the river dried up. In the vicinity of one of the largest wells, the channel has been filled and ploughed over. The waste water from the valley flows through sewers to the treatment works at Maple Lodge and thence into the River Colne. In recent years a campaign by old and new residents alike has demanded the revival of the flow in the Ver and the re-establishment of its wildlife and waterfowl. Unfortunately, with restrictions on expenditure, urgent demands for investment from new developments and some communities still lacking main drainage, there is no economic scheme available to allow the residents to have water both in their river and in their washing machines!

Technological change and an ageing infrastructure

London's ageing water infrastructure has four manifestations. First, most of the sewer collapses (320 in 1982–3) were in the small sewers of the 1930s and 1950s suburbs, where rapid speculative construction and frequent disturbance by other utilities combined to cause problems. Sewer problems in London are not caused by their age because the oldest sewers are large enough to have undergone regular maintenance. Modern developments in sewer repair and relining mean that it is not usually necessary to undertake excavations but the costs of maintenance and repair are heavy in a time of financial stringency and so the frequency of sewer collapses is likely to rise by 50 per cent between 1983 and 1987. Second,

drinking water has been adversely affected by rainwater entering service reservoirs. These are usually located in the tops of the small hills in the suburbs and serve to maintain pressure in the mains and to store water ready for supply. Clearly, the efforts of the waterworks are wasted if maintenance programmes on the infrastructure fail to halt contamination.

Third, up to 40 per cent of the water supplied by Thames Water leaks out of the mains before it reaches the consumer. This means that water resources have to be developed to feed the leakage, water works operating and pumping costs are inflated and sewage works receive increased inputs through subsequent infiltration into the sewers below the water mains. The 1983 plan on leakage control has a £5 million capital budget and aims to reduce leakage to 20 per cent, producing an annual saving of £3 million. This policy is a significant shift from the 1960s approach where the development of big new resources, for example the Wash Barrage, was seen as the solution to London's water supply problems. Finally, 13 000 properties in the region are liable to flooding by sewage at least once every ten years and 8 300 were actually flooded in 1982–3. This results from increased runoff from new buildings, infilling built-up areas and draining to existing sewers, and from increased water use which raises base flows and reduces the flood capacity of sewers. A solution will cost £275 million (more than half the cost of the Thames Barrier) and with restrictions on expenditure it will be more than 15 years before the problem can be solved.

Improvements in telecommunications, instrumentation, automation and computing will bring further benefits. The London Weather Radar Scheme will soon provide improved flood warnings on the highly urbanized watercourses in London. These short streams have a rapid rate of runoff from the paved areas in their catchments. The radar will provide a map of rainfall rate as the rain falls. This will be used by real-time computer models to forecast river levels and to provide the few hours of warning that are essential to emergency flood defence measures. In the rural west of the Thames basin, telemetry and automation make it possible to operate many small sewage works remotely without permanent staff on site and with only a fraction of the original maintenance staff. Similarly, the replacement sewage pumping station near the Isle of Dogs

Enterprise Zone has the latest technology to increase the efficiency of the mechanical and electrical plant as well as to reduce manpower requirements. Thames Water have allocated 6 per cent of their capital programme to increase efficiency and reduce costs. As a result, they expect to reduce manpower by a further 10 per cent during 1984–5 and to save £10 million in operating costs. The effect of these schemes will be a concentration of information and decision making at the Headquarters in Reading, a proportionate increase in white collar staff at the expense of manual operatives within a declining workforce, and around 1 000 people either seeking work or swelling the ranks of the prematurely retired.

Changes in the physical environment

The rising sea level relative to the land is the only natural trend to affect water management in London. The other changes; rising groundwater levels, improved estuarine water quality, rising nitrate concentrations in rivers, and exacerbated flooding because of urbanization, all result from man's action. Even the recent droughts do not represent a significant shift in climate.

Surge tide flooding

London suffers from an increasing risk of tidal flooding because high tides are rising by 0.85 m per century in London and record flood levels also show a progressive increase (Table 12.2).

Table 12.2   *Record flood levels at London Bridge (metres above) Ordnance Datum*

Year	Flood Level
1791	4.27
1881	4.91
1928	5.21
1953	5.41
Jan 1978	5.10
Dec 1978	5.22

The reasons are threefold. South-east England is sinking because of the continuing isostatic rise of the north and west following the melting of the Pleis-

The Thames Barrier was promoted by the GLC but largely funded by central government. Most of the money was spent on bank raising and other works along the river below the Barrier, between Woolwich and Southend.

tocene ice sheets. In addition, the over-pumping of the confined chalk aquifer has allowed contraction of the London Clay and consequent settlement. Second, sea levels are rising generally because of the melting of the polar ice caps. Third, dredging and the embanking of the former marshland of the estuary has modified estuarine hydraulics and caused a greater tidal range. London's tidal flood hazard arises from the coincidence of a high tide with a storm surge in the North Sea. The surges are caused by depressions that both lift water levels because of their low atmospheric pressure and drive the sea water into the Thames estuary with north-east gales.

The very serious risk of flooding in central London, which was likely once every ten years before the 1971 interim bank raising, has now been averted by the construction of the Thames Barrier and the associated raising of the walls and embankments in the whole of the outer estuary. The barrier has been designed to protect London from a once in 1 000 year surge tide during 2030. But, since the physical trends necessitating the barrier will continue, what type of flood protection will be available and required during the middle of the twenty-first century?

Water quality in the Thames estuary

By 1951, the Thames estuary was deoxygenated and black with a floating scum of filth. Investment in treatment works had not matched increasing sewage flows and thermal pollution from power stations had worsened the situation. Following the report of an investigatory committee, the Port of London Authority was given wide powers to control pollution and a massive investment was made in the sewage works at Beckton and Crossness. A minimum dissolved oxygen concentration of 10 per cent of saturation and a three month average of over 30 per cent was achieved by the beginning of the 1980s (Fig. 12.3). This dramatic improvement in quality has reinstated the Thames as a salmon river, with 116 adult salmon being taken in 1982–3, brought a wealth of wildlife, including mullet, whitebait, shelduck and dunlin back to the estuary, and has facilitated the re-establishment of a large scale eel fishery after a break of 150 years. Improvements to estuarial water are now included in Thames Water's lowest priority category, and no investment for further improvement is programmed for 1984–89.

Nitrate in surface waters

Concern exists over the rising concentrations of nitrate in the Thames and Lea (Fig. 12.4) because the World Health Organization has set 11.3 mg/l as the limit in drinking water. Excess nitrate causes blue baby syndrome and is suspected of having a link with stomach cancer. The reason for the rising levels of nitrate has not been conclusively demonstrated but artificial fertilizers and changing agricultural practices are prime suspects. Speculation that the World War II ploughing-up campaign may have released a slug of nitrate into groundwater which is only now reappearing, has arisen because the ploughing of grassland releases nitrate and recent springflow has been dated as having fallen as rain in the 1940s. In any event, most authorities conclude that the concentration of nitrate in rivers is likely to continue rising in the future.

The effect of this rise on London's water supply is, however, less severe than was once thought. Nitrate can be removed from drinking water, although at a cost, and many sewage treatment works have been modified cheaply to reduce the

Figure 12.3   *Changes in the water quality of the Thames estuary and the return of Wildlife (after information from the Thames Water Authority)*

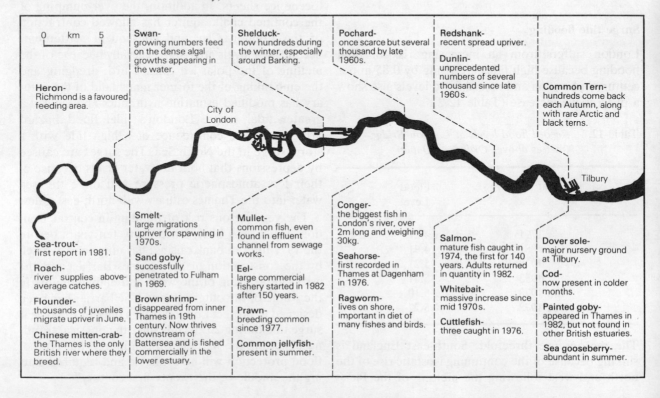

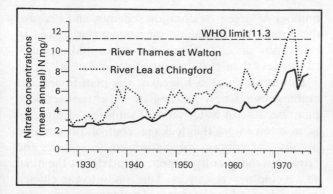

Figure 12.4 *The rising concentration of nitrate in the Thames and Lea.*

nitrate concentrations in their effluent. The discovery of this innovative method was made at a works in the Lea valley. The storage of water in the large reservoirs feeding London also greatly reduces nitrate concentrations by natural biological activity, and well water is usually low in nitrate. Thames Water has therefore prepared drinking water of acceptable standard by mixing water from a variety of sources by the use of their interlinked works. The rising nitrate levels in rivers will not require any substantial expenditure by Thames Water and so it is unlikely to cause problems for London.

Urbanization and floods

The urbanization of a river catchment renders much of its surface impermeable, creating rapid runoff via sewers. Fourfold increases in flood peaks and a 50 per cent reduction in the lag time between rainfall and runoff have been reported at Harlow New Town as a result of a 16.6 per cent impermeable cover. Within London, new housing and industrial estates in the catchment of the Silk Stream in north London produced a threefold increase in flood peaks. In the neigbouring Dollis Brook, no significant change in river floods resulted from substantial building because it was infill in a built up area, and storm runoff was throttled by the existing sewer network. Where extensive new schemes are built, for example Graham Park Estate in Hendon, runoff is retained on flat roofs or in lakes designed to have landscape appeal as well as helping flood alleviation. Where watercourses are of inadequate capacity, hydraulic improvements can be made by their enlargement, straightening or lining with

concrete as in the case of the recent comprehensive scheme for the River Brent.

The droughts of 1976 and 1984

A downward trend of low statistical significance has taken place in autumn and winter rainfall for the last 100 years. However, recent apparent reversals of the trend question established explanations. Water specialists believe therefore, that future droughts and spates will be similar to those already recorded. Droughts in London are intimately related to groundwater storage in the Thames basin. This is recharged only during the winter months when rainfall exceeds evapotranspiration. Riverflow originates from surface runoff and groundwater in roughly equal amounts in winter but groundwater flow dominates during the summer. Consequently, a dry winter and a dry summer are required to produce a drought in London unlike the impermeable areas of the South West and Wales which suffer after only a couple of months without rain. The droughts of 1976 and 1984 illustrate the significance of groundwater storage to London. Rainfall for the Thames basin in the 1975–6 drought was around 50 per cent of average and is likely to occur only once every 1 000 years. However, the low river flows have a much higher frequency because they are the result of an interplay of factors which may combine in different ways to cause minimal discharges. Figure 12.5 confirms that, for low flows at Teddington, 1975–6 was no more severe a drought than those occurring in other dry spells during this century. London was not seriously affected by the 1984 drought because groundwater recharge was substantial following very wet weather during the winter. Indeed the only restrictions imposed by Thames Water was a hosepipe ban around Swindon.

Future problems?

During the ten years since its formation, Thames Water has produced a genuinely integrated multifunctional approach to the management of its large and densely populated river basin. London has seen the reinstatement of the Thames as a salmon river thanks to measures to reduce pollution in the estuary, a reversal of dramatic declines in groundwater levels, and virtually complete protection from

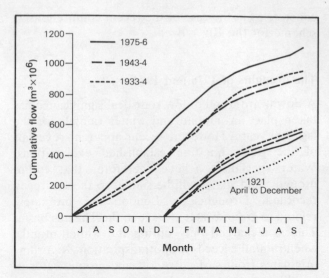

Figure 12.5   *The 1975/6 drought and earlier droughts in the Thames basin.*

tidal flooding thanks to the GLC's Thames Barrier. Moreover, the quality of the freshwater Thames has been safeguarded and London has been continuously supplied with its water through one of the severest droughts this century. Thames Water now operates as a business-oriented public utility rather than as a 'taxing' quasi-local authority. It has held its charges to less than the rate of inflation since 1979 and planned to continue this policy until at least 1987; although in 1985 the Chancellor of the Exchequer decided to raise charges substantially above this. The authority has increased its efficiency markedly through the utilization of automation and telecommunications, through two organizational restructurings in ten years and, most important of all, by shedding huge numbers of staff. If present trends continue, it is conceivable that the public may soon be invited to buy shares in a privatized Thames Water PLC dedicated to profitability, as were the early seventeenth century water companies.

In the 1984 Corporate Plan, Thames Water say that the Government's financial limits have caused capital expenditure to be cut below the level necessary to maintain levels of service in the longer term. Some areas with new development underway may suffer a temporary decline in service whilst in other areas the present unacceptable risk of sewage flooding or water supply failure will persist. Continuing financial restraint will give rise to an increasing number of urgent restoration schemes and because the annual rate of capital investment has halved in real terms since 1974, the planned capital expenditure is less than the amount of depreciation!

Despite these dire forecasts, the plan forsees no embargoes on new housing or industrial development because of water services shortages. Emphasis is also given to the leakage control programme because it reduces distribution costs, reduces the growth in the quantity supplied, and defers the need to develop new resources. This is a welcome change to the demand-led resource development prevalent in the 1960s and early 1970s. It will be needed in the Thames Water area in the future because of the growing per capita demand for water, rising population numbers and the increasing number of smaller households. The relatively greater population increases in the centre and upper parts of the catchment compared to those occurring in London, will require the movement of water up the catchment in contrast to the historic policy of using the water one or more times as it flows by gravity to the sea.

Further reading

A modern and comprehensive review, with an emphasis on hydrology and water management schemes, is found in:
Kirby C (1984) *Water in Great Britain* Pelican

A hydrology text with a wealth of UK examples and good chapters on water quality and water resources is provided by:
Rodda J C, Downing R A and Law F M (1976) *Systematic Hydrology* Newnes-Butterworth

A full report of the Barrier scheme is contained in:
Gilbert S and Horner R W (1984) *The Thames Barrier* Thomas Telford

A searching review of water management policies and structures which poses the question 'Who is water planning for?' is contained in:
Parker D J and Penning-Rowsell E C (1980) *Water Planning in Britain* Allen and Unwin

Essential reading for those seeking a little insight into 'real' water management for London is:
Thames Water *Annual Reports* 1974/5 to 1983/4

13 Central London

Gerald Manners

More than one million jobs

For centuries central London has adapted its functions and land uses to the industrial and commercial opportunities of the day. In parallel with a steady decline in residential population, its manufacturing activities have slowly contracted and its wholesale markets – most recently Covent Garden and Billingsgate – have decentralized to more spacious and convenient sites. Simultaneously, a range of higher value land uses, such as offices, specialized shops, hotels, medical services, educational establishments and central government activities, have expanded in response to market and institutional opportunities. The central area has experienced a slight decline in its overall employment in recent years. However, despite the problems of national and international recession, the economies of both the City and West End have remained remarkably buoyant. They continue to provide the largest concentration of jobs in the metropolis – estimated at 1 250 000 in 1981 – and they are, of course, the locus of high income employment.

An important contrast persists between the evolution of the City of London, on the one hand, and of the West End, on the other. The former still retains a few residual manufacturing activities in its northern and eastern parts, the renowned printing industry of Fleet Street to the west, and a hint of its earlier commercial functions in the meat market of Smithfield. In recent years it has re-established a minor residential role and has acquired important cultural activities through the redevelopment of the Barbican. Today, however, the City is dominated by office-based activities. Indeed in 1980 almost 70 per cent of its entire floor space was given over to nearly 5 000 000 m^2 of offices. More than half this space is concentrated in just one-quarter of the 'square mile' that has the Bank of England at its core. Here is to be found a unique combination of national and international financial services, especially the head offices of domestic clearing banks and merchant banks, major branches of foreign banks and, of course, the Stock Exchange. The mix of activities changes to the east of the Bank of England, and is more biased toward international trading functions, including commodity markets, insurance broking and shipping. To the west the specialization is towards professional services, particularly accountancy, the headquarters of large companies, economic consultancy and, in the Inns of Court, the law. The enormous national importance of the financial services provided by the City of London is reflected in the fact that in 1982/83 they generated some £4 400 million net of overseas earnings.

Activities in the West End had their origins in the Court and Parliament rather than in trade and commerce (see chapter 4). The Court spawned an important high-income residential role which, with the assistance of a distinctive pattern of land ownership and rigorous planning controls, still persists today. It also gave rise to the siting of overseas representation in the form of embassies, consulates and trade missions. These residential and international roles laid the foundations of the West End's distinctive range of specialized retail services (for example in Regent Street and Knightsbridge) and the growth of an exceptional range of entertainment and cultural facilities. Parliament, on the other hand, has led to the growth of a large complex of offices to house the civil service, and to the attraction, within easy reach of the Palace of Westminster, of a wide range of institutional and business activities that perceive an advantage by being located close to the centre of the nation's political power. The West End also has a distinctive role in the provision of medical services (for example Harley Street and famous teaching hospitals), the university, other institutions of higher education, and many museums and galleries.

The central area of London, roughly defined by an imaginary line between the major rail termini (Fig. 13.1), performs an important range of economic and social roles, which together employ approximately 1 250 000 people. However, the central area houses only about 225 000, no more than half of whom are active members of the workforce. Hence, most employees in the City and the West End come into the central area each day. They travel from neighbouring communities of inner London, from the suburbs and from an extensive zone in the outer metropolitan area. It was the physical and economic problems posed by managing this huge daily flow of people in and out of the central area, which reached 1.26 million at its height in the 1960s, that first prompted the government to adopt policies of 'planning restraint'.

Figure 13.1   *London's central area (updated from K. Clayton, 1964).*

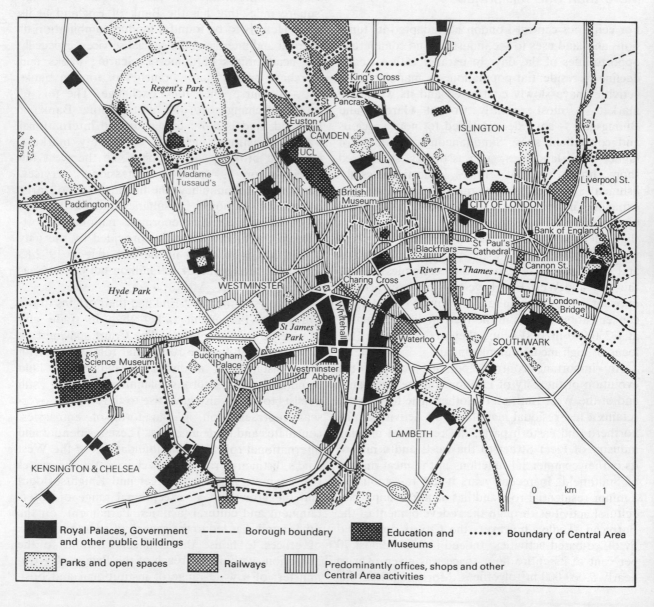

First, the Cities of London and Westminster individually, then the local authorities collectively, through the policies of the LCC, and finally in the 1960s central government decided to intervene in the process of land-use and employment change in the central area to restrain the growth of jobs and commuting, in the hope of easing 'congestion'. This was particularly the case with respect to growth of office employment. Indeed, from 1945 onwards successive plans were approved for the City and the West End in which the construction of further office buildings (and implicitly the generation of new office jobs) was severely controlled.

Moreover, for some fifteen years after 1963, central government, with the help of its Location of Offices Bureau (LOB), encouraged office activities to move from the central area to suitable places elsewhere in Greater London (see chapter 14) and in the rest of the country. In contrast, tourism-related activities which form another major and indeed faster growing source of employment in central London have never been subjected to comparable planning restraint. Yet they pose no less testing a challenge to the management of the central area. It is instructive to examine these two substantial bastions of central London's economy, to consider the problems they have posed, and to note the policies adopted in response to them.

The changing dynamics of office employment

Office employment in London's central area grew from 612 000 in 1951 to 754 000 in 1961, declining slightly thereafter to 732 000 in 1971 and 680 000 in 1981. In fact, some new office development during the last twenty years 'spilled over' onto cheaper but still convenient sites just beyond the central area (for example in north Southwark and south Islington); the significance of the decline in office employment in the central area is therefore limited. Much more important is the recognition that market forces have long encouraged the creation of new office jobs in the centre of London while also displacing other office activities.

The process of job creation is rooted in the concentration in central London of many industries and occupations that are in growing sectors of the economy. A wide variety of financial services, business consultancies, legal and accountancy activities,

corporate headquarters functions, and (until the 1980s) branches of the civil service have increased in economic importance and have found the environment of central London highly conducive to their efficiency and success. This is due to the presence of a cluster of key functions, such as the Bank of England, the Stock Exchange, Lloyds of London, the so-called terminal or commodity markets, and government itself, plus the relative ease with which knowledge can be acquired, processed and acted upon in an 'information-rich' environment that is without parallel elsewhere in the UK.

A price, of course, has to be paid for these benefits. So great are demands to exploit the opportunities of the central area that land and office space are much more expensive there than elsewhere in the country. In 1981 prime office space near the Bank of England commanded a rent of £225/m^2; in the West End the price of new 'prime' space was somewhat lower at, say, £170; in suburban Harrow the price was only £80; and in the outer metropolitan area (for example Basildon or Bedford) new offices were often available to rent at £35–45/m^2. In parallel with high commercial rents, office users in central London also have to pay much higher local authority rates than in the rest of the UK. They have, moreover, to pay wages and salaries that can meet the considerable expense of London housing and the increasing real cost of travelling to work. These costs are partially reflected in the 'London allowance' paid to public sector employees and in the pay and salary structure of many private companies.

For many enterprises the expenses incurred in having an office in central London are offset by the benefits of undertaking business there. Many, if not all, of the firms operating there take the view that high costs simply have to be afforded. Other office users, in contrast, find the expense of central London too burdensome, and over the years have looked for alternative locations where their activities can be pursued with equal or even greater efficiency but at lower cost. As a generalization, it has been firms that employ large numbers of people in fairly routine work that have been the most active decentralizers; the insurance industry in the 1960s and early 1970s was a classic example. Decentralization has also involved firms that were expanding and needed to acquire more space and more labour. The relative importance of different explanations of

Table 13.1 *Main reasons for office decentralization from central London* (%)*

Economy – the search for lower rents and rates	31
Expansion – the search for more labour and space	27
Expiry of lease – the search for new space	16
Integration with other parts of the firm	10
Staff recruitment – the search for labour	7
Traffic congestion and parking problems	2
Staff welfare and shorter journey to work	1
Other	6
Total	100

* given by firms leaving London with the assistance of the LOB

office decentralization in the 1960s and 1970s is recorded in Table 13.1. It was firms and activities with these attributes that were influenced most readily by the LOB and were in part priced out of the central area by planning policies.

The LOB was established in 1963 to promote the advantages of decentralization and followed from the government's belief that the growth of office employment in central London was imposing too great a strain on public transport and on the capital's labour and housing markets. Between 1963 and its abolition in 1979, LOB assisted the movement of some 5 000 firms and 150 000 jobs. Central and local government together aided this process by refusing to give permission for new offices to be built in many locations in central London. However, they did favour applications for developments near main rail termini and at sites where they offered to provide a wider public benefit, a so-called 'planning gain', such as a refurbished underground station or an improved road lay-out. But government resisted the construction of new office blocks in many other locations, particularly where residential areas needed protection from the encroachment of higher valued commercial uses. By reducing the potential supply of office space in this way the planners steadily raised the market worth of those offices that were already available for rent in central London and thereby added impetus to the process of decentralization.

The net outcome of both market forces and government policies is summarized in one sense by the aggregate office employment data mentioned

earlier. However, the reality was far more complex since it was the more routine and less skilled types of work that tended to be decentralized, while more specialized managerial and professional activities remained in the central area. Over the years central London's office employment has gradually been upgraded, as fewer jobs remained in clerical and junior administrative grades, and an increasing number appeared in senior, better-paid categories.

The amount of office space in the City and West End has increased steadily despite government constraints and the contraction of office employment there since the early 1960s. For example, at mid-century it was estimated that central London had 10.7 million m^2 of office space; by 1980 there were over 18.6 million m^2. The explanation of these divergent trends was that the average amount of floor space used by each office worker increased from 14 m^2/worker in the early 1960s to 28 m^2 in 1980 and it will probably continue to rise in the future. In the City of London's tallest office building, the National Westminster Tower, which houses roughly 2 500 employees, the average amount of floorspace is 29 m^2/worker. It is arguable that this improvement in the spaciousness of the employees' environment would have been even greater had there been fewer restrictions on constructing new office buildings.

The relationship between growth in office employment, decentralization of office activities, and public policy may be judged to have been reasonably satisfactory in the past. But many questions have been raised about the most likely balance between these forces in the future. The dynamics of office location could well be changing, and for two reasons in particular (see chapter 8). First, the economic advantages of decentralization could begin to appeal to an increasing number of firms and activities, as telecommunications and information technologies improve; the advantages of the physical juxtaposition of present central area activities could be lessened thereby, and high costs of operating in central London re-evaluated. Second, the economic advantages of decentralization could be further endorsed by changes in the preferences of management regarding the most desirable places to work. As in many North American metropolitan areas, top management and employees could increasingly prefer to conduct their business from decentralized offices. Thus, the rate of new job generation in central London could be further slowed. Third, the increase of civil service jobs that was sustained in the 1960s and 1970s has been put into reverse. Fourth, it seems unlikely that many existing large office firms in central London, especially those serving the manufacturing sector, will increase their workforce. And, fifth, the growth of office automation will lead to the substitution of word-processors, computers and advanced telecommunications for clerical labour. This trend should reduce unit costs and thereby increase market size for some types of office service; it could also slow down the rate of new job creation.

On the other hand, many small and medium-sized firms in the City and the West End undoubtedly will grow. Central London could also attract an increasing number of internationally footloose office activities, especially in banking and insurance, and also in the form of regional offices of multinational corporations with a manufacturing and/or a sales presence in the UK. Sustained activity in the exploration and production of British oil and natural gas also seems likely to provide a further increase in jobs in central London. And, of course, if the largest firms in the City and the West End do not increase their labour needs significantly, the principal motor of decentralization that operated in the 1960s and 1970s will be throttled back.

Opinions on the most likely trends in the scale and nature of office employment in central London are, not surprisingly, varied, while the speed at which the office floorspace/worker relationship will change is equally unclear. Partly in consequence, central and local government policies towards office construction and development have become increasingly opaque. The GLC would now like to concentrate further office development in a narrowly defined 'central activities zone' inside the central area, partly to protect surrounding residential areas from the gradual encroachment of commercial uses. Meanwhile, central government has adopted an agnostic attitude on strategic questions and now seeks to judge each planning dispute over office development solely on its merits. Certainly, the earlier policy of encouraging decentralization has been set firmly aside.

The growth of tourism

The growth of office employment has levelled off in recent years but jobs related to tourism continue to increase apace. In 1964 central London had only about 44 000 tourist bedrooms; ten years later the figure had risen to 130 000; and by 1982 had reached 154 000. These hotel and guest-house facilities, plus the museums, historic buildings, restaurants, theatres and concert halls, shopping facilities in the West End, and transport services used by tourists, generated an estimated income of over £2 200 million from overseas visitors alone in 1983.

Tourists can be defined as non-residents staying overnight. They may be visiting substantially for business reasons, or wholly for pleasure. They may come from other parts of the UK, or from abroad. They may be staying for a day, or much longer. They may be booked into hotels, or residing with friends. In 1950 London attracted an estimated 500 000 tourists; by 1960, there were twice that number. The 1972 figure for overseas visitors alone was 5.6 million and by 1978 it had risen to 8.4 million. Thereafter the number of tourists visiting London declined somewhat with the world recession and a relatively high value of sterling, but by 1984 it had risen to a new record level, exceeding 9 million from overseas (out of a national total of 13.5 million), plus a further 9 million from other parts of the UK visiting London for purposes other than business.

The benefits of tourism in the form of employment, earnings, and – for international visitors – the promotion of British culture are immense. Nationally, an estimated 1.4 million people work in the industry and the number of jobs is growing steadily. Of this total 3–400 000 are associated with London tourism and a significant proportion of these with the hotels, shops, restaurants and facilities in the central area. The Tower of London, Science Museum, National Gallery, Madame Tussaud's and the British Museum, to name but a few places, are among the nation's major tourist attractions (Table 13.2). The business generated by English tourism in 1984 was some £9 000 million. Just under half of this was from overseas visitors, making the tourism industry the country's largest invisible exporter. As we have seen, central London generates a substantial part of these earnings. Yet tourism is a mixed blessing. Alongside its many benefits it poses a number of challenging problems. Some of these can only be solved or minimized by the industry itself; others impinge on public policy.

Table 13.2   *Major tourist attractions in the UK, 1983*

	Visitors (millions)
Science Museum	3 346
National Gallery	2 897
British Museum	2 845
Windsor Castle*	2 800
Natural History Museum	2 534
Tower of London	2 182
Madame Tussaud's	1 996
Victoria and Albert Museum	1 817
Alton Towers*	1 600
Jewel House (Tower of London)	1 669
Wickstead Park*	1 250
Tate Gallery	1 270
Kew Gardens*	1 058
Botanic Gardens, Edinburgh*	1 039

NB Only five attractions * with more than 1 million visitors
each year are outside central London.

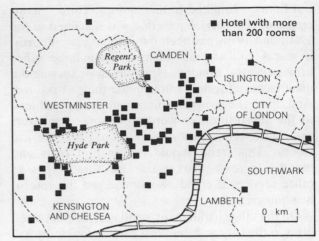

Figure 13.2   *Location of large hotels in central London.*

Seasonality and annual fluctuations in the tourist trade are the most readily acknowledged problems facing the industry itself. The provision of hotels, restaurants and transport to meet peak tourist demands during the third quarter of the year, when about 40 per cent of the trade normally occurs, means that for much of the time many facilities are under used. In response, the industry and the tourist boards have skilfully promoted low cost 'out of season' holidays to extend the international tourist trade well into the autumn and spring. Theatre and special interest tours have also been promoted during the winter months and it has been argued that a major international conference centre, capable of handling 5–10 000 delegates at one time, is required urgently to make a further impact on this problem.

Fluctuations in the annual level of tourism began to pose difficulties in the early 1970s when a burst of hotel construction (Fig. 13.2), aided by public subsidy, was followed initially by a fall in international tourism after the first oil shock, and then a slower market growth than had originally been forecast. Improving economic circumstances and then the Silver Jubilee celebrations combined to accelerate the growth of tourism once again in the late 1970s. But the second oil shock in 1979–80, followed by an increased international value of sterling, held back the growth of the industry for a few years until revised currency values and an improving international economy ushered in another tourist boom in 1983–4. There is no ready way in which the industry can successfully counteract these market fluctuations which are beyond its control. They can be ameliorated, however, through containing the industry's costs; through a willingness to vary the price of its services and the size of profit margins in the light of changing market circumstances; and through seeking increasingly to attact and serve the 'upper' rather than the 'lower' more price-sensitive end of the tourist market.

It is government and particularly local government that has an obligation to react to several other problems that have challenged the growth of the industry. The first concerns physical congestion in the central area. Increasing amounts of coach and vehicle traffic mean that each day during the peak summer season about 4 000 coaches are used to transport tourists between airports and hotels, to major places of tourist attraction in and around the capital, and to restaurants and entertainment in the evenings. It might be argued that some of this traffic, along with tourism generally, should be diverted to other parts of the South East and to other regions of Britain. Yet the fact remains that most tourists are first-time visitors, who express a clear preference to see the main London sights. The problems of circulation and congestion in the central area are substantially matters of traffic management. They require a degree of differential pricing to spread visits more evenly between different attractions, and the fullest encouragement of public transport through pricing policies and quality of service.

A second problem involving public decisions concerns land-use conflicts that exist between the hotel industry and residential functions. High returns to tourist accommodation in boom years encourage not only the construction of new hotels but also the conversion of older residential space into small hotels, guest houses and bed-and-breakfast accommodation in localities surrounding central London. Many streets in Bloomsbury, Bayswater and Pimlico, for example, have experienced this change. To the extent that housing is relatively scarce in central London, this trend can compound other social problems (see chapter 10). To the extent that tourist accommodation generates activities and traffic that are discordant with a residential environment, objections to expansion are properly raised. It has been up to the planning authorities to exercise their powers of control to try to manage this situation, by seeking to decelerate the speed and determine the location of residential conversions to tourist use.

A third problem of tourism, and one that has occasioned periodic disquiet from both local and central government, concerns the nature of the jobs that it provides. Many tourist facilities are labour-intensive but much of the labour employed is seasonal, low-paid and lacking in career structure. In consequence, a significant proportion of the men and women employed by the tourist industry are from overseas and often live in inferior accommodation in London. This dimension of employment in the tourist industry contributes only indirectly to lessening the capital's unemployment problems. Moreover, the central London boroughs have periodically felt it necessary to monitor and comment upon conditions of work in the industry, in the hope of improving them and finding ways whereby tourism might afford more job opportunities for the capital's own workforce.

There is public interest in all these issues but generally speaking, local and central government attitudes toward tourism have not hardened sufficiently to produce what might be called a tourist policy for the capital. The central 'sponsoring' Department – Trade and Industry – has responded to the industry's difficulties slowly and diffidently. Only in its search for a site for a third London airport, the need for which is closely related to an expected growth in tourist traffic, has the department taken a consistently supportive stance. Local authorities, on the other hand, similarly eschewing an overall policy, have devoted their interests and actions largely to the industry's 'pressure points', notably the congestion of traffic near major attractions and land-use conflicts involving residential localities. The significance of these policy issues is likely to grow in the future, as central London comes to rely increasingly on its touristic opportunities.

Further reading

The economic context of central London is examined in:

Barras R (1981) *The Office Boom in London* Centre for Environmental Studies, London

Dunning J H and Morgan E V (eds) (1971) *An Economic Study of the City of London* Allen and Unwin

Planning issues in central London are discussed in:

Central London Planning Conference (1976) *Advisory Plan for Central London* CLPC

Greater London Council (1969) *Greater London Development Plan* GLC

Greater London Council (1975) *Modified Greater London Development Plan* GLC

Greater London Council (1984) *The Greater London Development Plan: as proposed to be altered by the Greater London Council* GLC

Problems and potential of tourism in the capital are analysed in:

British Tourist Authority (1984) *Annual Report* BTA

English Tourist Board (1984) *Annual Report* ETB

Greater London Council (1973) *Tourism in London* GLC

Greater London Council (1978) *Tourism: a paper for discussion* GLC

14   Suburban London

Richard Dennis

The nature of suburbia

Medieval suburbs were places outside city law, socially as well as geographically marginal, places where upstanding citizens sought adventure and entertainment. But by the nineteenth century suburbia had acquired the characteristics with which it is popularly associated today: security, respectability, conservatism, and uniformity to the point of monotony. To Sir Walter Besant, writing in 1909, the suburb offered 'as dull a life as mankind ever tolerated'. To F M L Thompson (1982), suburbia is 'an unlovely, sprawling artefact of which few are particularly fond' (p 2). Yet most Londoners live in suburbia, many for their whole lives. Are they simply the prisoners of economic forces, obliged to live there against their better judgement? It seems more probable that most of them enjoy the regularity and predictability of suburban life. Certainly, suburbia provides an appropriate built environment for the private, family-centred and socially selective lifestyle espoused by most Londoners.

Some of the history of suburban development between 1815 and 1939 has been outlined in chapter 5: the roles of land owners, speculative builders, improved methods of public transport – steam trains, then electric trams, the underground, and motor buses – and the economic conditions of the 1930s when high rates of unemployment depressed building costs, and private capital, 'surplus' to the needs of declining heavy industry, was invested in building societies which could lend at very low interest rates to those who *were* in work. Provided you had a regular job it was relatively easy to become an owner-occupier in suburban London in the mid-1930s. The house occupied by the author of this chapter, worth around £60 000 in 1984, cost

£900 when built in 1935. This was a superior 3-bedroom semi. More modest versions, with smaller rooms or built by less established builders, cost only £500, or £25 down and a weekly repayment of around 15/-(75p). This was at a time when clerks earned about £5 per week, skilled manual workers about £4.

Very rapidly, and with a minimum of planning controls, semi-detached London grew to absorb previously free-standing suburban towns. Between 1921 and 1931 the population of Greater London increased by 9.7 per cent, but the built-up area virtually doubled. The population resident within the LCC area (roughly what we now call inner London) fell marginally, while that of many suburban districts more than doubled. For example, Harrow Urban District (with the same boundaries as the present London Borough of Harrow) grew from 49 000 inhabitants in 1921 to 190 000 by 1939. Most new building was for owner-occupation but some very large council estates (Fig. 14.1) were also constructed (for example Becontree, with 116 000 inhabitants and St Helier, with 40 000, in 1939).

Suburban 'sprawl' stopped abruptly with the outbreak of war. After World War II new estates were still constructed around the edge of London, but the creation of a statutory green belt, the introduction of more general planning controls, and the construction of new towns beyond the green belt, all helped to reduce the rate of expansion of the continuous built-up area. The earthworks of railways, under construction in 1939 but never completed, provide a lasting memorial to the expectation of sprawl, for example at Mill Hill to the north and Chessington to the south-west of London.

Since 1945 suburban development has involved increasing densities, infill of open space, often the

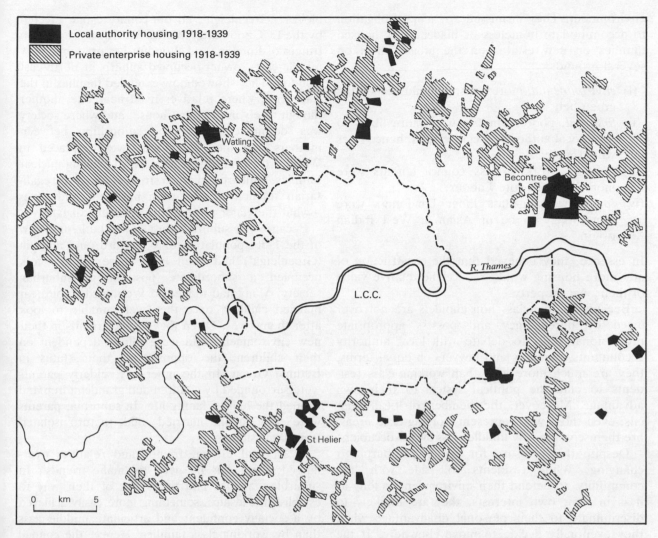

Local authority housing 1918-1939

Private enterprise housing 1918-1939

Watling

Becontree

R. Thames

L.C.C.

St Helier

0   km   5

Figure 14.1   *Construction of housing beyond the LCC, 1919–39, (after P. Abercrombie, 1945).*

demolition of the oldest suburban villas and their replacement by several new houses or small blocks of flats. As its component parts are replaced or renewed at different rates, so suburbia becomes more varied. The classic ecological models of urban geography – Burgess' model of concentric growth and Hoyt's sector theory – both assume continuing processes of invasion and succession. Recently arrived migrants or poorer households move out from the inner city, perhaps under the pressure of commercial expansion at the centre, in turn displacing the better-off into newer and more distant suburbs. So today's suburbs may become tomorrow's 'inner city'. In modern British cities, the details of these processes may not however be as

Burgess or Hoyt described – the rich may move to 'heritage homes' in deepest countryside, or they may return to gentrify inner-city areas. More importantly, ecological processes may be disrupted by the resistance to change organized by many middle-class suburban communities.

Most suburban housing is owner-occupied, and it is a commonplace that home ownership promotes conservatism (see chapter 10). Owners naturally wish to maintain the value of their property and this they do by excluding any social or environmental changes that might tend to reduce house prices. In his book on *Urban Politics* (1979), Peter Saunders shows how the middle-class residents of suburban Croydon combined to preserve the quality of their environment. They dismissed any moral obligation to accommodate homeless or inadequately housed families on new estates on the urban fringe on several grounds:

  (i) *environmental*, more housing would despoil the green belt;
 (ii) *financial*, poorer families were more likely to need local authority social services, hence rates would increase;
(iii) *political*, working-class council tenants were more likely to vote Labour;
 (iv) *racial*, working-class inner Londoners were more likely to be of Asian or West Indian origin.

In essence, they believed that the construction of any more housing would reduce the relative value of their own property.

Because middle-class householders are not over awed by bureaucracy and possess appropriate professional skills to debate with local authority accountants, planners and lawyers on equal terms, they are much more able than working-class residents to play the political system to their own advantage. Moreover, the members of local councils, even those who represent working-class areas, are themselves mostly middle-class owner-occupiers.

Despite this pressure for stability, suburbia *is* changing. While residents will side with 'the community' to defend their environment as long as it is in their own interests, they are unlikely to discriminate to their personal disadvantage when they eventually decide to move elsewhere. If the best offer for their house comes from a developer intent on converting it into flats, or from a family whose ethnicity or social status differs from their own, they are unlikely to reject it in solidarity with their erstwhile neighbours.

Suburban society

The classic work on suburban society in London was undertaken in the 1950s by two sociologists, Michael Young and Peter Willmott, and published in two very readable books, *Family and Kinship in East London* (1957) and *Family and Class in a London Suburb* (1960). Young and Willmott found dramatic differences between family life in Bethnal Green, still dominated in the 1950s by privately rented Victorian terraced houses and tenement blocks, 'Greenleigh', an out-county estate erected by the LCC soon after World War II on the eastern fringes of London, and Woodford, a predominantly middle-class, owner-occupied suburb in north-east London. They showed how extended families in the East End, where relatives lived near one another though rarely in the same house, and where society was dominated by the relationships between mothers and their daughters, were replaced in Woodford by more private, inward-looking nuclear families, built around much stronger and more egalitarian relationships between husbands and wives – what they later termed 'the symmetrical family'.

Because the suburbs were newly built, and few of the 1950s population of Woodford (and none in 'Greenleigh') had been born there, elderly folk occupied a subordinate position in suburban society. Many had moved to Woodford to be near married children once they were unable to look after themselves. Often they lacked friends in their new environment, and were totally dependent on their children, the opposite of their status in Bethnal Green. In the inner city, elderly parents were surrounded by children and grandchildren and formed the hub of family life. In suburbia, parents were close to one married child, in turn isolated from their siblings.

In Bethnal Green, friends and relatives overlapped; there was no need to 'make friends'. In suburbia, families had to go out of their way to establish friendships, something more easily achieved by a socially confident and articulate middle-class than by working-class families. Hence, the council tenants of 'Greenleigh' (and, especially, non-working wives, confined to the estate during the day) complained of its isolation and unfriendliness, while the self-assured residents of Woodford reported, perhaps contrary to our usual stereotype of suburbia, that 'They're very friendly round this district' and 'I think it's a wonderful community in this part'. Nonetheless, friendship and acceptance demanded conformity to expected standards of dress, tidiness (of house and garden) and respectability.

Because people were born into social relationships in Bethnal Green, there was little need for clubs and societies to facilitate social interaction. Among the more mobile residents of Woodford, a vast range of social, political and religious organizations provided newcomers with entrees into community life. Even Woodford was not wholly middle-class, but many of the Woodford working class lived there because they aspired to middle-class standards. Yet they found themselves rejected by the established middle-class who saw their presence as a sign that the neighbourhood was 'going downhill'. In the words of one man, Woodford was now 'well, you might say like Leytonstone'. Potential for class conflict was limited, because the middle-class was so dominant, and because the working-class hoped to emulate them. Nevertheless, the area was experiencing a form of social class succession.

In contrast to the focus on 'community' in the 1950s, themes of change and conflict dominated research in the 1960s. The geographical focus also shifted, from suburbia to the urban fringe, where a 'spiralist' middle-class was perceived as threatening to overwhelm established rural communities in the green belt. Locals and newcomers were regarded as vying for leadership of the community, for access to limited housing resources, for rights to determine the level and type of service provision. An influx of newcomers inflated house prices beyond the means of local residents, who instead demanded more council housing. The newcomers, usually middle-aged, probably 2-car families, had no need for public transport or local shops, or for state schools, since their children were either past school age or educated privately. They were concerned to keep the rates down, and to preserve the environment in an artificial state, free from modern developments, such as estates of mass-produced, identical houses, which they had hoped to escape by moving to the country.

All these studies were undertaken when basic differences in the wealth of working-class and middle-class families affected the way they spent their time and their ability to keep in touch with friends or relatives who did not live locally. In 1955 only 32 per cent of households in Bethnal Green, but 65 per cent in 'Greenleigh', possessed television sets. Not surprisingly, the residents of Bethnal Green sought their entertainment on the streets and in local pubs; the residents of 'Greenleigh' stayed at home. There were only 13 telephones per 1000 residents in Bethnal Green, 88 per 1000 in 'Greenleigh'. There was a similar contrast in levels of car ownership. And in each case, rates for Woodford were much higher.

Material differences still exist, but they are less likely now to affect patterns of social interaction. Four-fifths of Londoners have a telephone, over 90 per cent a television. In 1981, 64 per cent of outer London households owned at least one car, compared to 41 per cent of inner Londoners. But the proportion with two or more cars, critical for reducing the isolation of women and children where the husband uses the car for work, still varied dramatically: over 20 per cent in some outer boroughs, 7 per cent in inner London (and only 4 per cent in Bethnal Green). Moreover, there are still differences in social skills which make it easier for professional people to cope with situations of high mobility.

Housing and demographic change

The only 'incomplete families' in which Willmott and Young showed any interest were old people living on their own. But the nuclear family of two parents and their children is no longer the dominant household type in suburban London. By 1981, one and two-person households comprised 55 per cent of the total in outer London. The young parents of 1950s Woodford and 'Greenleigh' have grown old and their children have left home. In Harrow, for example, one-fifth of the population is now of retirement age, and 6 per cent are aged over 75. This has critical implications for both the provision of social services and the management of housing.

Three-fifths of dwellings in Harrow were built in the inter-war period; most are owner-occupied, three-bedroom, semi-detached houses. In 1981, 43 per cent of these dwellings were occupied by household heads aged over 65. While these householders will now be outright owners of their homes, having repaid mortgages that they took out in the 1930s or 1950s, they still have to pay rates and maintain their houses in good order. Many are no longer sufficiently active to do their own decorating or routine maintenance, but cannot afford to employ outsiders. Yet their houses now need not just repainting but rewiring, replumbing and reroofing. Hence the problem of a deteriorating housing stock, even in the owner-occupied sector. About 12 per cent of the entire housing stock in outer London needs repairs costing more than £4 200 per dwelling (1984 prices).

In council housing, maintenance may be handled by the local authority, but there is still a problem of under-occupation, i.e. one or two persons occupying dwellings designed for families of four or more. To encourage elderly tenants to move, suburban local authorities are concentrating their efforts on the provision of sheltered housing in small (usually one bedroom) units. Housing associations also cater for this part of the housing market, and most recently, sheltered owner-occupied housing has been built to encourage elderly home-owners to move into more manageable dwellings.

At the other end of the life cycle, suburbia is being colonized by increasing numbers of young one and two-person households: single adults who once would have lived with parents now expect a place of their own; groups of single sharers, now eligible for joint mortgages from building societies; childless couples, seeking a suburban house while both part-ners are working full-time, in the knowledge that when they start a family it will be much more difficult to afford the move from a flat to a house, especially if one partner gives up paid work. In the past, many of these households would have rented from a private landlord, probably in inner London. But as the supply of rented accommodation dries up, there is little alternative to suburban owner-occupation (see chapter 10). Indeed, much of what privately rented accommodation remains is situated in inner suburbs like Wembley and Ealing. In 1981, 289 000 households in inner London and 231 000 in outer London rented from a private landlord. By 1991 it is quite likely that the absolute size of the privately rented sector in outer London will exceed that in inner London. Hamnett and Randolph (1983) present a scenario of a socially polarized inner city, divided between gentrifying owner-occupiers and a residual local authority sector. 'Those groups excluded from this process may be displaced into outer London where many inner suburban areas may become transformed into lower value ownership mixed with much of what will be left of the private rented sector. The net result therefore will be a stabilizing but polarized inner city and a declining suburban ring. In the process "inner city" problems may become gradually displaced into the suburbs' (p 164).

The colonization of suburbia by 'non-family' households involves:

(i) piecemeal conversion of large Victorian and Edwardian villas into flats;
(ii) replacement of large old houses by small blocks of purpose-built flats, especially around commuter railway stations, for example Stan-more and Edgware in north London, Sutton and Wallington in south London;
(iii) groups of single adults renting furnished terraced and semi-detached houses, for example students in Wembley or Tooting;
(iv) conversion of owner-occupied houses into pairs of self-contained flats.

In 1980 Harrow Council approved 32 cases of the conversion of houses into flats; in 1983 there were 131 approvals. The borough plan envisages increasing numbers of conversions in the future, regardless of the consequences for on-street parking or the environmental degradation involved in converting front gardens into additional parking spaces.

Most small families (two parents + one child) would not think of themselves as 'under-occupying' a three-bedroom house. They are more likely to worry that the birth of a second child will make them 'overcrowded', by their own expectations, if not by official space standards. So, at the same time as conversions create smaller dwellings, home extensions are booming, the addition of an extra bedroom over the garage or in the roof adding further architectural variety to roads that had never been as uniform as their critics imagined.

Ethnic minorities in suburbia

Most research on ethnic minorities has examined working-class groups (see chapter 18). Less atten-tion has been directed at middle-class immigrants and their efforts to establish themselves in suburban communities. Yet suburbia has long been the destination of second or third-generation migrants: one version of Burgess' model defines the ring beyond the 'zone in transition' as the 'zone of second-generation immigrant settlement'. In London, Jewish immigrants settled in parts of the East End in the 1880s, but during the present century their children and grandchildren have moved out, first to inner suburbs like Stamford Hill, later to Golders Green, Redbridge, Hendon and Kenton.

More recently, large numbers of Asian families have settled in suburbia, especially in west and north-west London, usually without a prior stop in the inner city. While many live in relatively cheap owner-occupied property in Southall, working in manufacturing and services on west London industrial estates, or as baggage handlers, cleaners, catering staff and transport workers in and around Heathrow Airport, there are also large numbers of middle-class Asians employed as secretaries, clerks, accountants and managers, or running their own small businesses. Their ideal location is near enough to Southall to benefit from specialized Asian shops, entertainment and cultural facilities, but sufficiently far to demonstrate superior social status.

In Harrow, the proportion of the population living in households where the head had been born in Pakistan or the New Commonwealth increased from 6 per cent to 15 per cent between 1971 and 1981. Approximately 60 per cent are East African Asians, forced out of Kenya and Uganda during the late 1960s and early 1970s. Most live in middle-income, owner-occupied houses in the south and east of the borough (Fig. 14.2). The occupational profile of male East African Asians is similar to that of the total male population, and not dissimilar from their status prior to migration, although fewer are self-employed and more have had to take junior non-manual or skilled manual jobs than was the case in Africa (Table 14.1).

Socially and culturally, however, Harrow East African Asians have preserved their ethnic identity. In an interview survey in 1979, between seven and eleven years after migration for most families, Shaw (1982) found that 60 per cent claimed their closest friends were all or nearly all Asians and 54 per cent spoke only or mostly their mother-tongue at home. The self-employed were least likely to adopt an English lifestyle, perhaps reflecting their lack of informal contact with non-Asians at work. Even if they ran small businesses which depended on non-Asian customers (and it would be very difficult to survive commercially in Harrow catering only for other Asians), they did not mix *informally* in the way that manual or office workers did.

Ethnic identity is reinforced by a range of cultural organizations, some caste-based, catering for specific Punjabi or Gujarati groups, and helping to maintain the way of life followed in East Africa or India, facilitating arranged marriages, celebrating religious festivals, and teaching children their mother-tongue; others, more outward-looking, represent the political and economic interests of Asians, but are still almost exclusively Asian in their membership.

East African Asians in Harrow are united by their middle-classness, their culture, their common experience as forced migrants, and their colour. They are 'self-segregated' in that they have chosen to live together for positive, cultural reasons. Yet, if they wanted to disperse, they might find themselves forced by hostility and discrimination to stay 'self-

Table 14.1   *Socio-economic status of adult males in Harrow*

	All economically active males in Harrow, 1981 (%)	East African Asian male household heads in Harrow, 1979 (%)	East African Asian males in East Africa prior to migration (%)
Employers, managers and professional workers	31	33	30
Self-employed	8	11	22
Skilled manual and foremen	21	23	6
Other non-manual	26	20	9
Semi-skilled manual	9	9	1
Unskilled manual	3	0	0
Other	3	4	1
Students	–	–	30
		East African Asian sample size = 140	

Sources: Shaw, H M (1982)
         1981 Census

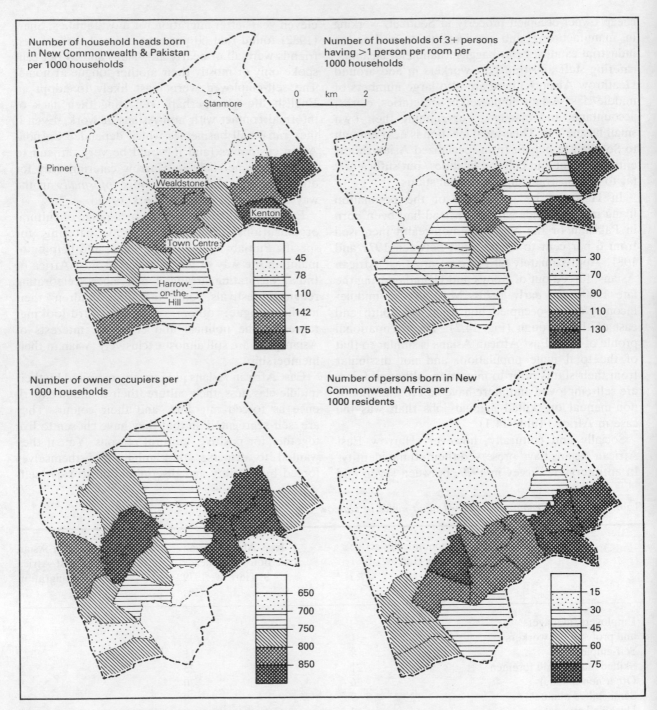

Figure 14.2   Aspects of the social geography of Harrow.

segregated'. Already, among young Asians with little or no experience of life before migration, the preservation of ethnic identity is at least partly a reaction to hostility.

Employment in suburbia

I have concentrated on suburbia as a place where people *live* and certainly boroughs like Harrow are predominantly residential. In inner London, domestic rates in 1981 contributed 27 per cent of local authorities' total rate income; the rest comprised rates paid by commercial and industrial ratepayers. But in outer London, domestic rates contributed 52 per cent, in Harrow 62 per cent, of all rate income. Another indication of the dormitory character of suburbia is the job ratio: the ratio of the population seeking paid work to the number of jobs available locally. In Harrow, the economically active population numbers about 97 000, the number of jobs only about 55 000, yielding a job ratio of under 0.6. In practice, fewer than half of Harrow's economically active population are employed there; 20 per cent work in adjacent London boroughs, and nearly as many commute to central London.

Harrow's manufacturing base is tiny and, as *everywhere* in London, fast declining. Even before the worst of the recession, manufacturing jobs had diminished from 14 350 in 1971 to under 12 000 by 1978. Since then, Kodak, the principal employer in the borough, manufacturing photographic materials on a 22 ha site in Wealdstone, have reduced their workforce from over 5 000 to 4 000, while in adjacent west London boroughs, major manufacturing plants like Hoover (domestic appliances) at Perivale, AEC (motor vehicles) at Southall, and Rockware Glass at Greenford have all been replaced by warehousing (Fig. 14.3).

In Harrow the number of office jobs is also below the average for outer London, while jobs in retailing are threatened as small shops in neighbourhood centres succumb to competition from discount warehouses, often located on industrial

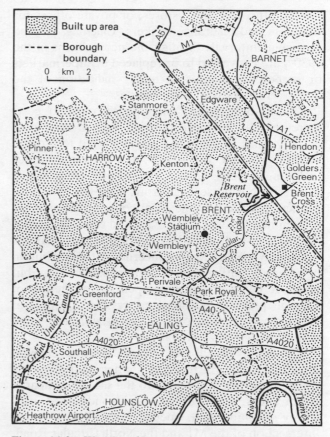

Figure 14.3   *West London.*

estates (for example around Wembley Stadium and at Park Royal), and urban fringe hypermarkets. Neighbourhood food shops and newsagents are acquired by Asian family businesses, prepared to work long hours for proportionally low returns (Table 14.2); other local shops become building

Table 14.2   *Asian retail outlets in Croydon, 1978*

Type of Development	Total outlets	Independent outlets	Asian-owned outlets	Asian-owned as % all independent outlets
Groceries	328	227	78	34.4
Newsagents, confectioners, tobacconists	352	307	58	18.9
Clothing and footwear	495	345	20	5.8
Other	1 485	1 166	58	4.9
Total	2 600	2 045	214	10.4

Source: Mullins, D (1979)

society offices or video stores, or private offices for solicitors and insurance brokers. Cinemas, planted at regular intervals through the new suburbs in the 1930s, are converted to or replaced by supermarkets or carpet warehouses, a telling indication of the home-centredness of suburbanites.

Yet, as both public and private transport costs increase, and as more married women seek paid employment, so there is a growing need to provide jobs in suburbia. In Harrow, new industrial estates include 'nursery units', a seed-bed from which successful businesses can grow, while an enterprise agency, financed by the local council and chamber of commerce, dispenses advice and encouragement. A few high-tech firms have moved in (for example Hitachi in 1981), mostly concerned with distribution or research, rather than routine manufacturing, but nowhere near enough to compensate for the loss of jobs on pre-war industrial estates (for example at Wealdstone in Harrow) or at established, large scale firms, such as Kodak.

Elsewhere in suburbia more positive changes have occurred. Harrow's stagnation as a shopping centre is partly attributable to the success of nearby Brent Cross, a fully enclosed, air-conditioned, two-storey shopping mall, opened in 1976, close to the intersection of the M1 and the North Circular Road. Although Brent Cross has good public transport links, it caters primarily for shoppers in private cars. Its 'quality' supermarkets, the range of consumer durables on offer, and the extended opening hours (until 8 pm each weekday evening) all reflect its appeal to affluent, mobile, two-income households.

In Croydon, the pre-GLC County Borough began a vigorous campaign to attract new offices in the 1950s. Croydon was perceived as a prestige location by senior executives who could work within relatively short commuting distance of several desirable residential areas. By the late 1960s, 20 000 office workers were employed in Croydon, 50 per cent in offices that had moved from central London. Half a million m² of offices were built, along with an extensive shopping precinct (the Whitgift Centre) and an educational and entertainment complex (Fairfield Halls). In time, wage rates and office rents increased to central London levels, central government imposed restrictions on office-building throughout London, and new development slackened. Local councillors had assumed that what was good for business must be good for Croydon. But

while the borough's rateable value increased by 20 per cent, and domestic rates could be held at a low level, not everybody benefited. Small shopkeepers lost out to town-centre multiples, homes were demolished in favour of ring roads, a flyover and multi-storey car parks. Croydon's new skyline is certainly dramatic, but architecturally mediocre. There is no coherent plan. Business has been attracted on business' terms.

Suburban futures

Recently, feminist geographers have argued that social scientists have examined urban structure from an exclusively male perspective. Planners have zoned 'residences' away from 'workplaces'; geographers have explained residential locations in terms of the trade-off between housing costs and transport costs for male households heads. But over 40 per cent of the labour force is now female. In Harrow, 38 per cent of the economically active population is female, including 59 per cent of married women aged 16–59; 53 per cent of working wives are employed full-time, including many with young children. For them, the separation of residential areas from employment areas is often inconvenient, especially since in practice most working wives still undertake more than their fair share of domestic tasks, such as shopping and taking children to and from school. Planning policies which located shops, schools, homes and workplaces in the same areas would reduce stress and help to support family life.

Another feminist criticism of geographical research, that 'work' is always equated with 'paid employment', is also relevant to our understanding of suburbia. Far from being just a dormitory, suburbia is the locale for the social reproduction of labour – it is where children are brought up, educated and socialized to perpetuate values acceptable to their elders – and it is a major centre of production and services in and around the home – cooking; washing, making and mending clothes; flower and vegetable cultivation; do-it-yourself activities; car maintenance; voluntary service; community action. All these activities are likely to grow as:

(i) new technology facilitates more elaborate forms of domestic production;

(ii) computer networks allow managers, accountants, administrators and typists to work from
home, visiting their head office (which may also
be in the suburbs) only occasionally;

(iii) long-term unemployment or, more optimisti-
cally, shorter working hours mean that more
time is spent at home.

The reality that mass unemployment is here to
stay unless we dramatically recast the shape of the
working day, year and life, demands a new definition of 'work'. Many of the voluntary, educational
and leisure activities currently undertaken in
suburbia should be considered just as vital and
productive as 'paid employment'.

According to one optimistic scenario, future
suburbs will at last become 'fully fledged communities'. Their daytime populations will be much
larger and more representative of the total population than they are now. New services, currently
associated more with the City and West End, will
move to suburbia:

'The large empty office blocks in the city centres
will stand in the year 2000 as a monument to last
year's technology whilst suburban life will have
a bustle and vitality unbelievable today.' (Guide
to career development, *The Times*, 16 February
1984)

A brave new world, but even if we find it attractive,
some major rethinking by politicians, planners *and*
suburban residents will be needed to bring it about.

Further reading

The history of suburbia is discussed by:
Dyos H J (1961) *Victorian Suburb: a study of the
growth of Camberwell* Leicester University Press
Jackson A A (1973) *Semi-detached London* Allen
and Unwin
Thompson F M L (ed.) (1982) *The Rise of Suburbia*
Leicester University Press

An extended case study of interest groups and local
politics in Croydon is found in:
Saunders P (1979) *Urban Politics* Hutchinson

Also on suburban society, see:
Willmott P and Young M (1960) *Family and Class
in a London Suburb* Routledge and Kegan Paul
Young M and Willmott P (1957) *Family and
Kinship in East London* Routledge and Kegan
Paul

The urban fringe is discussed by:
Connell J H (1978) *The End of Tradition: country
life in central Surrey* Routledge and Kegan Paul
Pahl R (1975) *Whose City*? Penguin

Recent changes in housing tenure are examined in:
Hamnett C and Randolph W (1983) 'The changing
tenure structure of the Greater London housing
market, 1961–81' *The London Journal* **9**: 153–64

The material on East African Asians in Harrow has
been drawn from:
Shaw H M (1982) *Immigrant preference and
suburban location: a case study of East African
Asians in Harrow* Unpublished Ph.D. thesis,
University of London

See also the journal, *New Community*, published by
the Commission for Racial Equality. Table 14.2 is
taken from:
Mullins D (1979) 'Asian retailing in Croydon' *New
Community* **7**: 403–5

A provocative discussion of suburban design from
a feminist perspective is presented by:
Women and Geography Study Group of the Institute of British Geographers (1984) *Geography and
Gender* Hutchinson

15   The Metropolitan Green Belt

Richard Munton

Green belt: a debate

Strong support for green belts as a means of restricting the outward growth of towns and cities is of long-standing, and no more so than in the case of London. Throughout the first half of the twentieth century many argued that only a green belt could contain the physical expansion of London while providing access to the surrounding countryside for those living in the capital. After a number of false starts, the first significant steps towards creating a green belt were taken in the inter-war period. In the absence of effective planning powers, local authorities began purchasing open land on the edge of London, declaring it green belt or land upon which development would not be permitted. They still own most of this land (approximately 24 000 ha), about half of which was acquired with financial assistance from the London County Council, and much of it lies within the area of the GLC or on its immediate boundary.

Following the introduction of comprehensive Town and Country Planning legislation in 1947, local planning authorities have been able to maintain a substantial green belt through the use of their powers of development control. This 'statutory' green belt – the Metropolitan Green Belt (MGB) – has been promoted enthusiastically by a wide range of local interests and, for the most part, its retention has been supported by central government as well. It should not be assumed, however, that those in favour of the MGB have necessarily held the same view of its purpose. It has been endorsed as a means of eliminating urban sprawl, protecting agricultural land from urban development, meeting the recreational needs of city dwellers, and providing attractive residential environments. It is not too difficult to appreciate the local self-interest

implicit in most of these arguments and critics of green belt have been quick to point this out. They have also gone on to suggest that green belts reduce the supply of residential and industrial development land in areas of high demand, thereby increasing the price of land and the cost of homes and factories throughout the region; that green belts merely protect local amenities, and so safeguard the value of houses in green belt areas for those fortunate enough to own them; and that they should be dispensed with, since green belts have not been able to ensure the full and effective use of all land in the urban fringe.

The large areas now covered by green belts help to explain why views of their purpose have become so diffuse and liable to local interpretation. In particular, green belts have become part of local planning folklore, never to be challenged or reduced in extent, and this local perspective conflicts with many of the original arguments made in support of green belts which asserted that they should be seen as strategic planning instruments contributing to a well-defined *regional* strategy for urban growth. Thus, for example, with the wish to disperse population and industry from London to other parts of the South East during the post-war period, the MGB was to provide the break between the built-up area of London and a number of new towns to which people and jobs would be decentralized (see chapter 6). The MGB would help to mould the spatial pattern of urban development in the region. Unfortunately, regional planning has never been a strong instrument of public policy and has now been watered down even further following the abolition of the Regional Economic Planning Councils in 1979. Strategic planning concepts have been submerged increasingly beneath local interpretations of their purpose, a process encour-

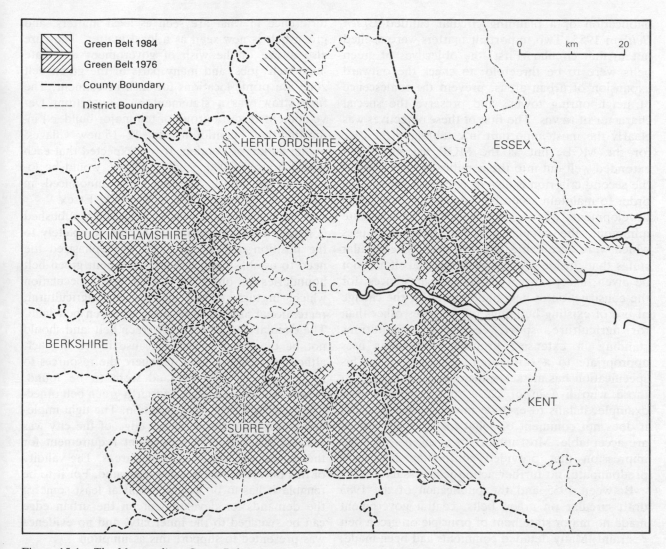

Figure 15.1   *The Metropolitan Green Belt.*

aged by central government in its recent re-allocation of planning powers and responsibilities, taking these from the counties and giving them to the districts or boroughs.

The MGB today extends into more than 60 district, borough and county planning authority areas (Fig. 15.1). Views within district and borough authorities emphasize the protection of green belt land from any form of development, almost irrespective of local circumstances, and the importance of enhancing amenities within the MGB for the benefit of local people. The only exceptions are some minor modifications to local policies to accommodate new job-creating enterprises, and the development of a few country parks. Strategic objectives,

such as the redistribution of the region's population or the deliberate attempt to provide recreational facilities for those living in inner-London, are accorded a low priority by most local planning committees.

Green belt policy

Before examining changes to the MGB, it is necessary to review the evolution of green belt policy. Green belt policy was widely debated during 1983–84 following the publication of a draft circular on the matter by the Department of the Environment. As seen by central government, the purpose of green belt restraint has changed little since the publication of a planning circular entitled *Green Belts* in 1955. Two important matters were spelled out in that circular. First, the objectives of green belts were to be threefold; to check the outward expansion of urban areas, prevent the coalescence of neighbouring towns, and preserve the special character of towns. The first of these objectives was clearly the most important in establishing the case for the MGB, but as the MGB has now been extended well out into the counties around London the second criterion is also of relevance. Second, in order to maintain green belts as areas where urban development was to be kept to an absolute minimum, the circular specified those land uses which were acceptable in green belts. The circular states that 'Inside a green belt approval should not be given, except in very special circumstances, for the construction of new buildings or for the change of use of existing buildings for purposes other than for agriculture, sport, cemeteries, institutions standing in extensive grounds, and other uses appropriate to a rural area' (paragraph 5). This specification has attracted increasing criticism from those who live in or close to green belts. For example, it fails to exclude mineral extraction and it does not comment on what *forms* of agriculture are acceptable. Most important of all, it leaves the impression that provided conforming land uses predominate, no further action is necessary.

Between 1955 and the publication of the 1983 draft circular on green belts, central government made no major statement of principle on green belt restraint. Many detailed comments had been made, of course, on particular proposals in local development plans. Nevertheless, in spite of the fact that the 1983 draft circular was based on the main principles laid down in the earlier circular, a public outcry followed its publication and it had to be withdrawn. In strategic planning terms the changes proposed in the new draft were minor but because they included the possibility of a small amount of green belt land being developed for private housing there was a major rumpus. The Department of the Environment had completely misunderstood the local significance of green belts. They had failed to recognize that *any* weakening of restraint, however slight, was locally unacceptable.

The strength of the adverse reaction to the draft has to be judged in a broader context. Local authorities are sensitive to central government in-terference in what are seen as local matters, and green belt is now seen as a local matter. They are also aware of the wish of government to create 'high-tech' jobs, and many parts of the green belt zone are prime locations for such investment. The final straw was a statement by Consortium Developments Ltd. (a group of ten major builders) indicating their intention to build 12–15 new 'villages' within 80 km of London. It was expected that each would house 15 000 people and five would be located in the MGB. The first to be announced, in 1985, was Tillingham Hall in Sturrock, Essex.

A revised circular was subsequently published (Circular 14/84). It retreated almost completely to the position outlined in 1955. It emphasized the need to establish and defend permanent green belt boundaries in order to reduce land speculation which, in turn, should maintain the agricultural, recreational and amenity value of green belt land. The circular also argued that green belt land should not be developed merely because it lies derelict, although it did not indicate where the resources to re-develop this derelict land were to be found. Finally, the circular added a fourth green belt objective – assisting urban regeneration. The tight implementation of restraint on the edge of the city was seen as a necessary if insufficient requirement for the regeneration of inner-urban areas. The validity of this objective was not demonstrated. For it to be tenable it has to be assumed that at least some of the demands for development on the urban edge can be switched to the inner city, and no evidence was presented to support this assumption.

Recent evolution of the Metropolitan Green Belt

Following the approval of local development plans in the 1950s, a statutory green belt 8–15 km wide came into being around London. Along with some minor additions, mainly in Surrey and Buckinghamshire, the statutorily approved MGB extended to just over 3000 km² by 1974 (Fig. 15.1). But improvements to rail communications and rapid growth in the region's population in the 1950s and 1960s (see chapter 6) meant that the planned overspill towns were unable to accommodate all those extra people who wished to live in the region outside London. As a result, suburban development took place rapidly in towns just beyond the green belt with good communications with the capital. In an endeavour to slow down the rate of growth of these towns, the shire counties proposed major extensions to the MGB in the late 1960s and early 1970s. For a long time central government could not decide whether to accede to these requests because of the implications they held for limiting the supply of residential and other development land. Firm decisions only followed the approval of county structure plans between 1979 and 1982. In total, the counties had requested that the area of the MGB be doubled, but by the late 1970s government was becoming increasingly concerned with the creation of jobs and the attraction of new investment. It compromised, creating a green belt no more than 20–25 km wide, except along certain axes of development where towns were in danger of coalescing (as along the A1(M) in Hertfordshire between Hatfield and Stevenage – see Fig. 15.1), thereby increasing the area of the MGB by about half.

Even this degree of enlargement threatens to create major planning conflicts. A substantial amount of private residential development is anticipated in and around the MGB during the 1980s. The most recent estimates suggest that more than 50 000 housing units per annum will be built there in the first half of the decade, or 22 per cent of the new housing for the whole South East region. There is also some evidence that the amount of land allocated for development during the life of current structure plans (virtually none is green belt land) is being used up faster than anticipated, and at planning enquiries private developers now constantly challenge the housing land supply figures of local authorities. The release of green belt land may therefore become difficult to avoid later in the 1980s, expecially as the completion of the M25 Motorway, which runs wholly within the MGB, in 1986/will create additional pressures. These pressures are likely to be greatest close to motorway intersections (Fig. 15.2).

The formal position of government is that the M25 will have no impact on the MGB (other than its construction) as any pressures created by the motorway in 1986, which runs wholly within the MGB, will create additional pressures. These pressures are likely to be greatest close to motorway intersections (Fig. 15.2).

reducing pressures to the west of the capital around Woking, Maidenhead and Heathrow. Hard evidence

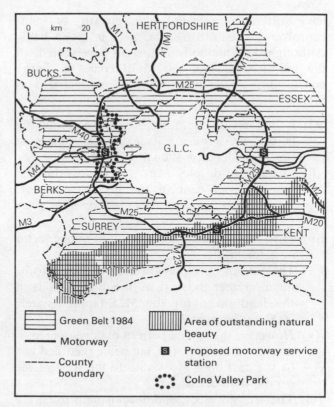

Figure 15.2   *Motorways and Environmental features in the MGB.*

has yet to be produced. The M25 confers similar advantages to both east and west, and the development control system is designed to regulate development, not prohibit it altogether. It is inevitable, therefore, that some changes to the MGB will occur. Service stations on the M25 are already proposed for just north of the Dartford Tunnel and at South Mimms in Hertfordshire close to the A1(M)/M25 intersection. And while the Department of Transport continues to insist that transport service areas must be provided at no more than 50 km intervals, at least two further sites will be required. In all probability these will be located in the Colne Valley Regional Park and in the Surrey Hills/Kent Downs Area of Outstanding Natural Beauty where they will have a significant impact on local amenity and recreational facilities (see Fig. 15.2).

The use and management of land in the MGB

In their analyses of green belt restraint, geographers

have often investigated the growth of non-conforming (i.e. urban) land uses in green belts. Although their methods of analysis have varied, all the major studies of the MGB come to similar conclusions. These may be briefly summarized as follows:

(i) Urban development has occurred continuously in the MGB during its existence. The most recent evidence is shown in Table 15.1.

(ii) The rate of development is slow, covering less than 0.2 per cent of the MGB each year. Development rarely takes place on sites away from the existing urban edge.

(iii) Most development is the result of public sector investment.

(iv) The rate of development does not seem to be much greater today than in earlier periods, if the land taken for the M25 (approximately 2000 ha) is excluded.

(v) *However*, the spatial pattern of development is uneven, a much faster rate being recorded just to the east and, especially, to the west of the capital than elsewhere.

(vi) There is sufficient land development to ensure a market in 'hope' value land, or land selling for more than its rural value in the expectation that planning permission will be granted at some time in the future.

Developers are prepared to pay extremely high prices for land with planning permission for residential, commercial or industrial development. In 1984, prices in excess of £500 000 per ha were commonplace, although the same land's agricultural value was in the order of only £5000–7000 per ha. Even after tax, the land's net value may be raised

40 or more times by planning permission. Speculation is inevitable in circumstances such as these and government only has to hint at a weakening of restraint for speculation to increase. Investors have already bought green belt land close to major intersections along the M25 motorway.

Some conforming land uses also bring planning problems. This is partly because the nature of these uses has changed dramatically since 1955. Agriculture, for example, has become very much more intensive in its use of land. Farms are often managed on industrial principles and farmers are intolerant of public access. Likewise, large numbers of people may visit popular recreation sites on summer weekends bringing traffic congestion, noise, trespass and litter in their wake. Mineral working, never prohibited in green belts, has not declined significantly in extent, and the nuisance it may cause to neighbours means that mineral operators and local people are frequently in conflict. The key, perhaps, to all these problems lies in the growth of concern among the population, and especially those living in outer suburbia, about standards of amenity and landscape conservation; and yet, in principle, these issues are unrelated to the objectives of green belt.

There is nothing in government circulars which says that open land in green belts *must* be put to productive use or be maintained in a way that is aesthetically pleasing, even if government would like to see this happen. This fact is not fully appreciated and leads to considerable confusion among local residents, and even local planners, about the purpose of green belts. Developers seek to exploit this confusion, arguing that areas of unattractive green belt land should be developed. This position

Table 15.1   *Development within the MGB between spring 1979 and spring 1981[1] (excluding the GLC area)*

Type of business	1979/80	1980/81	1981/82	Total	% Given on appeal[2]
Residential (units)	1 698	994	1 677	4 369	19.3
Industry/Warehousing/ Storage (ha)	13.37	31.10	8.63	53.1	38.3
Offices (m^2)	14 929	41 195	8 539	64 663	5.5
Shops (m^2)	8 814	10 484	4 704	24 002	19.8

[1] The periods returned by each country vary slightly.
[2] Appeal figures not returned by Buckinghamshire other than for residential units.

Source: Standing Conference (1983) *South East Regional Monitor 1982/83: The Metropolitan Green Belt*, SC 1891, London.

is tantamount to encouraging owners to run-down their land so as to improve their chances of acquiring planning permission. The best way to avoid this difficulty is to recognize that green belt restraint and environmental policies for urban-fringe land are separate but complementary. Green belt restraint should be seen as a means of retaining an area of land free from urban development, but for which countryside planning policies are then needed. This avoids the need to defend the inclusion of a particular piece of land in a green belt on the basis of whether or not it is being used satisfactorily. The main issue is then how to ensure that green belt land has an acceptable appearance and is maintained in some form of productive use.

It has long been recognized that parts of all urban fringes have a drab and unkempt appearance. This has often been dismissed as an unfortunate but inevitable consequence of the conversion of rural land to urban uses. It is a problem compounded by the fact that various undesirable land uses, ranging from refuse tips to public utility installations, congregate in the urban fringe because they are unacceptable in the urban area. The firm imposition of green belt restraint should minimize the secondary effects of land conversion but the very existence of a semi-permanent area of open land on the edge of the city attracts other unwanted land uses.

In one study two kinds of unwanted landscape in the MGB were identified and their extents mapped. These were termed 'damaged' and 'threatened'. Neither was defined rigorously but 'damaged' landscape consisted of areas of 1 km^2 or more which exhibited serious deterioration and required urgent treatment. It was often associated with gravel workings, industrial land uses and waste tips. 'Threatened' landscape was represented by zones of deteriorating agricultural or woodland management often linked to pony paddocks, piggeries, scrap yards and public utility installations. Substantial areas of 'damaged' landscape were identified in the Lea and Darent Valleys, in south Essex, and on the immediate western edge of the capital around Heathrow Airport. Major areas of 'threatened' landscape also existed to the north-west and south of Heathrow Airport, in pockets in north and north-west Surrey, and along the Colne Valley and the A1(M) in Hertfordshire. In a further study an attempt was made to measure the condition in which farmland was maintained. Two-thirds of the area investigated fell into Category I, land that was being adequately looked after. Nearly 30 per cent (Category II) showed signs of inadequate maintenance and 5.5 per cent lay derelict or semi-derelict (Category III – see Table 15.2). Disproportionately large amounts of poorly maintained land were adjacent to housing or owned by public companies which had little interest in the long-run future of farming, such as development companies and mineral extractors. Other features associated with low standards of maintenance were the use of land for horse grazing, and areas managed by hobby farmers or let on short, insecure leases. Standards of maintenance were universally bad on land let short-term *and* next to urban development.

Table 15.2   *Proportion of agricultural land in each land maintenance category*

	Maintenance category[1]	(% in each category)		
		I	II	III
Total Land		64.7	29.8	5.5
Land				
(a) let short term[2]		24.3	50.7	25.0
(b) adjacent to residential development		34.0	46.7	19.3
(c) let by public companies[3]		47.4	46.1	6.5
(d) occupied by hobby farmers[4]		41.8	51.3	7.0
(e) on farms with substantial horse grazing/keeping enterprises[5]		47.4	40.9	11.7

[1] The definitions used for the land maintenance categories are as follows:
Category I: Areas exhibiting high standards of crop husbandry and farm maintenance. Rough margins to fields, small patches of weeds etc. ignored. Field boundaries and farm roads well maintained; hedges fully stock-proof where appropriate. Woodland is managed; few signs of poor field drainage.
Category II: Areas indicating management problems. Crops may be thin, permanent grass deteriorating to rough grazing. Signs of poor field drainage; farm infrastructure inadequately maintained. Woodland receiving little or no attention.
Category III: Derelict or semi-derelict land. Field boundaries and farm roads badly maintained unless for the benefit of a neighbouring field.
Most areas exhibit more than one attribute characteristic of its category.

[2] Annual or shorter lets with no security of tenure for the occupier.

[3] Largely mineral or development companies.

[4] Obtaining 10% or less of their total gross income from farming.

[5] Occupiers keeping more than nine horses.

Given the difficulties of farming on the urban edge, it is only to be expected that some open land in the urban fringe will be badly maintained. Of greater significance for policy is the wide range of apparent causes of poor maintenance. Some reasons relate to planning considerations, some to the objectives of the owner and others to the competence of the occupier. It is with this consideration in mind that a brief analysis of the achievements of countryside management in south Hertfordshire completes the chapter.

Green belt in south Hertfordshire

In October 1975 the Countryside Commission, in cooperation with relevant local authorities, initiated an urban-fringe management experiment in south Hertfordshire/Barnet. In 1982 the scheme was incorporated into the countryside management programme of Hertfordshire County Council and Barnet London Borough. The area forms a highly urbanized part of the MGB and either contains or is bounded by several major towns including Watford, St Albans, Hatfield, Potters Bar and, to the south, London (Fig. 15.3). It is criss-crossed by numerous busy roads, notably the M1, M10, A1(M) and the M25. Over 60 per cent of the area is still farmed but does not have a predominant system of farming, traditional farming enterprises being regularly supplemented by the keeping of horses and the sale of farm produce at the farm gate. The number of horses kept in the area continues to increase. In 1978, for example, there were at least 110 stables and the largest 33 establishments alone accounted for over 1500 animals. It is estimated that at least 560 ha (3.4 per cent of the area) have been lost to farming since the 1950s mainly to road developments, housing and recreational facilities.

Countryside management is a local service designed to resolve conflicts of interest between those who live in and manage the countryside and those who use it for recreation. A small number of staff are employed to settle small-scale conflicts, for example between horse riders and farmers on a particular bridle-way, to mobilise local voluntary effort and to spend limited sums of money in carrying out management tasks on the ground, such as constructing stiles, coppicing and re-grading paths. The management service described here has been successful in reconciling local differences and

Farm Shop in the Green Belt.
Proximity to London ensures a thriving market for produce sold at the farm gate, much of which may not be grown on the farm or even on local farms. Example from Aldenham, south Hertfordshire.

improving access to the countryside. In spite of a small budget (£42 000 per annum at 1982/83 prices), numerous informal management agreements, woodland improvement schemes and nature conservation projects have been completed. At this level, cooperation has been forthcoming from all kinds of landowner and a special effort has been made to involve public owners (who own 25 per cent of the land) so that they can be seen to be leading by example. Much less progress has been made in changing the *general policy objectives* of landowners by, for example, getting them to put conservation objectives into their land management strategies, and it is worth quoting in full the Countryside Commission's own assessment of the limitations of countryside management. The Commission says:

In areas where there are underlying strategic land-use and land-management problems and where the overall climate is one of uncertainty and speculation, the potential of countryside management is limited and . . . there is even a danger that the resulting improvements, by obscuring the real nature of the problems, might be counter-productive, unless they are put in the context of a much more comprehensive planning and management framework. (Countryside Commission, 1981)

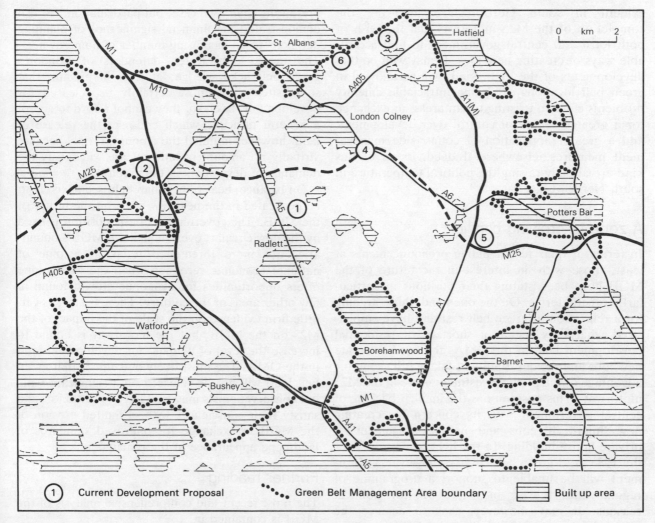

Figure 15.3   *The Urban-fringe management experiment, south Hertfordshire/Barnet.*

Examples of Current Development Proposals in South Hertfordshire Green Belt

1. Radlett Aerodrome: Former site of Handley Page (closed 1965); several applications for residential/industrial development refused except at southern end. Planning permission given in 1984 for progressive working of gravel but on condition that land be returned to agricultural use.
2. 'The Golden Triangle' – 60 ha of land severed by building of M25 and owned by the Department of Transport now (1985) being offered for sale to the highest bidder.
3. Proposed site for a leisure and technology park in a key piece of green belt between St Albans and Hatfield, put forward in 1984 by the Country Council Planning Committee as a means of creating jobs in 'high-tech'

industries.
4. Applications for industrial/commercial development expected on land sandwiched between the southern edge of London Colney and the new junction of the M25 and A6.
5. Proposed site of South Mimms service area for M25 likely to include filling station, service depot, facilities for heavy goods vehicles and motel.
6. Sale by Department of Health and Social Security of hospital land for development – likely in several locations, but notably 25 ha at Mill End Hospital, south of St Albans.

It is clear from this that the success of countryside management is highly dependent on local authority support, as reflected in local planning policies. Even then, in areas of strong development pressure, success will be tempered by a lack of resources and

powers. Countryside managers do not have the means to intervene in the land market to prevent owners running-down their land or speculating against the continued maintenance of green belt restraint.

Problems such as these may become increasingly

evident in south Hertfordshire following the completion of the M25 motorway and the wish of both local and central government to find acceptable ways of creating new jobs. It may well be that developments of the 'right kind' will be allowed in green belt locations exhibiting intractable amenity problems close to existing urban areas, in exchange for a greater degree of control over development, and a greater application of countryside management measures, elsewhere. Indeed, issues of this kind are already raising the political temperature in south Hertfordshire.

A zone of growing conflict

In terms of their recent public pronouncements at least, those with an interest in the future of the MGB have been stating their positions in particularly forceful terms. On the one hand, those arguing for a relaxation of green belt restraint have emphasized what they see as a shortage of residential development land in the OMA, the need to create new jobs and the desirability of taking full economic advantage of the public investment made in the M25 motorway. This position has the implicit backing of central government with its concern for creating new 'high-tech' jobs and its encouragement of private house building. In the light of the row over the 1983 draft green belt circular, however, government will be unable to support a programme of regular land release in the MGB for political reasons. It may, however, seek to achieve the selected release of land by overturning some local planning decisions on appeal. This is most likely later in the 1980s if the amount of land identified for development in structure plans continues to be used up more quickly than originally estimated. The first major test of the government's resolve to protect the MGB will, however, occur soon. Consortium Developments Limited are expected to seek planning permission for the first three of their 'villages' (two in the MGB in Essex) in 1985.

On the other hand, those opposed to the release of green belt land are well aware of these likely developments and will seek to counter them both locally and nationally through their own channels of political persuasion. The introduction of public participation into the planning process during the 1970s has increased the conservationists' bargaining power. Not only are they quite capable of skilfully

presenting their own case, but participation has also demonstrated the financial significance of planning decisions to an increasing number of home owners. The more sophisticated defenders of London's green belt acknowledge, at least in private, that some sites will almost certainly be released for development. Even so, they cannot afford to accept a general principle which endorses the release of land, however minimal the amount, if only because virtually no amount of land release will satisfy the demands of developers in the green belt.

On balance, heat rather than light seems likely to be generated in the next few years on the future of the MGB. The government's basic position is fixed by the new circular, even though the MGB's boundaries are more threatened today at a time of national economic recession when the MGB zone offers opportunities for economic growth found in few other areas of the country. There is also, as yet, little firm evidence on the scale of the impact of the M25 on the MGB, but the motorway is bound to increase the level of demand for development land in the OMA. The most likely outcome is that green belt land will not be released on a significant scale but conservationists may well have to settle for, and satisfy their consciences with, a limited erosion of the MGB in exchange for improved standards of landscape appearance in the remainder.

Further reading

The most recent and comprehensive analysis of the MGB is contained in:
Munton R J C (1983) *London's Green Belt: containment in practice* Allen and Unwin

An earlier book covering similar ground is by:
Thomas D (1970) *London's Green Belt* Faber

The most important official publications are:
Department of the Environment (1984) *Green Belts, Circular 14/84*, DoE London
Select Committee on the Environment (1984) *Green Belt and Land for Housing Vol I* HMSO

Two useful reports on environmental conditions in the MGB are:
Countryside Commission (1981) *Countryside Management in the Urban Fringe CCP 136* Countryside Commission, Cheltenham
Standing Conference (1976) *The Improvement of London's Green Belt* SERPLAN London

16   Parks and open spaces

Hugh Prince

London as a 'garden city'

Open space is an *integral* part of London's built-up area. Houses and gardens, terraces and squares, neighbourhoods and churchyards, districts and parks, a metropolis set among royal parks and commons, a conurbation encompassed by green belt and areas of outstanding natural beauty are motifs harmonizing bricks and grass, indoors and outdoors, man and nature. London's built environment is generously endowed with space. In no other city of comparable size is so large an area occupied by open spaces. Spaciousness and greenery have characterized building development since the beginning of settlement (Fig. 16.1).

Just as architecture in London has a history, so gardens, parks, squares, commons and recreation grounds have complementary *histories*. Period styles of medieval gardens, deer parks, eighteenth-century pleasure grounds, Victorian parks, metropolitan heaths and commons are readily identified and their distinctive appearances cherished. Protection and preservation constitute an important and, at times, a dominant theme in their history, but open spaces are not museums. They are lived in and subjected to change and reappraisal. Adaptations to changing population densities, to changing age structures in the population, to expansion of residential suburbs, to increasing car ownership, to growing tourist traffic, to new ideas and new ways of using space, as well as to changes in the physical environment, are no less important than the urge for preservation in an account of the historical geography of open spaces.

In general, open spaces have been acquired for public use by purchase from private owners or by transferring rights previously held by the Crown, lords or commoners, to trusts or to representative bodies. A large number of open spaces are privately owned and public rights range from controlled entry along particular paths at particular times to almost unrestricted freedom to cross any part at any time. On publicly owned land, use is regulated by statutes and by-laws restricting parking, prohibiting dumping of litter, forbidding fires and so on. During the past hundred years public interests have gained at the expense of private interests and public opinion has come to accept this as an inevitable and irreversible process. The late nineteenth-century view, enshrined in many acts of parliament, that land once dedicated as open space should be held in trust for all future generations, natural and unspoiled, is now a serious obstacle when pressure to change is mounting to bursting point.

Ideas of nature, beauty, amenity, heritage, conservation, recreation, access – all of which have been invoked in preambles to open space legislation – have changed and are currently changing. Since 1880 expectations have changed more rapidly and profoundly than changes in the character of landscape. Legacies from earlier periods no longer match contemporary images and park superintendents, labouring with small budgets under the terms of statutory enactments, have been severely restrained from modernizing the land in their care. Not only are many desired changes contrary to the purposes of the founding acts, but strict provisions are laid down to prevent subsequent alterations or evasions. In effect, many schemes designed in the nineteenth century or earlier have 'frozen' obsolete patterns of land use.

Pressure for change, erupting at the present time, springs partly from external sources, such as movements of population or shifts in the distribution of

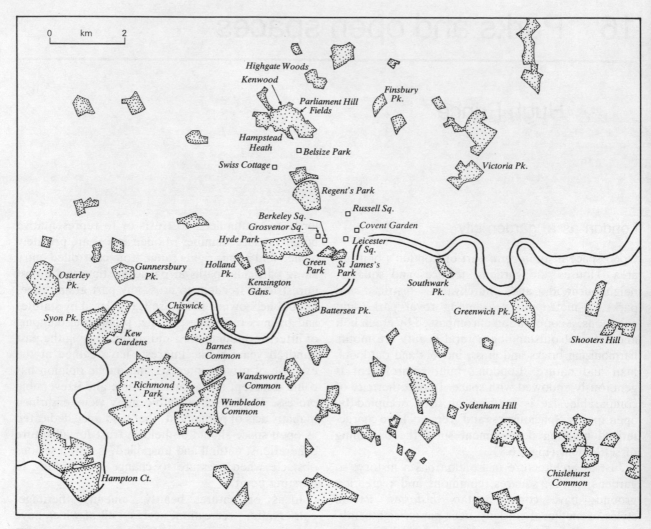

Figure 16.1   *London's parks and open spaces.*

wealth, and partly from internal processes generated by changing attitudes to nature, outdoor recreation, historic relics, visual amenities, entertainment and, above all, to the limits of private property and public rights. To understand where open spaces lie and how they are used it is necessary to trace their origins and development.

Open spaces in central London

The Romans gave the city plenty of room to expand within the walls and a few spacious medieval building plots were garnished with courts, gardens and orchards. Institutional inertia and tradition have conspired to spare one or two of these relict features. The 16 ha of gardens and vineyards surrounding Ely Palace, London residence of medieval bishops of Ely, have been built over, but street-names Saffron Hill and Plumtree Court are reminders of their former fruitfulness. Temple Gardens give a visual impression of the large size of courts once occupied by the Knights Templar, whilst College Gardens and Dean's Yard at Westminster offer glimpses of small cloistered gardens enclosed by collegiate buildings.

In the late sixteenth century the Crown attempted to stop the outward thrust of London's residential development by forbidding new building within 3000 paces from the city gates. Commoners united with the Crown in resisting encroachments by landowners and builders. In 1630 the Earl of Leicester was permitted to build a house on one side of

Leicester Fields on condition that the fields themselves were planted with trees, traversed by gravel walks and the area thrown open to the public. In 1631, Francis, fourth Earl of Bedford, paid £2000 to Charles I for a licence to build a classically designed residential neighbourhood on land formerly owned by Westminster Abbey. Covent Garden was not a garden suburb, but it was spaciously planned and its centre was laid out as a large *piazza*, a formal open space (see chapter 4). Later, estate developments created model villages around squares or circuses or greens, fragments of rusticity transplanted in town.

Most squares were private, in that they were surrounded by railings and residents possessed keys to enter them, but they were public in the sense that passers-by might enjoy the sight of spring flowers in St James's Square or listen to a nightingale singing in Berkeley Square. Promenades gave pedestrians limited access to Berkeley Square, Grosvenor Square, Russell Square and, in later centuries, gates of other squares were opened to non-residents.

Royal parks

The most extensive open spaces in central London are royal parks opened for state ceremonies and for informal enjoyment by the public. St James's Park was opened to the public by Charles II and was planned, in the manner of the gardens at Versailles, to cater for crowds of visitors. Green Park, an extension to the west, has remained less grand and more secluded. Beyond Green Park lies Hyde Park, nearly 250 ha in extent and occupying a larger area than all land newly built in the West End during the first half of the seventeenth century. The opening of such a large area to a small resident population in 1637 was premature and over-generous. It became notorious as a resort for duellists and armed robbers. Charles II attempted to control crime and give the park a stately appearance. But unruly crowds flocked to Tyburn to watch public executions, view firework displays or take part in political assemblies. The enclosure of Kensington Palace Gardens at the end of the seventeenth century stopped the westward advance of open space but was followed by fresh improvements in the park. A broad carriage drive, Rotten Row, along which gentry from the West End might exercise their horses, was planted and a large ornamental lake, the Serpentine, was constructed.

Further afield, Richmond possesses by far the largest royal park, almost four times the size of Hyde Park and Kensington Gardens put together, a semi-wild deer park that has survived virtually intact. Upstream at Hampton Court, Charles II and William III ordered a majestic formal garden to adjoin Christopher Wren's palace, whilst another 500 ha were enclosed as a deer park. About 5 km south-east of the city, seventeenth-century Greenwich was growing into a small town hemmed in between its Thameside wharves and the high wall of the oldest of London's royal parks. Stuart kings and queens commissioned a magnificent suite of residences and naval buildings, culminating in the Royal Observatory at the top of a hill. The park itself was laid out anew in the grand manner. The royal parks provided wedges of greenery between expanding residential districts. They served not only as arenas for State pageantry but as grounds for public recreation.

Landscape gardens

Private gardens for eighteenth-century aristocrats and pleasure gardens run for profit were taken over as public open spaces when they were engulfed by the spread of buildings. In Kensington, Holland House was pulled down in the nineteenth century but its park, embellished with many seventeenth-century structures, was retained as an open space.

The banks of the Thames above Hammersmith are adorned with many fashionable pleasure grounds. Palladian Chiswick and Marble Hill are smaller and less extravagent than Capability Brown's Syon or Kew. Kew's fantastic eighteenth-century architecture, its exotic flora introduced from 1759 onwards, its nineteenth-century Palm House and Temperate House attract hundreds of visitors every day in the year. In lilac time, celebrated in Victorian song, it is one of the most popular resorts for Londoners. Other private parks such as Osterley, Gunnersbury, Claremont and Kenwood have subsequently passed into public guardianship. They preserve an arcadian atmosphere and sense of proportion created by eighteenth-century landscape designers. Many vestiges of lost pleasure gardens survive; other landscapes have vanished but are commemorated in such names as Arnos Grove, Swiss Cottage or Belsize Park.

Kenwood, Hampstead Heath.
The grounds of Kenwood House were laid out in the late eighteenth-century as a private landscape garden for a wealthy law lord: It is now public open space adjoining Hampstead Heath.

Nineteenth-century urban lungs

At the beginning of the nineteenth century the total area of open space in London was very large but the spaces themselves were unevenly distributed. The West End possessed not only the most spacious squares but the largest royal parks, most numerous landscape gardens and best-kept noble residences. Crowded slums in St Giles' in the Fleet valley and in Shoreditch were distant from large parks. To the east of the city and to the south of the river, where building was active along the waterfront, near newly opened docks and canals, open spaces were few and small in size. The inequality of provision between West End and East End was broadened and further widened after the coming of the railways with the rapid outward expansion of residential suburbs. Crowded inner districts were walled in by railways, by factories and by thousands of new houses. Farmland, woods and marshes were built over and open country receded further and further from the city's meanest streets (see chapters 4 and 5).

From 1833, following the publication of a report by a parliamentary select committee on public walks, the government began to intervene to protect commons, obtain land for public recreation, abate the nuisance of smoke, prevent the fouling of streams and restore, as far as possible, an ambience of rurality. Between 1836 and 1845, general enclosure acts made provisions for the preservation of commons within 16 km of Charing Cross and authorized the allotment of land for gardens for the urban poor. The establishment of effective municipal government and, in 1855, the inauguration of the Metropolitan Board of Works, gave fresh impetus and summoned new authorities to take over open spaces (see chapter 5).

The making of parks to afford working men and their families 'means of healthy exercise and cheerful amusement' became an objective of parliamentary legislation. Acts were passed to set up Victoria Park in 1841, Battersea Park (1844), Southwark Park (1857) and Finsbury Park (1860). These spaces were planned to accommodate large numbers of visitors, who were encouraged or ordered to keep to clearly designated gravel walks. The playing of games, drinking alcohol, playing music, or holding meetings were either prohibited or strictly controlled. Notwithstanding these restrictions, the new parks were immensely popular.

Metropolitan commons

The demand for outdoor recreation could not be satisfied by creating municipal parks alone. Tidying disused churchyards and converting them into public gardens relieved the pressure in old, congested inner districts but most extensive additions were to come from village greens and common pastures on the outskirts of the metropolis. These spaces were secured for public use in the face of fierce and persistent competition from developers and speculators. The Crown itself and public agencies, including the War Department and Church Commissioners, were busily engaged in planning to build, or grant leases for building, over many tracts of common land. In 1865, to oppose a powerful array of vested interests, a society for the preservation of commons in the metropolis was formed by George Shaw Lefevre (later Lord Eversley). By sustained efforts in parliament and later in the London boroughs, further encroachments on commons were halted. Following an act of 1866, but mainly after a stronger measure in 1877, Wimbledon Common, Barnes Common, Wandsworth Common and hundreds of other open spaces were brought into public ownership. The largest areas provided space for playing fields, for children's playgrounds with swings and roundabouts, for boating ponds, band stands, horse troughs, drinking fountains and public lavatories. Management was inobtrusive and permissive, and designs were less formal than those imposed on early municipal parks.

One of the most highly publicized struggles was fought to preserve Hampstead Heath. The lord of the manor, Sir Thomas Maryon Wilson, after repeated attempts to break a family settlement that prevented him from developing his estate, threatened to exercise his right to grant leases over parts of the heath. In 1856, the Metropolitan Board of Works acknowledged the great lasting advantage that would be gained by preserving Hampstead Heath but declared that the Board had more urgent and desirable improvements to carry out and therefore resolved 'not to entertain the question of the purchase of land for the purposes of a park'.

In 1860, Hampstead Heath station was opened and tens of thousands of artisans and clerks thronged to the Heath for fresh air and relaxation. The lord of the manor could neither prevent this mass invasion nor could he make individuals pay for trampling on his soil; but he imposed entrance charges on club excursions and levied tolls on itinerant vendors and keepers of ponies and donkeys. He also charged fees for brick-making, and in 1865–7 the Midland Railway paid an enormous sum

for extracting sand and gravel from quarries on either side of Spaniards' Road. Each year the prospect of building on the Heath drew nearer but no public body possessed the legal power or financial resources to purchase the manorial rights.

In 1869 Sir Thomas Maryon Wilson died and his successors immediately offered to sell the manorial rights for £45 000. After two years of negotiations, an agreement was drawn up conferring possession of the Heath on the Metropolitan Board of Works. Between 1886 and 1889 a further £300 000 was subscribed by various bodies to add East Heath Park and Parliament Hill Fields to the area of open space. The Metropolitan Board of Works had no wish to convert the Heath into a municipal park. They planted a few oaks to screen the squatter settlement in the Vale of Health and scattered gorse seed over scars of recent gravel diggings, but no paved walks were laid out and the natural growth of plants was interfered with as little as possible.

Back to nature

As the built-up area expanded and population increased, Londoners sought to escape to wilder, more solitary places. This growing interest in unspoilt woods and heaths is reflected in efforts taken by different authorities to prevent suburban chimney pots rising above the wooded heights of Shooters Hill and Sydenham Hill, in extramural activities financed by the Corporation of the City of London in acquiring Highgate Woods and in winning public rights of access to places as far from the city as Burnham Beeches in Buckinghamshire and Chislehurst Common in Kent.

The most celebrated triumph for the City was the acquisition of Epping Forest for the enjoyment of Londoners. The action was precipitated by a fear that the Crown Commissioners might repeat in Epping a programme of enclosures similar to that which had converted most of the adjoining forest of Hainault into farmland in 1851. The City bought commoners' rights and proceeded to contest in the courts all encroachments and piecemeal enclosures. In 1878, the Epping Forest Act transferred the freehold of the forest to the City Corporation who were to appoint conservators to manage it as public open space. The Act required the conservators to 'preserve the natural aspect of the forest'. Whilst commoners continued to exercise their ancient

Connaught Water, Epping Forest.
A popular beauty spot. The eroded shore, exposed roots and stag-headed growth of the trees reflect the effects of heavy recreational use.

grazing rights, the practice of lopping and chopping trees was abolished and little effort was made to prevent trees colonizing the plains and forest glades. As a result, a close canopied high forest has grown up, the quantity and value of the herbage has declined and the diversity of plant species has been reduced. The amenities of the forest for ramblers and horse-riders have neither been impaired nor greatly enhanced (see chapter 17).

A small group of influential, energetic and highly committed Victorian reformers and philanthropists succeeded in bringing into public ownership lands that had belonged to or had been misappropriated by many individuals and corporate organizations. The objectives of managing the newly acquired commons were to extend freedom of access to all citizens and to preserve for future generations natural beauties of heaths and woods. The aim of restoring natural wilderness was incompatible with the continuation of such customary activities as gravel digging and the cutting of firewood. The most important legacies from the late Victorian era are numerous societies for protecting commons, promoting rambling, studying natural history and recording antiquities. Many of these societies are still strong and active in guarding threatened groves of trees and ancient earthworks.

Twentieth-century recreation grounds

Early twentieth-century reformers cherished an idyllic vision of village life as healthier and less stressful than metropolitan existence. Above all, they were preoccupied with restoring the townsman's health and fitness by vigorous outdoor exercise. Assessments of open space requirements accorded higher priority to the provision of playing fields and sports grounds than to protection of scenes of natural beauty or preservation of sites of historic and scientific interest.

Individual sports and team games were considered to make important contributions to improving the quality of life in inner London. The National Playing Fields Association, founded in 1925, aimed at providing 2.4 ha per thousand people of properly equipped recreational space, excluding golf courses, school playing fields and common land. Total open space requirements, including beauty spots and historic sites, were estimated at 4 ha per thousand people. Higher scales of need were put forward by Abercrombie in 1941, by Parker Norris in 1961 and by Dower in 1965 – all based on increasing expectations of numbers wishing to play team games.

Apart from the initial success of the National Playing Fields Association's campaign to acquire hundreds of new sites and reclaim derelict land for football pitches and in spite of investment by local authorities in constructing outdoor swimming baths or lidos, efforts to expand *public* recreational facilities have been meagre. Private or commercial organizations, including football clubs, cricket clubs, tennis clubs, golf clubs and many private firms have brought a far larger area of land into recreational use than public agencies.

Sports grounds reserved for use by schools have multiplied many times following the Education Act of 1918. The 1944 Act imposed on every local education authority a duty of providing adequate facilities for outdoor recreation and physical training in all schools and colleges. Some of these playing fields are now being loaned to local clubs and to other interested groups and individuals.

Since 1960, the most extensive public schemes, launched by consortia of local councils, have been the Lea Valley Regional Park and a similar project in the Colne valley. Being distant from residential neighbourhoods and having large areas of disused, flooded gravel workings, these regional parks have been able to cater for water sports and also absorb the noise and mess of car and motor cycle scrambling.

For the walker, cyclist and motorist, real country is the strongest magnet and green belt legislation has assisted in keeping open some woods, downs and fields within 30 km of the centre of London. The primary purpose of green belt proposals has been to contain and restrain the outward spread of the built-up area, to limit the ultimate size of the conurbation. A secondary, largely unfulfilled objective has been to protect landscape amenities beyond the urban fringe (see chapter 15).

As early as 1901, Lord Meath sought to establish a green belt that would offer Londoners access to open country. Under a green belt act in 1938, the Home Counties were empowered to purchase land to prevent building encroaching on their rural preserves. The LCC contributed funds in the expectation of securing access to pleasant countryside for the benefit of London's citizens. In the inter-war period the National Trust acquired beauty spots at Box Hill, Ivinghoe Beacon, Frensham Common and in the 1950s these properties were given additional statutory protection within Areas of Outstanding Natural Beauty covering the North Downs and the Chilterns. At the same time, many private parks were converted into golf courses, whilst others were taken over by public bodies as cemeteries, colleges and institutions that granted limited access to ramblers and horse-riders.

The most serious problem arising from increased use of the countryside by day visitors has been a growing demand for space for car parks. In addition, picnic areas, litter bins and toilets have to be provided and damaged fences and trampled crops repaired. Twentieth-century concern for physical fitness is reflected in a massive growth in all forms of outdoor recreation and accounts to some extent for the weekend exodus to country cottages, caravan tours and day trips to picnic spots. The city's youth and those who have cars now have a choice of playing sports, visiting the countryside or going to a London park. The third option is the least attractive and year by year declines in popularity.

Further outlook

In open countryside, beyond London's suburbs, private interests of houseowners, the value of whose property is enhanced by its rural surroundings, coincide with objectives upheld by green belt lobbyists, by local preservation societies, national amenity societies and scientific trusts. They are united in their endeavours to prevent gravel working, house building, motorway construction, and new airports and are repeatedly attacked by central government departments seeking sites for these and similar developments. At the same time the quality of the environment is being harmed by motorists, long distance commuters, campers, golfers and hordes of other invaders. Both village life and wildlife are suffering and being changed (see chapters 15 and 17).

In inner London, in the East End and south of the river, local residents, many of whom have no car or means of reaching open countryside, suffer from a chronic deficiency of open air amenities. Land might be obtained from British Rail in Somers Town and from dockland owners in Stepney and Rotherhithe for additional space to provide playgrounds for young children, resting places for the elderly and, not least, some green foliage and stretches of clear water.

Meanwhile, royal parks in west central London are visited by increasing numbers of foreigners and transient residents, and fewer local long-term residents find them accessible or attractive. As lifestyles change and London decentralizes, the uses to which the city's diverse legacy of open spaces are put, also change. New ideas about the future roles of the parks and commons of London need to be examined. Perhaps more land should be set aside within Regent's Park. Hyde Park and Greenwich Park for car parks, sports stadia, playing fields, cafes, terrace restaurants, small theatres, art galleries and dance halls, to give back the festive spirit that has been ebbing away from inner London since 1960?

Further reading

A valuable insight into London as a 'garden city' is provided by:
Rasmussen S E (1960) *London: the unique city* Pelican (Chapters 5, 8, 9 and 13 are especially interesting)

Further details of London's parks are found in:
Thurston H (1974) *Royal parks for the people* David and Charles

17 Wildlife and the city

Carolyn Harrison

A place for wildlife

Over the centuries the countryside close to London has been transformed through the processes of city growth. Woodlands, heathlands, downlands, marshes and bogs have disappeared and have been replaced by residential and industrial areas. As a result many plants and animals that were once common in the London area have been lost (Fitter, 1945). The extension of the built-up area has also meant that many Londoners now have to travel much longer distances to enjoy the pleasure of the countryside and the wildlife it supports. Gone are the days when John Stow was able to record in his *Survey of London* (1598) that:

> On May Day in the morning, every man, except impediment, could walk into the sweet meadows and green woods, there to rejoice their spirits with the beauty and savour sweet flowers, and with the harmony of birds praising God in their kind.

Today, people who live in the central areas of London have to undertake a car journey of over an hour and a half to get to the countryside and the journey by public transport is much longer. Not surprisingly, few people who live in the inner city undertake such a journey regularly and most people who grow up in London depend on open spaces close to their home to provide them with the countryside pleasures extolled by Stow. Thus, in the case of London, the use of wild areas within and close to the city for purposes of nature conservation and recreation are closely linked. Indeed any rationale for urban nature conservation is based upon the recognition that many people gain enormous emotional, physical and intellectual satisfaction from being in close contact with wild areas. More-

over, the present richness of the flora and fauna of the capital owes much to the efforts made to secure open spaces for use by the public – steps that were taken long before the provision of Nature Reserves and other protected areas became the statutory role of the Nature Conservancy Council in 1949.

There is a place for wildlife in London, but, as with any city, open land within and on the edge of the built-up area is subjected to all kinds of pressure from competing land uses and as long as there is a demand for new houses, factories and roads, the long-term security of these habitats will always be in doubt. The central objective of this chapter is to determine what security of tenure wildlife habitats have in London. The chapter starts with a brief description of the evolution of the present pattern of wildlife habitats and their nature conservation status and then moves on to explore what form development pressures take. A number of examples are used to examine how effective different legislative and management measures have been in conserving habitats and the chapter concludes with a brief appraisal of the place wildlife might come to occupy in the future.

The pattern of wildlife habitats and their nature conservation status

The sheer physical extent of the built-up area means that London cannot offer wildlife a very hospitable home. All the trappings and products of an urban society mean that open land which can support semi-natural communities is restricted in area and distribution, and what remains is subjected to all kinds of disturbance and development pressure. Nevertheless, within the GLC area, a surprising range of plants and animals can be found. The recently published *Flora of the London Area*

(London Natural History Society, 1983) provides a geographical and historical account of flowering plants and ferns found within 32 km of St Paul's Cathedral, and the *Atlas of Breeding Birds of the London Area*, published by the same society in 1977, provides a similar account for birds. Both these studies show the wealth of wildlife that inhabits the urban area; over 2000 plant species grow in Greater London and over 100 different kinds of birds breed there regularly. Not unexpectedly the number of species is lowest in the inner city and highest in the outer suburbs and the green belt, but fragments of many semi-natural habitats occur throughout the built-up area. These range from long-established areas of encapsulated countryside such as the large urban commons of Hampstead Heath and Wimbledon Common, to new, transient and often heavily modified plots of derelict and wasteland that occur in greatest abundance in the inner city.

The value of each of these areas as wildlife habitats is influenced by a number of factors, such as size, geographical location, proximity to other habitats, degree of naturalness and permanence. So, for example, the larger the area, the greater the habitat diversity and the larger the number of species supported. But, while the largest areas of a habitat are of most value as wildlife reserves, the total number of species varies according to habitat type.

Chalk grassland, for example, contains many more species than a comparable area of heathland on the Greensand or Pebble Gravels or of grassland on the sticky London Clay, and some of the richest habitats are remnants of the ancient deciduous woodland that formerly extended over much of the London basin. Likewise, the grazing meadows of the valley bottoms of the Rivers Lea and Colne support a rich and varied flora and fauna.

Over time the number of species supported by an area is also a function of how long it has been separated from similar habitats, and its management history. The longer a habitat island has been isolated from a potential source of colonizing species, then the lower the chances that lost species will be replaced. Similarly the greater the distance between two habitat fragments, the more difficult it becomes for recolonization to occur. So while we know that there have been recent improvements in the physical environment of London, as for example in air quality, many of the sensitive species of moths and butterflies which were lost in the eighteenth and nineteenth centuries have not been able to recolonize because suitable habitats are often isolated and are beyond the dispersal capabilities of existing colonies. In a general way, therefore, the theory of island biogeography proposed for oceanic islands by MacArthur and Wilson is likely to hold true for the artificial island habitats of the urban area. In

Table 17.1   *Changes in the flora of Hertfordshire since the mid-nineteenth century*

	Recorded in 1851	Added by 1881	Added by 1967	Total	Presumed extinct or very rare	% presumed extinct or very rare
Woodland	116	3	6	125	8	6.6
Hedgerow	51	5	9	65	1	1.5
Calcareous pasture	106	1	5	112	8	7.1
Acid pasture	69	2	2	73	13	17.8
Neutral pasture	85	0	6	91	1	1.1
Aquatic	38	4	6	48	6	12.5
Riverside	53	2	2	57	2	3.3
Marshes etc.	123	4	4	131	29	29.8
Walls	17	2	2	21	3	14.3
Arable land	97	5	4	106	26	24.5
Waste land	61	13	27	101	1	1.0
Garden throw-outs etc.	73	62	265	400	–	–
Total	888	104	338	1 330	–	–

Source: Dony J C (1974) Changes in the flora of Hertfordshire, *Transactions of the Hertfordshire Natural History Society*, 27(6).

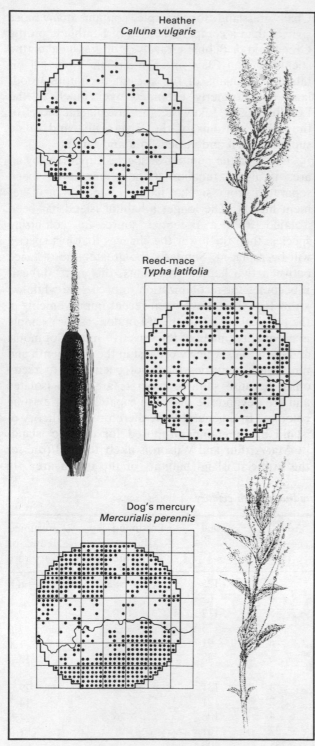

Figure 17.1 *Distribution of heather (Calluna vulgaris), dog's mercury (Mercurialis perennis) and reed mace (Typha latifolia) in the London area (partly after London Natural History Society, 1983).*

practice, however, it is difficult to disentangle the effect of isolation and size from other environmental changes.

On balance, overall losses in habitats favoured by native species in the London area have not been redressed by the creation of new habitats. Table 17.1, for example, shows how the flora of Hertfordshire has changed during a period of rapid urbanization when the population of the county grew from 100 000 in 1801, to over 250 000 in 1901 and about 1 million in the mid-1970s. Such changes are typical of those experienced around London and show that most of the gains to the flora have come from garden throw-outs and wasteland species which are exotic plants or introductions to the flora. Losses have been greatest among the native plants which thrive in aquatic and marsh habitats and in arable and pasture land. Even where good historical records such as these exist, it is often not possible to attribute changes in the distribution and abundance of plants and animals to a single cause because the inter-relationships between plants and animals and their changing urban environment are subtle and varied. The complexity of these inter-relationships is illustrated by the history of three well-known plants shown in Fig. 17.1.

Historical ecology of some popular plants

Common heather or ling: *Calluna vulgaris* is very restricted in its distribution and occurs only on some of the acid heaths that are found in London. It was once present on Iver Heath, Thornton Heath, Blackheath and Colney Heath. Many of these heaths have been built over or have succumbed to the plough, and heather can no longer be found even on those heathlands which have survived. For example, the single plant recorded in 1927 on Hampstead Heath was last seen in 1942 and *Calluna* only just about holds its own on Wimbledon Common. As with many of the heathlands in London, changes in the grazing regime of urban and rural commons have led to the invasion of scrub and bracken. The Londoner who wants to see heather in all its purple glory in the summer months now has to make do with the sorry display of a few plants or has to undertake a long journey out to the heaths of Surrey and beyond. The history of heather is repeated for many other heathland plants such as bilberry (*Vaccinium myrtillus*), cross-leaved heath

(*Erica tetralix*) and bog plants such as sundew (*Drosera rotundifolia*) and the bog bean (*Menyanthes trifoliata*).

Dog's mercury: Mercurialis perennis is commonly found in woods and hedgerows and recent studies have shown that this plant, which spreads by horizontal rhizomes, colonizes new areas only very slowly. Hence, the presence of dog's mercury in suburban gardens and along roadsides is likely to give a fairly accurate indication of the presence of a former woodland cover. Its absence from the central area of London does not, however, mean that woodland never grew there, but merely reflects the lack of suitable habitats and the inability of suburban plants to spread into the new woodlands found in parks and on abandoned waste ground.

Reed-mace: The distribution and history of *Typha latifolia*, the reed-mace, contrasts with that of the other two species because it shows how a once uncommon species in the London area has been able to establish itself as a relatively common sight around ponds and watersides. In part the rise in the fortunes of the reed-mace can be attributed to the recent vigilance of commoners and local naturalists in preventing the loss of local ponds, but it is also a function of the colonizing ability of the species itself. In the past when ponds and rivers were used as watering places by livestock, the reed-mace had few opportunities to become established at the water's edge. With a decline in this use and the heavy trampling that accompanied it, *Typha* was able to become established. Now, with an ample supply of potential seed sources, the wind-blown seed can be dispersed throughout the capital and *Typha* is one example of an attractive and well-loved plant that is now easier to find and enjoy than had previously been the case.

The history of these three species cannot do justice to the complex range of responses of plants and animals to pressures of urbanization. They do serve to show the varied nature of these responses and how precise ecological requirements have to be met before any one species can become established and replace itself. Moreover, they serve to show why it is difficult to ensure the survival of a particular species in a particular place, and help to explain why habitat protection is regarded as the single most effective way of ensuring that wildlife has a place in the city.

Habitat protection and development pressures

Some of the most important habitats for wildlife have been afforded statutory protection by their designation as Nature Reserves and Sites of Special Scientific Interest (SSSI). Twenty-six sites are currently scheduled in the London area under these designations by the Nature Conservancy Council (NCC), and others are in the process of being notified, for example at Oxleas Woods in Greenwich (GLC, 1984). Yet others have been acquired by wildlife trusts, for example Upper Woods in Dulwich and the Gunnersbury Triangle in Chiswick. In total the protected sites cover only some 2200 ha (excluding the London parks and the Thames itself) with just over a third of this area in woodland, 30 per cent in heathland, 23 per cent in open water and much smaller amounts in grassland, meadow and mineral workings. The recently formed London Wildlife Trust would like to see some seventy such sites afforded protection and in 1984 the GLC commissioned the trust to undertake a systematic survey and evaluation of sites in the GLC area with a view to establishing a more comprehensive and representative series of wildlife reserves than is currently protected.

In practice, of course, no site can be given full protection and in the case of urban areas the pressures from development are greater than elsewhere. In fact, the recent history of the damage suffered by SSSIs nationally is salutory (NCC, 1984) and the intensity of development pressures on protected habitats in the case of London and the South East can be seen from the study completed by Barton and Buckley (1983). This showed that two-thirds of the SSSIs in the six counties around London had been subject to harmful development proposals since their designation, and in Kent this represented a mean of 45 proposals per annum, approximately one each week. There was a strong correlation between the type of threat posed and population density.

Urban threats (housing and industrial developments) increased with higher densities, while in areas of low population, rural threats were stronger (for example agricultural reclamation, drainage improvements). Interestingly, however, the number of *successful* applications was lower for urban than for rural developments and paradoxically SSSIs in the urban area were better protected by conventional development control procedures than comparable sites in the countryside. At the time of the study, before the Wildlife and Countryside Act of 1981, existing development control procedures were, therefore, totally inadequate for protecting wildlife habitats, even when they were notified as SSSIs and, moreover, sites in the countryside were at greater risk than protected sites in the urban area. This study demonstrated the scale of rural and urban threats and it remains to be seen whether the new act will ensure better protection for SSSIs. Successful protection will depend upon the NCC's ability to compensate owners financially in circumstances where no agreement about proposed development can be reached, and upon their ability to monitor changes in management practices such as grazing pressure and fertilizer application.

Legislative changes alone will not prevent development threats from arising and we can expect most protected sites in and close to London to be the subject of new development proposals in the future. In the short term, threats are likely to fall most heavily on open land in the outer suburbs. These are the areas which have experienced the most rapid growth in population and offer the house-builders and developers the most sought-after and attractive locations. The completion of the M25 will further add to these locational advantages. The fact that these threats will be made to some of the richest wildlife habitats close to London is itself a cause for concern but the more so, because suburban habitats are increasingly regarded as refuges for species that are at risk in the wider countryside. For example, urban foxes and badgers are common in the suburbs of the southwest and their abundance is, in part, a reflection of the exchange that takes place between the rural and urban populations of these animals. Other sectors of outer London, such as Essex and Kent, are less well endowed with semi-natural areas and this dearth of habitats is reflected in the low numbers of urban fox and badger populations in adjacent suburbs.

Beebee's studies (1979, 1981) also emphasize the functional interdependence of urban and rural habitats for the conservation of British amphibia but, in addition, they reveal how habitat management on a local scale can influence the status of animal populations. These studies show, for example, that although frogs and toads were once much more abundant in the Sussex countryside, successful colonization of ponds in suburban gardens and parks has partly compensated these rural losses. However, not all amphibia have been equally successful at colonizing these new habitats and colonization reflects the influence of habitat management. For example, the presence of fish in garden ponds is no deterrent to frogs and toads but it is so to smooth and crested newts, and the presence of sizeable areas of scrub and woodland in the vicinity of ponds also affects success rates. The niches favoured by the amphibia are more complex than this because each species responds differently to other variables such as water quality. Nevertheless, Beebee suggests that, with appropriate management techniques, ponds in parks and suburbia could provide the means of stemming the general decline that has taken place in frogs, toads and smooth newt. The future of the amphibia is thus closely dependent upon both the widespread availability of habitats and their sympathetic management. In the absence of either, some species would become extinct.

The history of the British amphibia exemplifies many of the problems encountered in the conservation of plants and animals in the London area. Moreover, because the conservation of much of London's wildlife depends upon areas of unofficial countryside, such as parks, gardens, cemeteries, sportsgrounds, golf-courses and wasteland, most of which have to serve a number of purposes, management becomes a particularly exacting task. Conflicting interests constantly arise and never more so than on sites such as Epping Forest which play an important role both in recreation provision and nature conservation.

Epping Forest: conflicts of interest

Epping Forest comprises some 2430 ha of woodland and grass, together with small patches of heathland, marsh and bog; it extends from Wanstead Flats in the south to a little beyond Epping in the north, a distance of about 19 km. It represents one of the few remaining examples of large-scale wood-pasture, a type of land use formerly widespread on commonland and in parks in which productive woodland and pasture co-existed side by side (Corke, 1978). In 1953 it was designated as an SSSI and its status as a nationally important woodland habitat was confirmed in the *Nature Conservation Review* of 1977. The forest has long been used by Londoners as a pleasant place for a day out. When in 1878 the Epping Forest Act made the Corporation of the City of London conservators of the forest, after a long battle between protagonists of public access and the landowners, the rights of the Crown and the landowners were abolished and the conservators were charged with the duty of managing the forest as a public open space. They promptly exercised their powers and terminated the right of woodcutting. The many thousands of pollarded beech and hornbeam that were the product of a tightly managed productive woodland therefore remained uncut. Whereas previously the ground flora had benefited from the alternating pattern of light and shade of a 10–15 year cycle of pollarding (whereby trees were cut at 4–5 m above the ground), it soon declined under the heavy shade cast by the dense canopy of uncut trees.

Other changes have occurred since 1878 that were largely outside the control of the conservators. Grazing of the plains and grasslands which had formed an integral part of the woodland-pasture system declined because of the loss of local farms to urban development. Other grasslands and heathlands were left unmanaged and reverted readily to scrub. The extent of scrub encroachment since the 1920s can be seen in Fig. 17.2. The net effect of these ecological changes has been to create a forest which is much more uniform in its range of habitats, a cause of concern to wildlife conservationists (Ranson in Corke, 1978).

The fact that the forest has also been used for recreation during the same period means that some changes have also been attributed to the presence of visitors. Until the middle of the nineteenth century most visitors congregated on a few sites such as High Beach and Chingford Plain. By the mid-1930s more people lived closer to the Forest and the motor car brought it within easy reach of the northern suburbs. The effects of recreational use are to be seen in the eroded banks of Connaught Waters, the heavily trampled ground of High Beach and in the wide and muddy paths of parts of the forest. Some plants may have been depleted through excessive picking and certain shy birds may now be less common than they used to be as a result of disturbance. According to some observers who have had a long association with the

forest, however, more species have been lost from the shrub and field layer because of the increased shade than through increased human pressure.

The forest has changed in the last hundred years and the desirability of these changes from the point of view of particular users needs to be assessed by the conservators. For most visitors, the forest has largely changed for the better, but in comparison with other forest areas of similar national status, such as the New Forest and Sherwood Forest, surprisingly little attention is still given by the conservators to the needs of both the casual and committed visitor. For example, rides are way-marked for horse-riders but not for walkers. The Information Centre itself is poorly sign-posted and car-parks and picnic areas are disguised so discreetly as to be easily missed. Visitors who arrive by public transport are no better served, for there are no maps or directions at stations or bus-stops. In many respects the forest presents a number of missed opportunities as far as recreation is concerned, even though it is well placed to serve many potential visitors. The completion of the north-eastern stretch of the M25 and its link with the M11 means that Epping Forest is now less than an hour away from any part of the metropolis and the surrounding suburbs. Undoubtedly there will be an increase in new and inquisitive visitors and it will be instructive to see how the conservators respond to this new challenge and to that posed by the nature conservationists who wish to see a greater diversity of habitats reinstated.

The future of wildlife in the city

The realization that cities can offer a hospitable home to wildlife has grown in recent years. It owes much to the work of the urban wildlife groups founded in the West Midlands conurbation in the 1970s and to the activities of other groups in the voluntary sector. In London, for example, the London Wildlife Trust transformed a small area of derelict railway sidings near St Pancras station into an educational reserve which will be used by local schools. The Ecological Parks Trust also manages a number of other wildlife reserves in the urban area. Such activities have also received the support of the Nature Conservancy Council, and the council itself has done much to promote a greater awareness about the benefits of urban nature conservation.

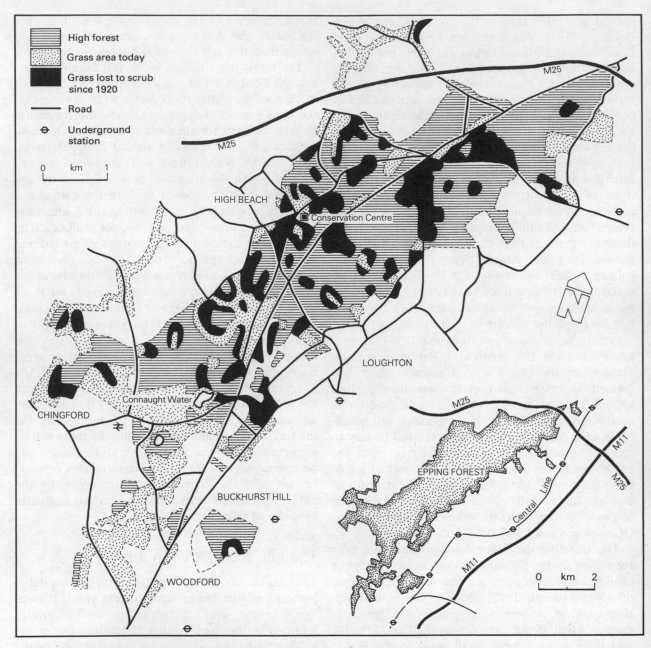

Figure 17.2 *Scrub enroachment in Epping Forest since 1920 (after D. Corke, 1978).*

Perhaps of most importance to the future of wild-life in the city is the NCC's realization that the purpose of wildlife conservation in Britain is primarily determined by cultural objectives (NCC, 1984). In the city more than anywhere else the main reason for conserving the natural heritage of plants and animals is their recreational, aesthetic and inspirational value as well as their scientific and educational value. This 'common ground' (Mabey,

1980) between nature conservation on the one hand and recreation and a sense of well-being on the other, is now becoming accepted as central to any discussion about the quality of life that might be achieved in the city. 'Think green' has become the slogan of many an urban wildlife group, residents' association, and voluntary organization.

Most recently, urban wildlife conservation has become recognized as a legitimate area for inclusion in local and strategic plans. So, for example, a few urban boroughs such as Lewisham and Tower Hamlets have taken steps to secure and manage unofficial open spaces as local nature reserves. On a larger scale, adjacent authorities continue to cooperate in the management of two London regional parks in the Lea Valley and the Colne Valley. And, at the strategic level, the proposed amendments to the Greater London Development Plan submitted to the minister for approval in June 1984 included, for the first time, a number of policies relating to the ecology of the London area. The overall objective of these policies is to encourage a diverse flora and fauna throughout the GLC by the definition, maintenance and extension of a continuum of habitats, not only within open spaces but also in association with housing (private gardens), industry and public utilities (space around buildings and vacant land) and transport (road verges, canals, railway land). In this respect London is following the lead established in the West Midlands conurbation, where a Nature Conservation Strategy has been agreed for the whole county. This strategy will be used to influence local plans and will be used as a material consideration in planning decisions and at planning enquiries conducted by the Department of the Environment. Were these new policies on ecology to be accepted and implemented in London, wildlife should have a more secure place in the city than it currently enjoys. At present piecemeal improvements in wildlife habitats in one area can be undermined by serious losses elsewhere. As long as local authorities in the urban area and in the green belt respond in differing ways to similar development proposals (chapter 15) and they continue to operate without the benefits of a strategic authority which could review the overall impact of development, wildlife and people will be all the poorer.

Towards a greener city

If the level of activity and membership of voluntary organization concerned with the conservation of wildlife in London is any measure of the commitment people have to greening the city, then London will be greener in the future. There is also some cause for optimism based on the achievements accomplished during the short life of statutory organizations like the Ecology Section of the GLC and the Urban Nature Conservation Section of the Nature Conservancy Council. At the same time however, development threats continue to be exerted against even the most highly-valued wildlife habitats. Without constant vigilance, the existing legacy of wildlife will be eroded and London may never regain the wealth of native plants and animals that once lived there.

Further reading

*Baines C and Smart J (1984) *A Guide to Habitat Creation* GLC Ecology Handbook No. 2

Barton P M and Buckley G P (1983) 'The status and protection of notified Sites of Special Scientific Interest in South-East England *Biological Conservation'* **27**: 213–42

Beebee T J C (1978) 'Habitats of the British amphibians (2), Suburban parks and gardens' *Biological Conservation* **15**: 241–57

Beebee T J C (1981) 'Habitats of the British amphibians (4), Agricultural lowlands and a general discussion of requirements' *Biological Conservation* **21**: 17–139

*Corke D (ed) (1978) *Epping Forest – The Natural Aspect?* Essex Naturalist 2 (available from the Epping Forest Conservation Centre, High Beach, Chingford, Essex)

Fitter R S R (1945) *London's Natural History* Collins New Naturalist

Greater London Council (1976) *The Greater London Recreation Study Part 3: The Supply Study* GLC Research Report No. 19

*Greater London Council (1984a) *Ecology and Nature Conservation in London* GLC Ecology Handbook No. 1

Mabey R (1980) *The Common Ground* Hutchinson London

*Nature Conservancy Council (1984) *Nature Conservation in Britain* NCC London

*The four most useful and accessible items.

18   Ethnic and social conflict

Peter Jackson

Setting

This chapter is concerned with the changing ethnic composition of London's population and in particular with the waves of civil unrest which broke out in many of Britain's cities, including London, in the 1980s. By exploring the history of British immigration and the social geography of immigrant areas in London, a very different perspective on these issues emerges from that which characterized most newspaper and television reports of the racial disturbances, street violence and civil disorders which took place in 1981 and 1985. The media have been so preoccupied with the riots that other instances of social and ethnic conflict have frequently been overlooked. In contrast, this chapter argues that the riots were instances of a more widespread feeling of unrest which arises from the latent racism of British society.

Once geographers begin to supplement their long-standing interest in patterns of immigration and ethnic segregation with research on housing and job discrimination, police harassment and racially-motivated attacks, they will inevitably confront the reality of racism in both its individual and institutional forms. For racism can be both direct and indirect, intentional and unintentional. One of its most pervasive forms undoubtedly exists in the policies of institutions, such as local authorities and the police, that work to perpetuate racial inequality whether or not this is consciously acknowledged. Before undertaking further analysis of contemporary patterns, however, we must first of all establish the historical and geographical context of recent social and ethnic conflict.

Immigration and ethnic diversity

London has always played a dominant role in

Britain's long history of immigration, serving as the major port of entry and one of the main centres of immigrant concentration. In the late seventeenth century, several thousand Huguenot weavers arrived in London fleeing from persecution in France and the Low Countries (see chapter 4). One of their churches in Spitalfields stands as a symbol of the succession of ethnic groups which has passed through London's East End. Built originally in 1743, the Huguenot church on Fournier Street became a synagogue in 1898 as Jewish sweatshop workers began to arrive from Eastern Europe. In

Fournier Street Mosque, Spitalfields.
Formerly a Huguenot church and then a Jewish synagogue, the Jamme Masjid mosque on Fournier Street now serves the Bengali community around Brick Lane.

1975 it reopened as a mosque for the Bengali community then growing up along Brick Lane.

Despite this long history of ethnic diversity, contemporary political debate on immigration is more immediately focused on the West Indian and Asian populations which have come to Britain since 1945. The reasons for this preoccupation are clearly racial as the Afro-Caribbean and Asian populations are distinguished from other immigrant groups by their skin colour. The black or coloured population in Britain is now approximately 1.5 million of whom about 500 000 (and probably nearer one half) are in fact the children of first-generation immigrants. This growing second generation makes census measures of the overseas-born population of doubtful validity in estimating Britain's black population which is increasingly indigenous (British-born).

Just as it is incorrect to assume that Britain's black population is entirely an immigrant population, so it is incorrect to assume that all Britain's immigrants are coloured. As the figures in Table 18.1 show, the largest overseas-born group are the Irish, although their numbers have fallen considerably over the last decade. There are also large numbers from the Mediterranean, together with a rapidly increasing population from the Far East.

At this point it should be stressed that the concepts of racial and ethnic group are not easily defined. However, racial groups are normally assumed to share biologically inherited characteristics, such as skin colour, whereas ethnic groups are more subjectively defined by feelings of common ancestry or by shared cultural attributes, such as language and religion. In any case, the 1981 Census asked no direct questions about race or ethnicity and the size of Britain's black population must be inferred from the number of people born in the New Commonwealth and Pakistan. This figure comprises about 3 per cent of the total population nationally and about 9.5 per cent in Greater London (up from 6.4 per cent in 1971). An alternative method is to count those people usually resident in households headed by members born in the New Commonwealth and Pakistan, which yields a slightly higher figure.

The rapid rise in the New Commonwealth population during the 1960s slowed down somewhat in the 1970s, reflecting the passage of various Commonwealth Immigration Acts in 1962, 1965 and 1971. During the 1970s, however, the relative concentration of London's black population was accentuated by the fall in the city's total population. It is still too soon to predict the precise effect that the 1981 Nationality Act will have on continued immigration from the New Commonwealth, although it is already abundantly clear that the new legislation will severely restrict both the number of New Commonwealth immigrants who are allowed to

Table 18.1   *Country of birth of residents of Great Britain and Greater London, 1971 and 1981 (in thousands)*

	Great Britain			Greater London		
	1971	1981	% change	1971	1981	% change
Total Population:	53 826	55 557	+3.2	7 237	6 609	−8.7
Irish Republic:	616	607	−1.5	236	199	−15.6
New Commonwealth and Pakistan:	1 297	1 513	+16.7	467	631	+35.5
Caribbean:	303	295	−2.6	165	167	+1.2
India:	323	392	+21.4	104	139	+33.8
Pakistan:	139[1]	188	+69.8	29[1]	36	+96.4
Bangladesh:		49	−	−	22	−
Mediterranean:[2]	118	130	+10.0	−	69	−
Far East:[3]	83	137	+65.7	20	38	+87.1

Notes:
[1] includes Bangladesh
[2] Cyprus, Gibraltar, Malta and Gozo
[3] Hong Kong, Malaysia, Singapore — No data

Source: 1971 and 1981 Census, Country of Birth Tables

enter this country and the rights of existing residents to continue living here.

Because of the controversy which surrounds the issue of immigration, it is worth looking at the official statistics in more detail. Whereas the population from Pakistan and Bangladesh almost doubled between 1971 and 1981, the Indian-born population increased by about one third and the number of those born in the Caribbean remained almost constant. There are also significant differences between the relative size of each group at the national level and in London. Thus, while the size of the Caribbean-origin population in London is stabilizing, it is still the city's largest New Commonwealth birthplace group, whereas in national terms the Indian-born population is considerably larger. This reflects the greater concentration of the various Asian-born groups in the West Midlands and northern textile towns.

Partly because of the inadequacy of census measures, there has been an unfortunate tendency to group together all the immigrants from the Indian sub-continent as a single 'Asian' population. Such a tendency ignores the diversity of language, religion, nationality and regional origin that is represented within the population. For example, Britain's 'Asian' population includes substantial numbers of Urdu and Gujarati speakers as well as many whose first language is Tamil, Punjabi or Bengali. The diversity of the 'Asian' population is further increased by differences in religion and area of origin which cross-cut each other in complex ways. Those from India include large numbers of Sikhs from the eastern Punjab as well as both Hindu and Muslim Gujaratis. The Pakistani Muslims include those who lived formerly in west Pakistan, particularly from Mirpur, as well as the Sylhetis from what is now Bangladesh. The Asian-origin population in Britain now also includes some 27 000 expelled from Uganda in 1972 together with others from Tanzania and Kenya.

As one might expect, this social diversity is reflected in the spatial pattern of ethnic minority settlement which reveals a high degree of differentiation between these sub-groups. The Afro-Caribbean population has an equivalent degree of 'internal sorting' by area of origin within the Caribbean. Residential patterns within London still reflect island-origins, with Jamaicans being most heavily concentrated south of the river and in Brent, Dominicans and St Lucians around Paddington, Anguillans in Slough and Montserratians in Stoke Newington, Finsbury Park and Hackney.

Changing patterns

Debates about immigration and ethnic conflict are frequently couched in emotive terms which refer to the prospect of 'British culture' being swamped by an uncontrollable tide of immigration from alien lands. Thus, to quote Margaret Thatcher: 'The British character has done so much for democracy, for law and order and so much throughout the world that, if there was any fear that it might be swamped, people are going to react and be hostile to those coming in' (*Daily Mail* 31 January 1978). As we have seen, however, immigration has already been severely curtailed and there is little genuine prospect of such a process actually taking place.

Much of the hostility which has been directed towards ethnic minorities has arisen from their geographical concentration in certain parts of the city as well as from fears about growing absolute numbers. In his book on *West Indian Migration to Britain* (1968), for example, the social geographer Ceri Peach, discussed 'the possibility of segregation' and the formation of ghettoes which he regarded as 'the geographical expression of social failure'. Academic debate was mirrored in political circles where, at about the same time Enoch Powell was voicing his disquiet about the inevitability of conflict, and right-wing political groups (such as the Conservative Monday Club) and neo-Fascist organizations (such as the National Front) were openly advocating induced repatriation.

It is worth pursuing the issue of geographical concentration for various reasons, not least because of the unstated assumption of much policy analysis that ethnic segregation is necessarily a bad thing. The Cullingworth Committee's report on council housing in 1969, for example, recommended that council house allocation be used to encourage the dispersal of immigrant groups. It is striking that similar views are rarely expressed about residential segregation on class grounds. Ethnic segregation is obviously to be abhorred insofar as it involves the denial of choice through the operation of negative forces such as racial discrimination. But geographical concentration also has a number of distinct advantages for minority groups, providing a threshold population for the provision of ethnic goods and services and a potential popular base for political organization. Geographical concentration also gives people the opportunity to maintain cultural practices, such as the ritual preparation of halal meat in Muslim communities, which find little support outside such groups. Finally, there is a territorial dimension to any ethnic minority's defence against external aggression. This was clearly shown in 1976 when members of the Bengali Housing Action Group attempted to have a council estate in Brick Lane, Spitalfields, reserved exclusively for them, following continual threats of physical violence and frequent outbreaks of racially motivated attacks. However, it is undeniable that London's black population is disproportionately represented in areas of poor housing and low economic opportunity. The main areas of immigrant concentration are in the inner city, in the area that E W Burgess termed the 'zone in transition'. In London, this is an area of generally poor housing where high-rise council estates stand alongside large deteriorating Victorian houses which have been subdivided as flats and furnished rooms.

Figure 18.1 shows the distribution of the main foreign birthplace groups (excluding the Irish) at the borough level. The Caribbean-origin population is heavily concentrated in the inner city in three main sectors: to the north, in Hackney and Haringey; to the west, in central and southern Brent; and south of the river, in Wandsworth, Lambeth, Southwark and Lewisham. The various Asian-birthplace groups are somewhat less concen-

Figure 18.1   *Distribution of selected foreign-born groups in Greater London, by borough, 1981.*

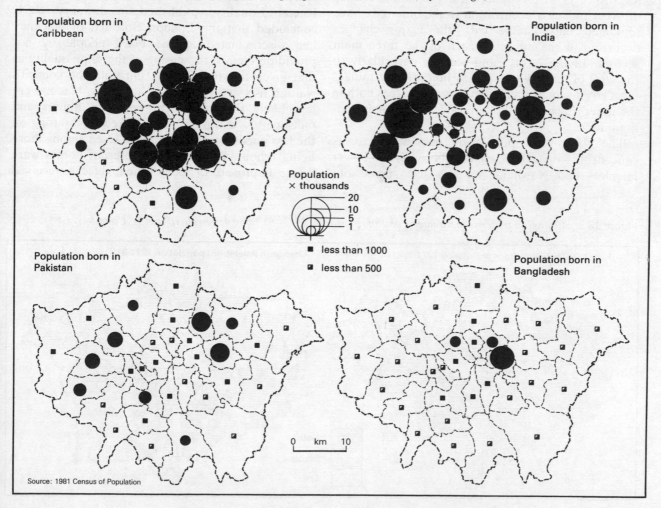

trated in the inner city (except for the Bangladeshis who are heavily concentrated in Tower Hamlets with lesser concentrations in Camden and Westminster). The Indian and Pakistani populations have a rather more suburban distribution with major concentrations to the west of London in Brent, Ealing, Hounslow and Harrow; to the north east, in Newham, Waltham Forest and Redbridge; and to the south of the river, in Wandsworth, Croydon, Merton and Greenwich. Each of these distributions is clearly related to different employment opportunities, such as the clothing sweatshops in London's East End and low-paid sevice work at Heathrort airport (see chapter 14).

Figure 18.2, which has been adapted from the recent *Social Atlas of London*, summarizes the changes which have occurred in the distribution of the Caribbean and Asian-born population at ward level since 1971. It is apparent that the main centres of West Indian concentration in the inner city have remained fairly stable with the major changes occurring at the edges of each of the three main sectors. In the intervening sectors, particularly to the west of the city, the proportion of West Indian-born has declined somewhat in several areas both in the inner ring and at the outer edge of the metropolitan area.

The Asian-born population has intensified its concentrations in the East End boroughs of Tower Hamlets and Newham but has also spread out further into Waltham Forest and Redbridge. To the west of the city, there have also been increases in the Brent, Harrow, Ealing and Hounslow sector. These increases have been balanced by declining proportions of Asian-born in the inner ring (particularly in Kensington and Chelsea, Camden, Haringey and northern Islington) and in scattered areas throughout the suburbs south of the river.

As previously suggested, these patterns represent the balance of forces between positive, voluntary reasons for geographical concentration and negative, involuntary constraints on freedom of choice. While the positive reasons have already been elborated, the constraints remain to be discussed.

Several recent studies have confirmed the presence of racial discrimination in both public and private housing markets. For example, although discrimination is notoriously difficult to prove, a recent formal investigation by the Commission for Racial Equality, published in January 1984, concluded that the London Borough of Hackney had discriminated against black people by not providing them with housing of the same quality as that given to white people. On both the council's waiting lists and among the homeless, blacks were less likely than whites to be given houses and maisonettes, and more likely to receive housing on the less popular high-rise estates. Even among those being rehoused because their present homes were being improved or demolished, blacks received

Figure 18.2　*Changing patterns in Greater London, by wards, 1971–81 (after J. Shepherd and P. Congdon, 1985).*

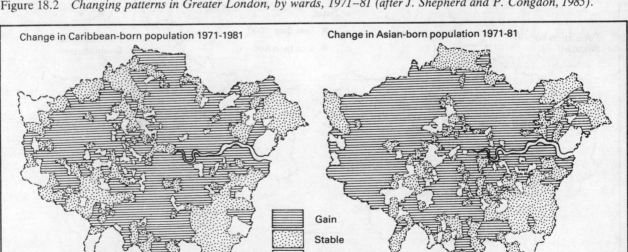

significantly fewer new properties when compared with whites. In the private market, too, a recent review of research on housing and race in Britain by Valerie Karn (1983) argued that priority should be given to the analysis of white society and white institutions as the generators of racial inequality. In both markets, she suggested that the *quality* of housing, in terms of age and state of repair, is now as important as inequalities of access and housing tenure (see chapter 10).

Having explored the geographical background to ethnic and social conflict at the broad, citywide scale, it remains to investigate the local context in which particular conflicts have arisen. In order to do this, two contrasting examples have been chosen. The first deals with an area of high West Indian concentration in Brixton; the second with a suburban Asian population in Southall.

Case study: Brixton

In 1981, the London Borough of Lambeth had a Caribbean-born population of around 17 000 or about 7 per cent of the borough's total population. The non-white population, including the second and third generations together with those of Asian-origin, was at least 25 per cent. This population is a young one and in central Lambeth, where Brixton is situated, approximately half of the teenage population is black.

Following earlier disturbances in St Paul's, Bristol in April 1980, the violence which took place in Brixton in the spring and summer of 1981 was part of a larger wave of civil disorders which occurred throughout Britain and which included major disturbances in Moss Side, Manchester, and in Toxteth on Merseyside. Violence broke out in Brixton on three separate occasions in 1981. On the weekend of April 10–12, rioting began as young blacks retaliated against two police officers whom they thought were mistreating a man who was suffering from stab wounds. The following day, violence recurred as police stopped and searched a taxi driver whom they suspected of drug offences. The rioting that ensued took the form of petrol bomb attacks on police, looting of shops and widespread destruction of private property. Over the three day period, 409 policeman and 49 members of the public were injured, 28 buildings were burned and damage was estimated at £6.5 million.

The second wave of violence occurred on July 10 when areas throughout London were hit by what *The Times* described as a 'rash of street violence and looting' (11 July 1981). Although the violence was more widespread than in April, only 80 arrests were made in Brixton. A few days later, on July 15, a third wave of disturbances occurred when hundreds of young people rioted in Railton Road and Effra Parade, following dawn raids by police in search of petrol bomb factories which they failed to find.

The rioting was some of the most violent ever experienced in mainland Britain with police resorting to water cannon and CS gas to quell the disturbances. Shortly afterwards the Home Office set up an inquiry into the Brixton disorders under the 1964 Police Act, led by Lord Scarman. The majority of the 150 page report, which subsequently became a best-selling paperback, was given over to criticism of policing methods. The report admitted that the police had been involved in triggering incidents in several of the major riots including St Paul's, Toxteth, Southall and Brixton. But Scarman was insistent that while instances of harassment and racial prejudice could occasionally be found among a few officers, the direction and policies of the Metropolitan Police were not racist. Similarly, while Scarman concluded that police attitudes and methods had failed to respond sufficiently to the problems of policing a multi-racial society, he steadfastly maintained that 'institutional racism does not exist in Britain'. His recommendations stressed the 'special needs' of ethnic minorities rather than a more radical programme of positive discrimination.

Clearly the police played a major role in provoking the disorders. Hard-line policing methods such as the infamous 'Swamp 81' operation employed in Brixton immediately prior to the riots, as well as insensitive handling of stop-and-search powers over a long period, undoubtedly antagonized a substantial number of local people and led to a complete breakdown of police–community relations. But there were deeper, underlying causes to the social unrest which occurred in Brixton besides the provocative policing methods currently employed.

Lord Scarman himself concluded that social conditions were not a *cause* of the disorders but that, taken together, they had created 'a predisposition towards violent protest'. Equally deprived areas elsewhere in the country had not experienced disorders, so no simple causal explanation could be upheld. However, social conditions in Brixton at the time of the riots were certainly very grave. Unemployment levels at the Brixton Employment Office in early 1981 averaged 13 per cent and ethnic minority unemployment, particularly among black teenagers, was considerably higher. Total unemployment in Lambeth, according to the 1981 Census, had increased from 6.1 to 13.2 per cent over the previous decade. It is therefore not surprising that of those arrested for riot-related offences in Brixton in the months of April and July 1981 the majority were young, black and unemployed. Of those arrested for threatening behaviour, theft, assault or affray, carrying an offensive weapon, or criminal damage, 67 per cent were black, 83 per cent were male and 63 per cent were unemployed (Metropolitan Police data, reported in *The Times* 23 November 1981). Since 1981, unemployment in Brixton has continued to rise.

Housing conditions were no less dire. The National Dwelling and Housing Survey in 1977/78 revealed a local authority waiting list of 18 000 households in Lambeth, with 20 per cent of total households currently homeless. Black households were particularly hard-pressed, comprising 37 per cent of the homeless. Overcrowding and deterioration were widespread, especially in the areas affected by the riots, including the Mayall/Railton Roads Housing Action Area.

No simple answer can be offered as to the ultimate cause of the Brixton riots. Social conditions, police behaviour and long-standing ethnic tensions all contributed to the eventual outbreak of civil disorder. These complex circumstances provide evidence of the abiding nature of both social and ethnic conflict in Britain, a conclusion that official sources have been reluctant to admit.

Case study: Southall

Despite its suburban location, some 15 km west of central London, Southall has had a socially and ethnically mixed population for several generations (Fig. 14.3). Today, the area's diverse population includes large numbers of immigrants: East African Asians, Pakistanis and West Indians are all represented but it is the Punjabi Sikhs who currently predominate. Employment conditions in Southall are markedly different from those in inner city areas of high Asian concentration, such as the East End, where the workforce is highly fragmented. In the East End, Asians are employed in restaurants and in the rag trade, working from home or in small sweatshops. In Southall, by contrast, the great majority of the Asian workforce is employed in half a dozen factories making bread, rubber goods and processed foods. Although the work involves long and irregular hours with few prospects, the localization of Asian workers in a handful of factories has been much more conducive to successful union organization than in the East End. The Indian Workers' Association was formed in Southall in March 1957 and has been involved in frequent industrial action, contradicting the racist stereotype of a docile and passive Asian workforce. The Race Today Collective has elaborated this argument in their pamphlet on *The Struggles of Asian Workers in Britain* (1983) where they argue that the Asian workforce has been 'disciplined, united and organized by the very mechanism of capitalist production'.

The concentration of a large Asian population in suburban Southall has had other consequences, such as the opening of a Sikh temple (*Gurdwara*) as early as 1959. Following the expulsion of East African Asians from Kenya in 1967 and from Uganda in 1972, the arrival of a middle-class population of Gujarati Hindus, many of whom already had experience of running small businesses, led to a proliferation of ethnic enterprises in Southall. Travel agents, food shops and clothing stores were quickly followed by estate agents, insurance brokers, banks and other financial institutions. The growth of the Asian Community in Southall has not gone without opposition, however, and ethnic conflict has frequently resulted.

Southall's recent history is punctuated by a variety of violent conflicts including racially-motivated attacks on Asian residents and business premises. Racial violence peaked first in the late 1960s, coinciding with the expulsion of Kenyan Asians in 1968, and again in the late 1970s in the wake of increased activities by the National Front and other extremist groups. On 4 June 1976, Gurdip Singh Chaggar was stabbed to death by a group of white youths. Tensions continued to smoulder during the next few years, reaching a climax again on 23 April 1979, when the National Front held a meeting at Southall's Town Hall. The Asian community undertook a massive sit-down protest having failed in their efforts to have the meeting banned. In the violent confrontation which ensued, a white school teacher, Blair Peach, was killed. In this and other incidents in Southall, the police have been heavily criticized for appearing more anxious to defend National Front supporters than to afford the same protection to Asian residents who constantly suffer racist attacks.

Violence has continued to flare. The most recent example occurred in July 1981 when several hundred Asian youths confronted a group of skinheads who had been taunting them and throwing stones from behind police lines. Several policemen were injured in the conflict which developed and the Hambrough Tavern, where the skinheads had retreated, was burnt down.

These episodes are not isolated incidents. In the Brick Lane area of East London in 1978, several deaths occurred as a result of racist attacks, coinciding with local elections in which several National Front candidates were standing. From these examples it seems clear that ethnic and social conflict cannot be divorced from its wider political context. Neither are these conflicts limited to specific geographical areas, occurring equally in the inner city and in more prosperous suburban areas such as Southall. In short, apart from its more conspicuous and widely publicized forms, conflict is endemic and widespread rather than occasional and localized.

New challenges

The extent to which the social and ethnic conflicts reported in this chapter reflect problems of recent change in London is a matter for debate. While the population of Caribbean and Asian origin is substantially a post-war phenomenon, Britain's ethnic diversity has a much longer history. Despite the British self-conception as a tolerant and fair-minded people, the hostility and suspicion which have repeatedly been shown to foreigners should not be ignored. Whether one is concerned with Russian Jews in Stepney, with Cypriots in Haringey, or with Chinese in Limehouse or Soho, ethnic tensions and social conflict are long-standing problems which reflect poorly on British attitudes and behaviour.

However, some new issues have arisen with the immigration to Britain of a substantial population from the New Commonwealth. For increasingly, in the future, Britain's ethnic minority population will not be an immigrant population but one that is born in Britain. The ideology of assimilation which confronted first generation immigrants has been unequivocally rejected by their British-born offspring. The consequences of these changes for public policy and urban affairs in general have yet to be satisfactorily resolved. But, as this chapter has attempted to illustrate, they are issues concerning which the geographer has a definite contribution to make, not only in the analysis of spatial patterns but also in understanding the geographical and historical roots of social processes such as racism and ethnic discrimination.

Further reading

On the nature of institutionalized racism in Britain, see:
Centre for Contemporary Cultural Studies (1982) *The Empire Strikes Back* Hutchinson

On the Brixton riots, see:
Benyon J (ed) (1984) *Scarman and After: Essays Reflecting on Lord Scarman's Report, the Riots and their Aftermath* Pergamon
Lord Scarman (1981) *The Brixton Disorders, 10–12 April 1981* Command no. 8427, HMSO, also published by Penguin
Burgess J (1985) 'News from nowhere: the press, the riots and the myth of the inner city', in Burgess J and Gold J (eds) *Geography, the media, and popular culture* Croom Helm

On the Asian community in Southall, see:
Campaign Against Racism and Fascism/Southall Rights (1981) *Southall: the birth of a black community*, Institute of Race Relations/Southall Rights, London

And for more specifically geographical work, see:
Herbert D T and Smith D M (eds) (1979) *Social problems and the city* Oxford University Press
Peach C, Robinson V and Smith S (eds) (1981) *Ethnic segregation in cities* Croom Helm

Examinations of housing and race are provided in:
Henderson J and Karn V (1984) 'Race, class and the allocation of public housing in Britain' *Urban Studies* **21**: 115–28

19   Community organizations

Jacquie Burgess

Problems and participation

Lifts not working in the flats, no safe play space for
the kids, derelict buildings, racist graffiti, mounting
unemployment, neighbourhood decline – what can
ordinary people do when faced with the day-to-day
reality of national recession and structural change
in the economy? How can they confront an ideology
that tells them there is no alternative to accepting
that the State can no longer 'afford' to support
education, public housing, health, social services
and the environment to the extent it did in the past?
What impact can they have on decisions which
affect their own localities?

The great variety of community organizations and
voluntary groups in London demonstrates the
strength of feeling that something can and must be
done to improve people's circumstances. Participation in community groups offers both tangible and
intangible benefits. At a personal level, people
become more confident, understanding more clearly
how political decisions are made as participation
increases their experience of being in more control
over aspects of daily life. Traditional voluntary
organizations meet the needs of such groups as the
elderly and disadvantaged in more direct and
informal ways than social service departments,
while community groups that are more concerned
with planning issues have been able to transform
patches of derelict land and improve environmental
conditions around their housing estates.

But difficulties also confront voluntary groups.
Increased volunteering can be used to cut public
spending; there is always the danger that the efforts
of volunteers will be used to cope with fundamental
social needs, rather than add to basic provision of
social services. There are problems in the represent-
ativeness of community organizations, especially

those committed to changing planning proposals.
Groups also face great difficulties over funding.
Many find that their goals must change to meet the
aims of the organization funding them, while the
State 'can incorporate community organizing
methods for deeply cynical and self interested
motives' (Cowley *et al*, 1977, p 13). Many groups
are worried about being co-opted into the administration through too close involvement with the
mechanics of local government.

In this chapter, I shall explore some types of
voluntary action in London, concentrating on local
community groups concerned with environmental
change. Interviews with community groups in Docklands will be used to identify differing attitudes to
community participation expressed by the GLC and
the LDDC. Since 1981 the GLC has been officially
committed to developing participatory forms of
local government. The LDDC, on the other hand,
is a government appointed authority, under no form
of control by local people, and has been slow to
recognize the need for local public consultation
about its major planning proposals. In the next
section of the chapter the voluntary sector and its
activities will be defined, then the critical effect of
dependence on state funding will be considered.
Finally, some expressions of community action in
Docklands will be explored.

Definition and purposes of the voluntary sector

The voluntary sector covers a wide range of activities and political orientations. Its backbone is
composed of major charities, such as Mind, Age
Concern and the Samaritans, which are both active
among the needy and also work to lobby government about their problems. Beneath this national

charitable umbrella, a multitude of different interest groups operate at the local level. The majority focus on relieving welfare problems but a significant proportion are committed to influencing local politics, housing, planning and the environment. Groups deal with two main types of issue. There are some that agitate in various ways to *improve the delivery of services*. Their activities may relate to the provisions made by local authorities, with respect to accommodation, planning or social facilities, or they may address the shortcomings of central government in providing services because of public expenditure cuts. The activities of other groups are orientated to *action within the local environment*. Environmental improvement schemes, running community newsletters, painting murals and fighting development proposals are the most tangible expressions of this kind of activity. Action groups are also to be found running community centres, playgroups, and day centres for the elderly and providing facilities for ethnic groups. Increasingly, the voluntary sector is becoming involved in job creation through cooperatives and community-based workshops.

Volunteering finds support right across the political spectrum. From the Conservative point of view, voluntary organizations embody the best principles of self help. By their own efforts, people can improve their circumstances and those of the more disadvantaged. At the same time, voluntary activities help 'roll back the State' by reducing the intervention of central and local government in people's daily lives. The case for self help, especially in environmental improvement, has been argued forcefully by Charles McKean (1977) in *Fight Blight*, where he insists that derelict land is a local problem that can be tackled locally. He maintains that the common interests of people to improve their environments are 'obfuscated by political irrelevance'. Those from the Left of the political spectrum question his determination to avoid involvement in the politics of environmental change. By confronting the inequalities and inherent contradictions of capitalist society, expressed in both central and local decision making, they believe that community action can challenge both the distribution of resources and power and variations in access to them (Paris, 1982).

Community organizations emphasize the home rather than the workplace, while the feminist belief that 'the personal is political' is very influential in the actions of voluntary groups. The strongest demands for community involvement in decision making have been expressed in local planning: 'the most readily visible and, once completed often the least reversible forms of social change, removing or rehousing familiar faces and destroying familiar places' (Gyford, 1976, p 144). For example, a survey of residents in North Battersea, found that residents were sceptical about the intentions of local authority planners and angry about local conditions (Beresford and Beresford, 1978). They wanted more services, better local shops, more social amenities, small houses with gardens, clean streets, more open space and the demolition of tower blocks. Yet they felt powerless and wanted more direct involvement in decision making. The successful campaign waged by community groups around Coin Street on the south bank of the Thames in Southwark, where property developers have finally withdrawn their proposals, illustrates the strength of feeling for local areas. The cartoons used in that campaign illustrate the importance of local buildings in creating a sense of identity and belonging.

Resources for the voluntary sector

Community groups need money for a variety of purposes, from administrative costs of small *ad hoc* groups, to support for ambitious projects that require premises, facilities and full-time paid workers. Funding is critical if alternative voices are to be heard. 'It is not possible to talk about wanting participation and healthy democracy if society is not prepared to allow people some practical help which will aid them in their dealings with the complex institutions of government and commerce, and in their community action and self help projects' (Butcher, 1979, p 200). Most groups, nevertheless, have to rely on their own resources. A smaller number have grants from local or central government, and a few obtain finance from charitable trusts.

At present, the pattern of funding for voluntary groups in London is complex. Support from central government comes through two different programmes. The Manpower Services Commission assists community projects but many groups are unhappy about the short period of employment for workers, the emphasis on low wages and part-time work. The second source of government funding in inner London is the Urban Programme administered by the Department of Environment (see chapter 8). Grants are allocated to three types of project: economic, environmental and social. The DoE meets 75 per cent of costs, while the local authority pays the rest. Since 1981 the Conservative government has insisted that more grants be allocated to economic and environmental projects rather than social ones, and has favoured capital investment rather than support for day-to-day expenses. This has 'encouraged' groups to buy and renovate buildings, for example, rather than pay full or part-time workers on projects. Grants to Urban Programme authorities in 1983–4 came to £288 million nationwide, of which £62 million went to voluntary groups. Projects run by ethnic groups received £27 million (9 per cent of the total) which partly reflects increased awareness of minority needs following the 1981 riots (see chapter 18). Urban Programme spending contributed £3.9 million to voluntary projects in London during 1983–4.

Groups can also turn to the London boroughs and the GLC for finance. The London Voluntary Services Council (LVSC) calculates that contributions to the voluntary sector in 1984–5 were as follows. The GLC allocated £47 million, including

£14.1 million for London-wide projects and £32.9 million for local projects. The 32 London boroughs contributed £26.6 million to projects within their boundaries. Additionally, organizations operating in Docklands can turn to the LDDC, which had a budget of £845 000 for community-based projects in 1983–4.

Which groups are likely to be funded by the London boroughs? Research has shown that councillors and officers favour certain groups rather than others. The more aggressive, flamboyant, radical or publicity-conscious the group, the less acceptable it is likely to be to councillors (Newton 1976). A recent survey by LVSC showed that all boroughs required the aims of groups to be consistent with council policy, although considerable variations exist between the policies of inner and outer boroughs. Boroughs like Camden and Hackney, committed to local socialism, are funding groups critical of council practice and have developed innovative approaches to women's projects and ethnic minority schemes (Boddy and Fudge 1983). In contrast, outer boroughs, like Bexley, only support traditional groups whose activities improve statutory social services provision. All the boroughs increased financial support for the voluntary sector during 1983–84, but central government control over local authority expenditure through 'rate capping' will jeopardize that support after 1984,

Table 19.1   *Distribution of grant budgets between various GLC committees in 1982–3 and 1983–4*

Grant unit	1982–83 Budget (£'000)	(%)	1983–84 Budget (£'000)	(%)
Finance and General Purposes (including voluntary services)	2 075	10.1	5 854	14.8
Ethnic Minorities	864	4.2	2 530	6.4
Women's Support Unit	384	1.8	6 389	16.2
Police	390	1.9	631	1.6
Industry and Employment	1 720	8.4	4 750	12.0
Greater London Training Board	730	3.5	2 905	7.3
Housing	1 723	8.4	2 680	6.8
Planning (including ecology)	681	3.3	967	2.4
Community Areas	5 520	26.9	3 980	10.0
Transport	–	–	595	1.5
Recreation and Arts	6 397	31.2	8 230	20.8
Docklands	18	0.08	–	–
Public Services and Fire Brigade	17	0.08	126	0.3
Total	20 519		39 637	

especially in the nine inner London boroughs, plus Brent and Haringey.

Turning to the GLC, support for community organizations has undoubtedly had a major impact under the Labour administration voted into power in 1981. The GLC had previously provided funds for voluntary groups on a modest scale (for example £427 000 in 1965–6, rising to just under £5 million in 1980–1). In 1981 the Labour group in the GLC committed itself to much greater funding of community and voluntary groups. This reflected a concern to redistribute resources from richer to poorer boroughs and to develop more participatory forms of local government, whereby people are able to express alternative views about policy decisions. It also reflected a belief that new solutions to rapid de-industrialization, experienced particularly in the inner boroughs (see chapter 8), could be found

Table 19.2 *GLC grant-aid for voluntary and community organizations*

In 1984 the GLC invited applications for funding from voluntary and community groups serving London. The main committees involved and the types of activity or group for which applications were invited are set out below.

☐ Arts and Recreation
☐ Community Arts Sub-Committee (publishing projects, community bookshops, photo-collectives, film and video resources; other art forms for local communities or communities of interest, e.g. women, the elderly, young people, people with disabilities, gay and lesbian groups)
☐ Ethnic Arts Sub-Committee (especially Afro-Caribbean and Asian arts groups)
☐ Sports Sub-Committee
☐ Ethnic Minorities (groups responding to special needs, London-wide initiatives and anti-racist projects)
☐ Greater London Training Board (especially high quality training schemes, pilot or innovatory projects)
☐ Police (monitoring of police activities and accountability)
☐ Planning (planning issues, ecology groups, community groups in Docklands)
☐ Transport (people with disabilities, pressure groups)
☐ Women's (on-going projects, projects seeking to redress double discrimination, e.g. black and ethnic minority women, lesbians, the elderly, women with disabilities, young and working class women).

through community organizations, including workers' and community cooperatives. The support given by the Popular Planning Unit of the GLC was vital to the success of the Coin Street action groups and played a major role in the People's Plan for the Royal Docks that will be discussed below. One of the major functions of the GLC funding was to support groups that would not, for a variety of reasons, be funded by their own borough.

Much of this expenditure was regarded as highly controversial (Carvel 1983). The GLC, nonetheless, expanded support to traditional groups offering services to meet local needs and helped groups serving black Londoners, women and gays. In 1984 the GLC was supporting over 2000 voluntary groups and had created over 1000 new jobs. Table 19.1 includes expenditure by various committees in the GLC concerned with voluntary organizations, while Table 19.2 summarizes a GLC advertisement in 1984 inviting community organizations to bid for its support and thereby gives a clear sense of its concerns and interests.

Community organizations in Docklands

'It's crucial to have an elected body which encourages consultation. There's little consultation about anything in Docklands. We're disenfranchised. It's like the GLC being abolished but it happened to us four years ago without many people noticing' (Ted Johns, Association of Island Communities, 1984). Since London's docks started to be closed in 1969, local communities have been subject to various political initiatives designed to regenerate the area. The extent to which local people have been consulted has fluctuated, reaching a participation peak in 1975–6 with discussion about the London Docklands Strategic Plan formulated with the Docklands Joint Committee (DJC) including representatives from Newham, Tower Hamlets, Southwark, Lewisham and Greenwich. The Docklands Forum, an umbrella organization representing the wide range of interests in the area, was a full member of the DJC and was able to express the views of local groups. After election in 1979, the Conservative government decided that the DJC was progressing too slowly and the Strategic Plan relied too heavily on public funds (£360 million at 1979 prices). The DJC was displaced by the LDDC which started operations in 1981 to regenerate the Docklands, primarily by attracting private investment (see chapter 8).

Docklands form an anomaly; a small island of development, increased spending and new investment in a sea of recession and cuts in public expenditure. Voluntary and community interests reflect this anomalous position, with people being deeply concerned about the new plans and changes being made to the area, the extent to which social structures are being changed, and the lack of consultation about what is happening. Traditionally, Dockland communities have been isolated one from another but the activities of the LDDC are uniting communities so as to express their opposition (for example over the marketing of sites, creation of new industries and employment that do not match the skills of local people, and development of housing for sale at prices that local people cannot afford – see chapter 10).

Environmental and social changes are always difficult experiences but the LDDC is implementing massive schemes for which it has no accountability to local people. For its first two years the LDDC concentrated on regenerating the physical environment and marketing the area to change its image among private investors. It neglected local needs. In 1983, however, the Corporation appointed a Community Liaison Officer. This tardiness revealed the LDDC's early priorities. Now its orientation has changed as it is seeking to persuade residents that regeneration is a process in which they can participate; participation does not, however, extend to changing policy decisions. The LDDC remains as remote and unaccountable as ever. Its Community Liaison Officer believes that community involvement gives people a new esteem and that they can be persuaded that the Docklands are changing for the better. The LDDC is supporting a large number of community projects, such as recreation facilities and equipment, training and employment initiatives, and community centres. In 1983–4, £845 000 was shared among 600 groups in Newham, Tower Hamlets and Southwark; however, like many London boroughs, the LDDC is not prepared to support groups that might be critical of its practices. It hopes that through experience of working together, a consensus will emerge and local people will feel greater loyalty and commitment to it.

How can the Dockland communities influence an unaccountable organization? How can they make their feelings known? How can groups opposed to the activities of the LDDC support themselves? Different groups have adopted different strategies. Three examples illustrate the problems. The Dockland Forum endeavours to work with the LDDC and reconcile the conflicting views that regeneration is raising among the various interests in the area. It is financed jointly by the LDDC and the GLC. The Joint Docklands Action Group (JDAG) actively contests the LDDC over its regeneration strategy and acts as a resource and research centre for local groups; it is financed by the GLC. Finally, Dockland Community Posters (DCP) is a group of designers financed by the community arts committee of the GLC. This politically conscious cooperative challenges the character of regeneration, helps local groups with publicity material, and collects material on environmental change.

Docklands Forum was established in 1974. Its members range from the London Confederation of British Industries and Chamber of Commerce, to the North Southwark Action Group. It had a seat on the DJC, representing the views of community organizations. Since the creation of the LDDC it has been deprived of power, now reacting to events rather than initiating ideas and proposals. Its function is to inform local groups and represent their views to the LDDC, primarily on planning, housing and training matters. It lodges objections to developments that it believes are not in the best interests of local people. In 1984 it was involved in proposals about the Dockland Light Railway and matters relating to housing, being unhappy about the number of newly converted luxury apartments along the Thames and the amount of private housing being built for sale, when so many families are on the waiting list for council housing (see chapter 10).

The Forum tries to maintain a consensus among its members but in 1984 two issues threatened this. The first, which divided the community groups themselves, was the STOLport proposal. Some groups felt that the airport would bring new jobs to the Royal Docks area and should be accepted. Others felt unhappy about its environmental impact and the low quality of jobs likely to be provided. The second issue was that of funding in the future. The LDDC might well finance the Forum but certain members, such as JDAG and North Southwark Group, will not accept money from an organization to which they are opposed irrevocably. The project

THE OXO TOWER, STAMFORD WHARF, S.E.1.

WHEN OXO WERE REFUSED PLANNING PERMISSION TO ERECT A NEON SIGN, IN 1929, THEY BUILT THIS TOWER AND NEATLY SIDE-STEPPED THE PLANNERS. THE WINDOWS, WHICH SPELL OXO, WERE ILLUMINATED FROM WITHIN AND COULD BE SEEN FOR MILES AROUND. IT IS NOW PART OF THE COIN STREET DEVELOPMENT SITE AND GREYCOATS (THE DEVELOPERS) WERE GOING TO DEMOLISH IT. THE LOCAL COMMUNITY PLAN WOULD RETAIN THE TOWER & WAREHOUSE AS SHOPS/FLATS/RESTAURANT/MUSEUM. AS A TOKEN GESTURE, GREYCOATS DECIDED TO RETAIN IT AMID THEIR MASSIVE OFFICE DEVELOPMENT

Oxo Tower Drawing.
One building in Southwark threatened by the South Bank redevelopment. The sketch is by Francis Boyle from his protest comic, 'Gannets'. © Francis Boyle 1981.

workers themselves are pragmatic. The LDDC is there; it has money; the Forum should use it.

JDAG is a federation of community interests with a much clearer political stance than the Forum. Its aim is to act for the benefit of local people against City-based development interests. It acts as a research organization and resource centre for local groups in their struggles over housing, employment, service provision and planning. Workers in JDAG are committed to community action and often engage with local groups in campaigns against proposals and in submission of evidence at public enquiries. They publish newssheets and *Dredger*, which is an alternative to the LDDC's newspaper. One function of the JDAG is to publicize property deals and market connections between members of the LDDC board and the City (Colenutt, 1984). JDAG feels that such marketing objectives are incompatible with social objectives of regeneration. This kind of activity is not replacing lost jobs with new employment suitable for the skills of the local population. Bob Colenutt believes that there is no history of Dockland-wide identity, but one is now emerging as people from Canning Town, the Isle of Dogs, Limehouse, Wapping and Bermondsey all experience a similar sense of exploitation as their neighbourhoods are redefined into marketable sites for property development.

Contrasting perceptions of the future for the Docklands by the LDDC, JDAG and other community groups were revealed in evidence to the STOLport enquiry in 1984, the airport scheme that had been announced two years earlier. Some people wanted to see something happen and, because no alternative was offered, felt that an airport in the Royal Docks was the only way to proceed. However, a campaign quickly emerged against it, as other local people began to ask what alternative developments there might be. With support from the GLC's Popular Planning Unit, JDAG and the Newham Dockland Forum consulted local people during the first part of 1984 and produced a comprehensive alternative plan. The People's Plan, submitted as evidence to the STOLport enquiry, envisaged regeneration serving mainly the needs of local people. It advocated part of the Royal Docks being reopened to port trade, another section being filled with public housing and gardens, and outlined many more ideas. JDAG was funded as a resource centre for Docklands after 1975 and employed half a dozen workers in 1984. Its grant is secure for 1984–5 but, as one worker said, 'the years after that will be a nightmare for everyone in the voluntary sector'. Staff are not optimistic that JDAG will be funded by the local authorities, whose limited budgets will be put under great pressure by claims from other voluntary groups that will lose support. And, of course, JDAG has a high profile that is perceived as 'political'.

An innovative, arts-based community group called Docklands Community Posters attacks the activities of the LDDC in a highly provocative, visually arresting way from premises actually inside the Enterprise Zone! DCP was founded in 1981 and has the aim of demystifying the process of regeneration, rather than hiding the interests that stand to benefit most, as brochures and glossy reports normally do. This cooperative now has seven workers whose activities link art, photography, design, environment and politics. Their photomontage posters catch the attention and raise fundamental questions about the nature of Docklands and its future. They are, in fact, powerful pieces of protest and are viewed with disfavour by the LDDC and those who endorse its aims. DCP has only been granted two display sites in the whole LDDC area: one was established before the LDDC was set up (Wapping Lane) and the other was only agreed

after a long wrangle (Market Road, Isle of Dogs). The other five sites are inside the Dockland boroughs but outside the area controlled by the LDDC. DCP is also establishing an archive that records changes in the local environment and is compiling an exhibition on life in the Docklands that can be taken to community centres and public enquiries. The cooperative is funded annually and its members fear that they will 'go to the wall' when the GLC is abolished. But in the meantime their activities are helping to energize the debate about what is happening in Docklands.

Photomontage, Dockland Community Posters.
Photomontage from the beginning and end of 'What's Going on Behind our Backs? © *DCP 1984.*

Facing the future

At the time of writing, the future of the voluntary sector in London is uncertain. Community organizations are caught up in the Conservative Government's attack on local government. The proposals to abolish the GLC, when combined with the statutory limits imposed on rates, will devastate the sector as it has emerged over the last few years. Reactions to the White Paper *Streamlining the Cities* (1983) from the voluntary sector were almost universally hostile. Of 418 submissions, 95 per cent opposed abolition; first, because they felt it would have a detrimental impact on the poor and needy in London, and second, because they believed that the alternatives proposed by government were unworkable. In the Bill now before Parliament, it is proposed to give the boroughs a maximum of £10 million to fund London-wide groups. Given the political divisions that exist between inner and outer boroughs, it is unlikely that joint funding arrangements will work satisfactorily. An additional £5 million is to be allocated for local voluntary groups but the local authorities must contribute 25 per cent to costs, despite average cuts in current expenditure of 12 per cent for rate-capped boroughs. This represents a cut of 70 per cent on current support available from the GLC. Innovative projects for women, industry and employment, ethnic minorities, gays and community arts will undoubtedly suffer most.

It is impossible to predict the outcome of likely changes but representatives from the voluntary sector are pessimistic. Many groups may well cease to function. Of those that remain, many will lose workers, facilities and premises, while expertise built up in the course of individual projects will be lost. The government wants to reduce the dependence of the voluntary groups on the public sector but there are few alternative sources for funds; the private sector is unlikely to increase its financial support for projects that lack visibility and prestige. The voluntary sector has traditionally been funded on the principle that its activities are not party-political. Now many community workers are unhappy that they have been dragged into a major battle between central and local government. But the experience of groups in Docklands reveals that a political dimension underlies all community action as soon as people begin to question and challenge decisions made on their behalf by higher authorities. Any form of participation is really a practical education in the politics of decision-making. In the words of Alinsky (1969), the founding father of community organizing, 'popular education . . . becomes a direct and intimate part of the personal lives, experience and activities of the people . . . knowledge then becomes an arsenal of weapons in the battle against injustice and degradation' (p 173). If environmental conditions and services continue to deteriorate and the government further reduces the opportunities for people to do something themselves, new forms of direct action and politicization may well find expression in London's local communities.

Further reading

Alinksy S D (1969) *Reveille for Radicals* Random House, New York

Beresford S and Beresford P (1978) 'Participation for whom?' *New Society* 17 August pp 351–2

Boddy M and Fudge C (eds) (1984) *Local Socialism? Labour Councils and New Left Alternatives* Macmillan

Butcher H, Pearce J, Cole I and Glen A (1979) *Community Participation and Poverty. Final Report of the Cumbria CDP* Papers in Community Studies, University of York

Carvel J (1984) *Citizen Ken* Chatto and Windus

Colenutt B (1984) 'London's Docklands: Regenerating Profits' *Community Action* **66**: 26–29

Cowley J, Kaye A, Mayo M and Thompson M (1977) *Community or Class Struggle?* Stage 1, London

Gyford J (1976) *Local Politics in Britain* Croom Helm

McKean C (1977) *Fight Blight* Kaye and Ward

Newton K (1976) *Second City Politics* Oxford University Press

Paris C (ed) (1982) *Critical Readings in Planning Theory* Pergamon

The People's Plan for the Royal Docks (1983) Available from People's Plan Centre, 10 Pier Parade, North Woolwich, London E16

Streamlining the Cities (1983) Command no. 9063, HMSO

Index